BRITAIN'S COAST

BRITAIN'S COAST

A TOUR IN HISTORICAL PHOTOGRAPHS

Compiled and edited by Eliza and Terence Sackett

with photographs from
THE FRANCIS FRITH COLLECTION

WEYMOUTH, THE PROMENADE 1918 68114t

CONTENTS

BRITAIN'S COAST

FRANCIS FRITH, founder of the world-famous photographic archive, was a complex and multi-talented man. A devout Quaker and a highly successful Victorian businessman, he was philosophical by nature and pioneering in outlook.

By 1855 he had already established a wholesale grocery business in Liverpool, and sold it for the astonishing sum of £200,000, which is the equivalent today of over £15,000,000. Now a very rich man, he was able to indulge his passion for travel. As a child he had pored over travel books written by early explorers, and his fancy and imagination had been stirred by family holidays to the sublime mountain regions of Wales and Scotland. 'What lands of spirit-stirring and enriching scenes and places!' he had written. He was to return to these scenes of grandeur in later years to 'recapture the thousands of vivid and tender memories', but with a different purpose. Now in his thirties, and captivated by the new science of photography, Frith set out on a series of pioneering journeys up the Nile and to the Near East that occupied him from 1856 until 1860.

INTRIGUE AND EXPLORATION

These far-flung journeys were packed with intrigue and adventure. In his life story, written when he was sixty-three, Frith tells of being held captive by bandits, and of fighting 'an awful midnight battle to the very point of surrender with a deadly pack of hungry, wild dogs'. Wearing flowing Arab costume, Frith arrived at Akaba by camel sixty years before Lawrence of Arabia, where he encountered 'desert princes and rival sheikhs, blazing with jewel-hilted swords'.

He was the first photographer to venture beyond the sixth cataract of the Nile. Africa was still the mysterious 'Dark Continent', and Stanley and Livingstone's historic meeting was a decade into the future. The conditions for picture taking confound belief. He laboured for hours in his wicker dark-room in the sweltering heat of the desert, while the volatile chemicals fizzed dangerously in their trays. Back in London he exhibited his photographs and was 'rapturously cheered' by members of the Royal Society. His reputation as a photographer was made overnight.

THE RISE OF FRITH & CO

Characteristically, Frith quickly spotted the opportunity to create a new business as a specialist publisher of photographs. He lived in an era of immense and sometimes violent change. For the poor in the early part of Victoria's reign work was exhausting and the hours long, and people had precious little free time to enjoy themselves. Most had no transport other than a cart or gig at their disposal, and rarely travelled far beyond the boundaries of their own town or village. However, by the 1870s the railways had threaded their way across the country, and Bank Holidays and half-day Saturdays had been made obligatory by Act of Parliament. All of a sudden the working man and his family were able to enjoy days out and see a little more of the world.

With typical business acumen, Francis Frith foresaw that these new tourists would enjoy having souvenirs to commemorate their days out. Frith's studio was soon supplying retail shops all over the country. To meet the demand he gathered together a team of photographers, and published

the work of independent artist-photographers of the calibre of Roger Fenton and Francis Bedford. In order to gain some understanding of the scale of Frith's business one only has to look at the catalogue issued by Frith & Co in 1886: it runs to some 670 pages, listing not only many thousands of views of the British Isles but also many photographs of most European countries, and China, Japan, the USA and Canada. By 1890 Frith had created the greatest specialist photographic publishing company in the world, with over 2,000 sales outlets.

POSTCARD BONANZA

The ever-popular holiday postcard we know today took many years to develop. The Post Office issued the first plain cards in 1870, with a pre-printed stamp on one face. In 1894 they allowed other publishers' cards to be sent through the mail with an attached adhesive halfpenny stamp. Demand grew rapidly, and in 1895 a new size of postcard was permitted called the court card, but there was little room for illustration. In 1899, a year after Frith's death, a new card measuring 5.5 x 3.5 inches became the standard format, but it was not until 1902 that the divided back came into being, so that the address and message could be on one face and a full-size illustration on the other. Frith & Co were in the vanguard of postcard development: Frith's sons Eustace and Cyril continued their father's monumental task, expanding the number of views offered to the public and recording more and more places in Britain.

Francis Frith had died in 1898 at his villa in Cannes, his great project still growing. The archive he created continued in business for another seventy years. By 1970 it contained over a third of a million pictures showing 7,000 British towns and villages.

FRANCIS FRITH'S LEGACY

Frith's legacy to us today is of immense significance and value, for the magnificent archive of evocative photographs he created provides a unique record of change in the cities, towns and villages throughout Britain over a century and more. Frith and his fellow studio photographers revisited locations many times down the years to update their views, compiling for us an enthralling and colourful pageant of British life and character.

We are fortunate that Frith was dedicated to recording the minutiae of everyday life, for it is this sheer wealth of visual data, the painstaking chronicle of changes in dress, transport, street layouts, buildings, housing and landscape that captivates us so much today. His images offer us a powerful link with the past and with the lives of our ancestors.

THE VALUE OF THE ARCHIVE TODAY

Historians consider The Francis Frith Collection to be of prime national importance. It is the only archive of its kind remaining in private ownership. The archive's future is both bright and exciting.

Francis Frith, with his unshakeable belief in making photographs available to the greatest number of people, would undoubtedly approve of the computer technology that allows his work to be rapidly transmitted to people all over the world by way of the internet. His photographs depicting our shared past are now bringing pleasure and enlightenment to millions around the world a century and more after his death.

INTRODUCTION

J A STEERS in his 1948 book 'The Coast of England and Wales in Pictures' estimates that the coastline of England and Wales runs to 2,750 miles in length. When you add in Scotland the figure jumps to an astonishing 6,000 miles! Steers points out, too, that it is rare to find the same kind of coastal scenery for more than ten or fifteen miles together.

This book aims at showing Britain's coastline in all its rich variety: the towering cliff that gradually gives way to a broad sandy bay; a rocky headland beyond which the land falls quickly to a sluggish, winding river creek; a remote fishing hamlet lying huddled around a break in the cliffs where the only sound is the crying of gulls; a flat ridge of tilled fields extending into the distance, stopping just short of the line of wet shingle; and still further on the gleaming towers and gantries of a great port rising into the blue sky, where ships from five continents jostle for space; and across the estuary the colourful pier pushing out into the sea, backed by the terraces of whitewashed hotels of a popular resort town.

The British have always enjoyed their reputation of being a maritime nation. They feel that the sea runs in their blood. However, the British love affair with the coast as a holiday destination is a relatively recent phenomenon. It was the spreading of the railways and the introduction of Bank Holidays in the 1870s that introduced the working man and his family to the delights of sand and sea air. Transport and free time away from work made it possible for them to enjoy days out and so see a little more of the world. A Victorian guidebook 'Round the Coast' published in about 1890 extols the delights of the seaside holiday: 'We love our haunts by the sea; the poorest among us regards his favourite resort pretty much as the rich man does his country seat – as a place of relaxation from the hurly-burly of life, and yet a home withal … How the eyes brighten at the sight of a familiar spot! And how vividly the old associations crowd back to the mind – memories of glowing, careless days, that gave new life to the jaded

worker, and caused the brain-weary to forget their ineffable tædium vitae.' Early on Francis Frith recognised that these new tourists would enjoy buying souvenirs commemorating their days out and happy times spent by the sea. He produced many thousands of fine photographs of coastal scenes that were keenly bought by the Victorians and pasted into family albums. It is from these pioneering images that much of this book has been compiled.

However, the coast was not just the place for leisure and pleasure; it was also the place of work for many thousands of Britons including merchant seamen, fishermen, herring gutters, whelkers, dockers, shipwrights, lighthouse keepers, ferrymen, kelp gatherers, millers, maltsers, and coal miners. Much of the work was hazardous, and Britain's fishermen risked their lives daily, venturing out in small boats into treacherous seas. Wrecks and drownings were all too common, and rescue by lifeboatmen never certain.

These Frith photographs are of particular interest to us today, for they show many sights from the past that could not be witnessed now: entire cliffs and villages that have long since vanished under the waves after relentless attacks by the sea; tranquil headlands now speckled with caravans and holiday cottages; and modest resort towns now bloated and smothering broad stretches of what was once open downland and shore.

The Frith photographs are deeply atmospheric and nostalgic, and offer us a fascinating insight into how our coasts looked a century or more ago. The many quotations from writers, poets and travellers down the ages add valuable insights into vanished people and places, emphasising the rich diversity of Britain's coastal history and heritage. Together they act as a moving testimony to a way of life now hugely changed.

The book has been arranged as a tour round the coast of Britain, beginning at Portsmouth in Hampshire, historic port and home of Nelson's famous ship the 'Victory'.

PORTSMOUTH

England's dockyard and home of Nelson's 'Victory'

RICHARD I was responsible for establishing a settlement on Portsea Island, and it was he who built the first dock at Portsmouth in the late 12th century. The Tudor kings, Henry VII and VIII, later constructed the first dry dock in the world here. A considerable amount of development took place here in the 17th and 18th centuries, including the building of naval establishments and factories. Most of the dockyard, where Nelson's flagship HMS 'Victory' has remained more or less intact since the Battle of Trafalgar, also dates from this time.

In the view of the Hard (22751t, opposite), carriages standing in front of an imposing line of banks, taverns and offices epitomise bustle, trade and commerce. The timber floating loosely in the dock has been off-loaded from a boat, probably one engaged in the Baltic trade; the wood is being stored in the dock to save quay space whilst awaiting further transportation. The many waterfront drinking houses – there are at least three in this photograph, including the Victoria and Albert in the centre – would have tempted Portsmouth's shifting population of sailors.

Opposite: **PORTSMOUTH, THE HARD 1890** 22751t

Above: **PORTSMOUTH, THE HARBOUR 1892** 30004

Right: **NELSON'S 'VICTORY'**

[The Victory's] only function now is to stand year after year in Portsmouth waters and exhibit herself to the festive Cockney

LORD NELSON

The dockyard, into which I was unable to penetrate, is a colossal enclosure, signalised externally by a grim brick wall, as featureless as an empty black-board. The dockyard eats up the town, as it were, and there is nothing left over but the gin-shops, which the town drinks up. There is not even a crooked old quay of any consequence, with brightly patched houses looking out upon a forest of masts. To begin with, there are no masts; and then there are no polyglot sign-boards, no overhanging upper stories, no outlandish parrots and macaws perched in open lattices. I had another hour or so before my train departed, and it would have gone hard with me if I had not bethought myself of hiring a boat and being pulled about in the harbour. Here a certain amount of entertainment was to be found. There were great ironclads and white troopships that looked vague and spectral, like the floating home of the Flying Dutchman, and small, devilish vessels whose mission was to project the infernal torpedo. I coasted about these metallic islets, and then, to eke out my entertainment, I boarded the Victory. The Victory is an ancient frigate of enormous size, which in the days of her glory carried I know not how many hundred guns, but whose only function now is to stand year after year in Portsmouth waters and exhibit herself to the festive Cockney.

HENRY JAMES, 'ENGLISH HOURS' 1905

SOUTHSEA

❝ *It would not be rustic or romantic enough for all tastes, but recommends itself to many by the stir of military and naval life.*

VICTORIAN GUIDEBOOK

Above: **SOUTHSEA, THE HOVERCRAFT c1965** S161123

Below: **SOUTHSEA, THE SANDS AND PIER 1921** 71472

IT WAS during the Victorian era that Southsea, Portsmouth's sister town, established itself as a fashionable holiday resort for the middle classes. It is not without its literary associations. H G Wells and Rudyard Kipling spent their formative years locally, and Arthur Conan Doyle established a medical practice in the town in 1882. He wrote his first Sherlock Holmes story, 'A Study in Scarlet', here in 1886, and eventually left Southsea in 1890.

About six years before photograph S161123 (left) was taken, the designer Christopher Cockerell was turning a drawing-board dream into reality with his invention of the hovercraft, a revolutionary new concept in passenger travel. The Suffolk boat builder took out 56 patents on the design, and the first experimental hovercraft crossed the English Channel in 1959.

COWES

THE DEEP and sheltered waters known as Cowes Roads, which lead to the small harbour at the mouth of the River Medina, were instrumental in the development of Cowes as a yachting mecca and of East Cowes for shipbuilding. Wooden ships were built at Cowes as long ago as the 16th century. Indeed, after the Spanish Armada ceased to be a threat, ships would drop anchor in the natural harbour to stock up with supplies before they made their often treacherous voyages across uncharted seas. The town's fame as a yachting haven was rapidly established after the formation of the Royal Yacht Squadron in 1833, and when in 1845 Queen Victoria bought Osborne House in East Cowes as a retreat, Cowes also became extremely fashionable as a holiday resort.

The pier, with its twin turrets at the entrance (50797b, above), was built in 1901 by the local council at a cost of £10,500, partly to attract business from the many pleasure steamers plying the Solent. From the seaward end of the pier there were excellent views of the harbour: passing ships, yacht racing, and regattas. The pier was in use during World War II, but was demolished shortly after.

Natural harbour and fashionable yachting haven

Left:
COWES, FROM THE AIR 1923 AF39662

Above:
COWES, THE REGATTA 1903 50797B

BLACKGANG CHINE

It has been duly domesticated; paths have been cut along its slopes, summer-houses erected; a bazaar bars the entrance; villas and an hotel have sprung up around it, and such charms as the place once possessed are almost dispelled … Many a good ship has been shattered among the breakers here, and the crew have not seldom perished. Gold-dust is said to have been sifted from the sand of the sea-shore.

VICTORIAN GUIDEBOOK

ROUNDING St Catherine's Point we reach the dramatic scenery of Blackgang Chine. Through millions of years, soft sands and clays slipped over the underlying gault clay to form the green and abundant world of the Undercliff, a haven for wild plant and animal life. Blackgang Chine is a great cleft in the bright yellow sandstone and blue clays of the cliff, plunging 400 feet (B113037). Popular with smugglers, it remained savage until tamed by the Victorians, and these gardens are a testimony to their achievement. This huge chasm was an early tourist attraction on the Isle of Wight, with its dramatic waterfall and eroded colourful cliffs. Entry was relatively expensive in Victorian times. One guidebook writer noted that 'entrance to the Chine is through a bazaar, where one must either make a purchase or pay sixpence before he descends to this great chasm, echoing the ocean waves that break on the beach below'.

Alum Bay lies just beyond the Old Battery (see line illustration below). Its coloured cliffs are one of the most enduring sights on the Isle of Wight. These cliffs are unusual in displaying the famous coloured sands, arranged vertically down the cliff face, created by water percolating through the surface over thousands of years, depositing chemicals in the process. Alum (sulphate of potassium) was first mined in 1561 for the paper making and tanning industry. The land rises 80 metres to Headon Warren tumuli, with Totland Bay beyond.

Above:
**ISLE OF WIGHT,
BLACKGANG CHINE
GARDENS c1955**
B113054

Right:
**ISLE OF WIGHT,
BLACKGANG CHINE,
THE CLIFFS c1960**
B113037

THE NEEDLES

THERE IS nothing very thin and sharply pointed about any of the three chalk stacks making up the Needles, the Island's most westerly point. The one stack that did resemble the sewing implement – the Needle Rock itself – disappeared after crumbling into a storm-lashed sea as long ago as 1764. The gap it left is obvious (26176, centre of photograph, below). The lighthouse (N7011p, left) stands by the most westerly of the Needles; 109ft high, its light can be seen from 14 miles away. It was built in 1859 to replace an 18th-century lighthouse on the cliff-top. Once manned by a keeper and two assistants, it was automated in 1994, and the coastguard operation is run largely from the other side of the Solent. Around 100 ships pass daily.

The Isle of Wight is at first disappointing. I wondered why it should be, and then I found the reason in the influence of the detestable little railway. There can be no doubt that a railway in the Isle of Wight is a gross impertinence, is in evident contravention to the natural style of the place. The place is pure picture or is nothing at all. It is ornamental only – it exists for exclamation and the water-colour brush. It is separated by nature from the dense railway-system of the less diminutive island, and is the corner of the world where a good carriage-road is most in keeping. Never was a clearer opportunity for sacrificing to prettiness; never was a better chance for not making a railway. But now there are twenty trains a day, so that the prettiness is twenty times less.

HENRY JAMES, 'ENGLISH HOURS' 1905

NEEDLES INTO SPACE

Needles Old Battery, 1861–63, was a main defence against the French. Two 12-ton guns were hauled up into position, while tunnels through the cliff led to a searchlight station and a parade ground. Thanks to its underground facilities, the site has been used in the space race: Saunders-Roe of Cowes developed a rocket programme here between 1956 and 1971. A site was laid out close to the Needles so that the Island company could test-fire the engines it had manufactured at East Cowes for the Black Knight and Black Arrow rockets. (The rockets themselves were later put through their paces in Woomera, Australia). Test firing on the Needles headland was carried out until the site – like the British space programme soon afterwards – was abandoned in the 1970s. It is now a ghostly, incongruous promenade to nowhere on the edge of the cliffs.

Above left: **THE NEEDLES, THE LIGHTHOUSE c1955** N7011p

Below left: **THE NEEDLES 1890** 26176

SELSEY

THE QUIET little seaside town of Selsey was once part of a small island. During the reign of William the Conqueror, Selsey was a larger town than today, with many important buildings and a cathedral built by St Wilfrid, who taught the local townsfolk to fish. However, much of it has been engulfed by the sea over the years. Today, Selsey is still almost entirely enclosed by water – the English Channel lies to the south-east and south-west, Pagham Harbour to the north-east, and a brook, known as the Broad Rife, to the north-west.

Right: **SELSEY, THE LIFEBOAT HOUSE 1930** 83449

The lifeboat station was established here in 1861. The lifeboat house, pier and slipway we see in 83449 (right) were replaced in 1960 by a larger version of the same design. The Lifeboat House is now a museum dedicated to the history and development of the RNLI.

The coastline is still eroding, and as each winter storm breaches the vulnerable unprotected beach, the sea threatens to make Selsey an island again.

THE TRAGIC LOSS OF THE 'ROYAL GEORGE' OFF SPITHEAD

The HMS 'Royal George' was renamed in honour of George II before she was launched in 1756. At 2,000 tons, she was the greatest warship of her time.

On 29 August 1782, while she was undergoing repair work at Spithead, she heeled over and began to take on water, which poured through her lower tier of gunports. More rapidly than anyone on board could take in, she capsized and sank with the loss of about 900 lives, including 300 women and 60 children who were visitors to the ship. An account of the disaster is given in Frederick Whymper's 'The Sea':

'A little child was almost miraculously preserved by a sheep, which swam some time, and with which he had doubtless been playing on deck. He held it by the fleece till rescued by a gentleman in a wherry. His father and mother were both drowned, and the poor little fellow did not even know their names; all that he knew was that his own name was Jack. His preserver provided for him.

One of the survivors, who got through a porthole, looked back and saw the opening 'as full of heads as it could cram, all trying to get out. I caught hold of the best bower-anchor, which was just above me, to prevent falling back again into the porthole, and seizing hold of a woman who was trying to get out of the same porthole, I dragged her out.' The same writer says that he saw 'all the heads drop back again in at the porthole, for the ship had got so much on her larboard side that the starboard portholes were as upright as if the men had tried to get out of the top of a chimney.'

A local fisherman reported that 'in a few days after the 'Royal George' sank, bodies would come up, thirty or forty at a time. A corpse would rise so suddenly as to frighten anyone ... [I] saw them towed into Portsmouth harbour, in their mutilated condition, in the same manner as rafts of floating timber.'

BOGNOR REGIS is fondly remembered for its sandy beaches, which are now more shingle than sand. Safe bathing and a host of traditional family attractions made Bognor a popular destination in the great days of British seaside holidays.

Queen Victoria referred to the place as 'dear little Bognor'. The suffix 'Regis' was added to the name of this seaside town in 1929 after George V spent some weeks recovering here following a major illness. Until the 1920s the bathing machines (22626, right) were ready for business at 6am with 'the conductor waiting' and were 'drawn (by a horse) to any depth required; at low water the bather may even go as far as the rocks; the ladies will find a female guide'. The most famous bathing machine attendant was Mary Wheatland who had her pitch with over a dozen machines occupying a prime site immediately west of the pier. She was a well-known character from the late Victorian years until the 1920s.

Rough seas were always popular with local photographers, and 25182b (below right) shows a spectacular sea crashing over the promenade to batter the Carlton Hotel.

BOGNOR REGIS

> ❝ *A quiet, mild, healthy watering-place, situate on a level in the face of the ever-restless Channel.* VICTORIAN GUIDEBOOK

Bognor was once the focus of ambitious plans to transform the once tiny settlement into a fashionable watering-place known as Hothamton, after Sir Richard Hotham. Sir Richard was a wealthy hatter who came here to recuperate in the 1780s. He saw the potential of the area as a seaside resort, bought land here, and began the development of what he hoped would be a fashionable town, including bathing facilities, terraces and crescents of smart houses, a hotel, and a home for himself. Visitors began to arrive in the 1790s, and no less a personage than the Duke of St Albans laid the foundation stone of a chapel for visitors in 1793. Sir Richard died in 1799, and somehow the new name of his resort never caught on.

Above: **BOGNOR REGIS, LOOKING NORTH-EAST FROM THE PIER 1890** 22626

Right: **BOGNOR REGIS, ROUGH SEAS BESIDE THE PIER 1890** 25182B

BRIGHTON

SHOREHAM'S POWERHOUSE

For years the harbour and sea have provided employment for many of Southwick's inhabitants, and in 1871 the increase in population at Southwick and Fishersgate was attributed to oyster-dredgers and other seafarers who resided there. The large shingle bank on the southern side of the harbour, formerly part of the parish of Lancing, became part of Southwick in c1900.

Southwick stands beside Shoreham Harbour, the point where the Adur emerges into the sea a mile and a half east of new Shoreham. The harbour is long and narrow, cut off from the sea by shingle spits. The west spit is occupied by the bungalows and inter-war houses of Shoreham Beach, and the east spit, nearer Southwick, is lined with warehouses. Here too stands the Shoreham B Power Station. Photograph S477072 (top) is dominated by the old power station; fed by coal barges, it dated from 1947–1948. Designed by G H Somerset, its two vast chimneys echoed Battersea Power Station in London. It used 15 million bricks and sat on over 6,000 reinforced concrete piles. It was demolished in the 1990s, and its successor (S477701) is a much lighter-looking building finished with a tall, elegant chimney – peregrines perch here today.

Top: **SOUTHWICK, THE HARBOUR c1965** S477072

Right: **SOUTHWICK, THE NEW POWER STATION 2003** S477701

> I like to go down on the beach among the fishing-boats, and to recline on the shingle by a smack when the wind comes gently from the west, and the low wave breaks but a few yards from my feet. I like the occasional passing scent of pitch: they are melting it close by. I confess I like tar: one's hands smell nice after touching ropes. It is more like home down on the beach here; the men are doing something real, sometimes there is the clink of a hammer; behind me there is a screen of brown net, in which rents are being repaired; a big rope yonder stretches as the horse goes round, and the heavy smack is drawn slowly up over the pebbles. The full curves of the rounded bows beside me are pleasant to the eye, as any curve is that recalls those of woman. Mastheads stand up against the sky, and a loose rope swings as the breeze strikes it; a veer of the wind brings a puff of smoke from the funnel of a cabin, where some one is cooking, but it is not disagreeable, like smoke from a house chimney-pot; another veer carries it away again, – depend upon it the simplest thing cooked there is nice. Shingle rattles as it is shovelled up for ballast – the sound of labour makes me more comfortably lazy. They are not in a hurry, nor 'chivy' over their work either; the tides rise and fall slowly, and they work in correspondence. No infernal fidget and fuss. Wonder how long it would take me to pitch a pebble so as to lodge on the top of that large brown pebble there? I try, once now and then.

RICHARD JEFFERIES, 'THE OPEN AIR' c1882

Left: **BRIGHTON, WEST PIER PAVILION FROM KINGS ROAD 1894** 33763

THE SEA bathing craze that overwhelmed genteel England in the 18th century probably began in Brighton – then the half-dilapidated fishing village of Brighthelmstone. The patronage of the Prince Regent catapulted the little village to the forefront of fashion, and it became the first seaside resort. The opening of the London to Brighton Railway in 1841 rapidly changed Brighton from a fashionable watering place into a centre of mass entertainment.

Piers allowed the visitor to obtain views which otherwise would be only possible from a boat, but without any of the attendant discomfort! The West Pier (33763, previous page and 48497, above) was designed by Eugenius Birch, who also designed Eastbourne's pier. Built between 1863 and 1866, it cost £30,000, and was one of the first piers built as an entertainment centre as well as a landing stage. The seaward end was widened in 1890 and the pavilion built; later in 1903 this was converted into a theatre. The central wind screen was also added in 1890. Pleasure boats were still available from the beach, as we can see from the photograph; these competed for trade with the paddle steamers. The 1896 storm that destroyed the Chain Pier badly damaged the West Pier, as picture B2085009 (opposite) shows, and the partly built Palace Pier.

> *It is a Piccadilly crowd by the sea – exactly the same style of people you meet in Piccadilly, but freer in dress, and particularly in hats.*
>
> RICHARD JEFFERIES, 'THE OPEN AIR' c1882

A walk to the end of the pier has been an essential ingredient in a Brighton holiday since the famous Chain Pier opened in 1823. This pier was designed as a landing stage for the cross-channel trade (Brighton to Dieppe was on the quickest route between London and Paris), but it was immediately popular with 'promenaders' who paid 2d or one guinea annually to walk the 13 ft wide, 1,154 ft long wooden deck. Brighton's Chain Pier was the first pleasure pier ever built, with kiosks contained in its towers and other attractions, including a camera obscura, at the shore end. It was completely destroyed in a storm on 4 December 1896.

Richard Jefferies described the art of promenading on the pier at Brighton in his book 'The Open Air':

'*Most people who go on the West Pier walk at once straight to the farthest part. This is the order and custom of pier promenading; you are to stalk along the deck till you reach the end, and there go round and round the band in a circle like a horse tethered to a pin, or else sit down and admire those who do go round and round. No one looks back at the gradually extending beach and the fine curve of the shore. No one lingers where the surf breaks – immediately above it – listening to the remorseful sigh of the dying wave as it sobs back to the sea.*'

Opposite: **BRIGHTON, WEST PIER 1902** 48497

Above: **BRIGHTON, THE PIER AFTER THE STORM c1896** B2085009

A PAVILION FIT FOR A PRINCE

A Lewes doctor, Richard Russell, published a treatise on the beneficial effects of drinking and bathing in salt water. It caught the mood of the times; Dr Russell moved to Brighthelmstone in 1754 to supervise his sea-water cures there. He publicised the little village, and some 30 years later the arrival of the Prince of Wales (later George IV) in Brighton glamorised it and secured its pre-eminence among resorts.

The prince developed his chief Brighton residence as the mock-oriental Royal Pavilion (B208018, below), and the town began to grow. The nucleus of the Pavilion was built in 1787 as a simple Georgian villa, but by 1821 it was transformed by Nash into the extravaganza we see today.

Queen Victoria found the pavilion not to her taste, and sold the redundant palace to Brighton Corporation for £50,000.

> *One would think St Paul's Cathedral had gone to Brighton and pupped.*
>
> SYDNEY SMITH (1771–1845)

BRIGHTON, THE PAVILION c1955 B208018

THE SEVEN SISTERS

EAST DEAN, BIRLING GAP, HOTEL BEACH c1960 E136035

CHALK CLIFFS, which run eastwards from the Seven Sisters to Beachy Head, dip to about 30 feet at the Birling Gap. Set in the magnificent chain of chalk cliffs, the hamlet of Birling Gap was an important landing place for smugglers in years gone by. For a long time East Dean, which is cupped in a hollow of the South Downs a little inland, was a haunt of smugglers and wreckers. Coastal erosion has always been a distinct problem hereabouts, counter-balanced by the silting up of other areas. The Birling Gap chalk has eroded back 20 yards in 30 years, and in 1999 the Beachy Head lighthouse was temporarily joined to the land when five thousand tons of chalk cliff fell.

There are ledges three hundred feet above, and from these now and then a jackdaw glides out and returns again to his place, where, when still and with folded wings, he is but a speck of black. A spire of chalk still higher stands out from the wall, but the rains have got behind it and will cut the crevice deeper and deeper into its foundation. Water, too, has carried the soil from under the turf at the summit over the verge, forming brown streaks … Another climb up from the sheep-path, and it is not far then to the terrible edge of that tremendous cliff which rises straighter than a ship's side out of the sea, six hundred feet above the detached rock below, where the limpets cling like rivet heads, and the sand rills run around it. But it is not possible to look down to it – the glance of necessity falls outwards, as a raindrop from the eaves is deflected by the wind, because it is the edge where the mould crumbles; the rootlets of the grass are exposed; the chalk is about to break away in flakes. You cannot lean over as over a parapet, lest such a flake should detach itself – lest a mere trifle should begin to fall, awakening a dread and dormant inclination to slide and finally plunge like it. Stand back; the sea there goes out and out, to the left and to the right, and how far is it to the blue overhead? The eye must stay here a long period, and drink in these distances, before it can adjust the measure, and know exactly what it sees.

RICHARD JEFFERIES c1880

BEACHY HEAD

❖ **The terrible edge of that tremendous cliff …where the limpets cling like rivet heads.** RICHARD JEFFERIES

BEACHY HEAD is the spot where the chalk range of the South Downs reaches the sea in magnificent chalk cliffs rearing almost vertically five hundred feet out of the sea. This view from the beach (64979p) looks out to the lighthouse, itself 153 feet high and yet reduced to the scale of a toy by the dramatic height of the cliffs.

It is amazing that this headland, notoriously dangerous and strewn with shipwrecks down the centuries, did not have any permanent lighthouse until the Belle Tout was erected on the cliff top in 1832. The lighthouse we see here replaced the Belle Tout; built between 1899 and 1902 on massive foundations of Cornish granite, it was constantly manned until 1983, and is now automated. Its distinctive red and white painted bands add a splash of colour at the foot of the friable chalk of the cliffs.

Above left: **SEAFORD, THE SEVEN SISTERS 1891** 28397
Above right: **BEACHY HEAD, THE LIGHTHOUSE 1912** 64979p

EASTBOURNE

EASTBOURNE, THE PIER 1910 62958t

Eastbourne – Empress of Watering Places

BEFORE about 1850 Eastbourne barely existed. Unlike most of the other south coast resorts, the 'Empress of Watering Places' developed late. This may seem odd, given its enormous physical advantages, but it comes down to land ownership (see box below). Nowadays the bustling town (often awash with French schoolchildren in the summer months as well as with other visitors) has a population of over 80,000 and has long swamped the four settlements from which it grew. Three of these, East Bourne, South Bourne and Sea Houses, stood along the Bourne stream, now largely underground, and the fourth, Meads, lay to the west.

In the early 1860s the Pier Company was formed, but infighting slowed the work. Eastbourne's pier, designed by Eugenius Birch, finally opened in 1872. In 1901 two grand salons were built midway along the structure. The theatre at the seaward end was built originally in 1888 and rebuilt in 1899, replete with a busy café and offices as well as a famous camera obscura. This was damaged by fire in 1970. The building is now a disco, bar and shop.

A DUCAL DETERRANT

One of the landowning families hereabouts was the Cavendishes, the family of the Dukes of Devonshire, whose principal seat is Chatsworth in Derbyshire. The Cavendishes acquired Compton Place and its park along with large acreages around it and, more importantly, much of the coastline. They kept Compton Place as a rural retreat where they could enjoy stimulating air and sea bathing. It is said that this desire for privacy held back the development of Eastbourne. There is a story that Decimus Burton, the great early 19th-century architect, arrived at Compton Place in 1833 to visit Lord Burlington (the Cavendish then in residence). Burton showed him plans for a resort to be called Burlington, but he was sent packing; instead he developed St Leonards further along the coast near Hastings. It was not until this Lord Burlington's grandson William inherited the title of Duke of Devonshire in 1858 that Eastbourne really got going.

Right: **HASTINGS, ECCLESBOURNE CLIFFS 1894** 34438

HASTINGS

WHEN Hastings and St Leonards are approached from the sea, their beauty is obvious. To the west of Hastings are the great cliffs of Ecclesbourne (34438, previous page), named after the eagles that perhaps once lived there; at over 600ft, they are the highest headlands on the Sussex coast, spectacular and dramatic. The coastal paths would have been used originally by customs officers seeking to curb the notorious smuggling gangs. Many local fishermen in past centuries involved themselves in 'the trade' as a way of supplementing their incomes. Even as late as 1831, a smuggling affray at Ecclesbourne led to the deaths of two men.

The fishermen's quarter of Hastings is seen at its picturesque best near the Stade, or landing place (H36021p, above). Unique buildings here are the tarred wood fishermen's huts (right), built for drying fishing nets and storing equipment. The fishermen had to pay ground rent, and therefore constructed these extraordinary buildings upwards to keep down costs. There are still over 40 of these tall thin weather-boarded gable-roofed net shops, but there were over 100 of them at the beginning of the 20th century. A fishermen's church, built in 1854 at a cost of £600, was used by seafarers before they undertook perilous journeys.

❝ *A bad shore for bathing, tho' there is always a summer company there.*

This town stands between two hills, and immediately upon the sea; but it is a bad shore for bathing, tho' there is always a summer company there. After walking the beach, we ascended the steep hill to the right, on whose summit are the poor remains of the castle built by William the Conqueror: in our way, and about its limits, searching many turf-traps set for wheatears, where the custom is to leave a penny for every caught bird you take away. Within the castle we seated ourselves for some time, delighted with the weather, the freshness of the sea-breeze and the cheerfulness of the scenery; till the shepherd came to survey his traps, when we paid him sevenpence for his capture of seven birds, whom we sat down instantly to pluck in preparation of our dinner spit; and it would have made others laugh to have seen us at our poulterer's work …

JOHN BYNG, 'RIDES ROUND BRITAIN' 1788 (EDITED D ADAMSON, FOLIO SOCIETY)

Above left: **HASTINGS, FROM EAST CLIFF 1891** 29039

Above right: **HASTINGS, THE BEACH AND THE CLIFF RAILWAY c1955** H36021p

❝ *The leafy, blossomy depths ... where on the famous Lovers' Seat one may sit on a rude oak bench and look out afar over the sea.* VICTORIAN GUIDEBOOK

The massive coastal landslides and deep glens between Hastings and Pett have been popular with tourists since the mid 19th century. The whole stretch of cliffs and glens provided cliff-top walks and wooded climbs and descents into secluded valleys, which were more easily accessed after 1902 by the East Hill Lift.

Victorians flocked to see the Lovers' Seat in the beauty spot of Fairlight Glen (22806, left). Tradition alleges that a naval lieutenant called Lamb trysted here with his sweetheart Miss Boys. Their relationship met with family disapproval, hence the secret meeting-place. The pair eventually married at St Clement Danes Church in London in 1786. The original seat was a long rock that tumbled away in a landslide. The Glen's Dripping Well was situated just below the famous Lovers' Seat, and was a favourite subject for both artist and photographer. Here the little stream cascades in a double waterfall over the two bands of hard sandstone rock, and has cut itself a narrow gorge within the wider glen.

Left: **HASTINGS, FAIRLIGHT GLEN, LOVERS' SEAT 1890** 22806

SOUTHERN BRITAIN'S SEA DEFENCES

The south coast of England was border country, constantly under the threat of raids or invasion from the Continent until the 19th century. Each age left its military residue, including the Iron Age hill-fort on Seaford Head, the Roman Saxon Shore fortress of Pevensey, and various Norman and later castles. Fear of French invasion led Henry VIII to build Camber Castle around 1540. The Napoleonic threat led to the building of a chain of 103 circular forts called Martello towers along the south-east coast between 1805 and 1810. Named after a formidable fortification on Martella Point, Corsica, these brick towers were massively strong; each tower was equipped with a 24-pounder cannon with a range of 1000 yards and manned by one officer and 24 men.

Right: **HASTINGS, A MARTELLO TOWER c1880** H36302

RYE, on the River Rother and now a few miles from the sea, was already a borough before the Domesday Survey, and King Stephen set up a mint here in 1141. By the 12th century Rye and Winchelsea had become so prosperous and important that they were invited to join the influential Cinque Ports; they were given Head Port status, having complete equality in all respects with the original five.

Today the River Rother takes a long curving course to the south east of the town and joins the open sea nearly three miles away (R77102, left). Despite all the reclamation of the marshland, Rye was fortunate that the Rother did not entirely desert her. The Quay is the historic seafaring mercantile area of the town (R77005, below). In the past, barges would sail up to Rye with cargoes of timber from the Baltic and coal from the Tyne. Reports from the late 19th century show that at least 50 fishing vessels were registered as using Rye harbour, situated some two miles south of Rye at the narrow and awkward mouth of the Rother. With the volume of tidal waters ever decreasing, nowadays a cargo of any type rarely comes up the River Rother, other than small individual fishing craft.

Left: **RYE, ROMNEY MARSHES c1955** R77102

Below left: **RYE, FROM FINDENS VIEWS OF THE PORTS, HARBOURS & WATERING PLACES OF GREAT BRITAIN 1841**

Below right: **RYE, THE HARBOUR c1955** R77005

❛ *The tidal river, on the left, wanders away to Rye Harbour and its bar, where the black fishing-boats, half the time at lop-sided rest in the mud, make a cluster of slanting spears against the sky. When the river is full we are proud of its wide light and many curves; when it is empty we call it, for vague reasons, 'rather Dutch'.*

HENRY JAMES, 'ENGLISH HOURS' 1905

HYTHE

THE Romney, Hythe & Dymchurch Railway is said to be the world's smallest public railway service. The 15-inch gauge line opened in 1927, and was the brainchild of Henry Greenly, Captain J E P Howey and Louis Zborowski. From Hythe to New Romney the line is double-tracked, so trains travelling in the opposite directions can pass each other. However, beyond New Romney the line is a single track to Dungeness with a passing place at Romney Sands. It is still running today, and serves both as a novelty for holidaymakers and as a commuter train for local schoolchildren.

At this time, nearby Dymchurch was a tranquil place; it attracted the author Edith Nesbit, who wrote 'The Railway Children'. Dymchurch's other literary son was Russell Thorndike; he penned the 'Dr Syn' series of novels, concerning the activities of Romney Marsh smugglers.

❝ *... Let nobody with corns come to Pavilionstone [Folkestone], for there are breakneck flights of ragged steps, connecting the principal streets by back-ways, which will cripple that visitor in half an hour.* CHARLES DICKENS, 'OUT OF TOWN' c1853

FOLKESTONE

FOLKESTONE developed as a resort when the railway arrived from London in 1843. The town was generally regarded as a rather superior, exclusive resort for middle-class visitors. Charles Dickens walked here while writing the opening chapters of 'Little Dorrit' in 1855. In Edwardian times, fashionably clad visitors took the air along the mile-long greensward of the Leas on top of the cliffs.

In 65007 (right), we see the impressive undercliff before the dramatic landslip of 1915, which altered the look of the cliffs nearest the camera, and swept away the idyllic pond near Warren Halt station. The station itself has now gone, although there is still a halt here for railway company staff.

Alive, alive o! Here's your fine cockles and mussels! Here they are! Only twopence a quart!

NOWADAYS, we tend to dress down for a day at the seaside in T-shirts and jeans, flip-flops and deck shoes. But when young east-enders went out on a Sunday outing to Folkestone in the 1960s (F35154), they very definitely dressed up. Bright prints, stylish bags and stilettos spoke of elegance rather than Essex. For men, a suit was still the prerequisite of formality, but it could be set off by a nonchalant slouch and greased, coiffed hair.

Opposite above: **FOLKESTONE, FROM THE AIR 1931** AF35415

Opposite below: **FOLKESTONE, WARREN HALT STATION AND ZIGZAG PATH 1912** 65007

Above: **FOLKESTONE, A COCKLES AND WHELKS STALL c1965** F35154p

❝ *What is that object that lies on yonder stretch of sand, over which the shallow water ripples, washing the sand around it and presently leaving it dry? It looks like a stone; but there is a fine scarlet knob on it, which all of a sudden has disappeared. Let us watch the movement of the receding wave, and run out to it. It is a fine example of the great spinous cockle for which all these sandy beaches that form the bottom of the great sea-bed are celebrated … They gather them in baskets and panniers, and after cleansing them a few hours in cold spring-water, fry the animals in a batter made of crumbs of bread. The creatures have not changed their habits nor their habitats, for they are still to be seen in the old spots just as they were a century ago; nor have they lost their reputation; they are, indeed, promoted to the gratification of more refined palates now, for the cottagers, knowing on which side their bread is buttered, collect the sapid cockles for the fashionable [visitors] and content themselves with the humbler and smaller species … Hundreds of men, women, and children may be seen plodding and groping over the sinking surface, with naked feet and bent backs, picking up the shell-fish by thousands, to be boiled and eaten for home consumption, or to be cried through the lanes and alleys of the neighbouring towns by stentorian boys who vociferate all day long, ' Here's your fine cockles, here! Here they are! Here they are! Twopence a quart!'*

FREDERICK WHYMPER, 'THE SEA' c1885

THE PORT of Dover, just 21 miles from the French coast, has always provided a convenient link from Europe to London and beyond. It has been a landing point since Roman times, but its importance grew with the building of the railways and the cross-channel ferries between Dover and Calais. Dover was designated a naval base and coaling station (48058, opposite). By 1914 the harbour covered 610 acres, parts of which were still 30ft deep at low water.

Perched on a lofty hill behind the beach (25699, left) stands one of the very finest fortresses in England. Dover Castle dominates the town and harbour below, with the top of the keep standing 465ft above sea level. The castle and the curtain wall were built by Henry II in the 12th century at a cost of £7000, but the first fortifications were constructed by King Harold in 1064. Further reinforcements were made over succeeding centuries, until it was regarded as impregnable.

After the Second World War, with the popularity of private car ownership and with the introduction of package tours and group travel, Dover expanded its port facilities. The large roll-on roll-off ferries made Dover one of Europe's busiest ports (D50069, below).

❝ *... Much bluster'd and buffeted by wind over the exposed hills, we came (leaving Shakespeare's Cliff at a small distance to our right) within sight of Dover Castle; and soon into the town of Dover, to the York Hotel; where, amidst noise and racket, we procured a mean dirty parlour for ourselves, and a kind of ship-hold for our horses. Bad specimen this, to the French, of English comforts! Bread and wine not to be endured; with a nasty brown fricassee and old tough partridges! A room fill'd with wind and ships' stinks!!*

JOHN BYNG, 'RIDES ROUND BRITAIN' 1790 (EDITED D ADAMSON, FOLIO SOCIETY)

Above left:
DOVER, THE BEACH 1890
25699

Above right: **THE ARMS OF THE TOWN OF DOVER**

Right:
DOVER, THE CAR FERRY TERMINAL c1965 D50069

Opposite top:
DOVER, ADMIRALTY PIER 1901
48058

Opposite below:
DOVER, SHAKESPEARE CLIFF 1908 60413

DOVER

'Stand still – how fearful
And dizzy 'tis, to cast one's eye so low!'

One of the best views of Dover Castle is gained from the western heights, the opposite boundary of the harbour. These heights are more lofty than the cliff on which the castle stands, and a deep valley divides them from Hay, or Shakespeare's Cliff – the character Gloucester pictures it dramatically in Shakespeare's 'King Lear':

'How fearful/And dizzy 'tis to cast one's eyes so low!/The crows and choughs, that wing the midway air/Show scarce so gross as beetles …/The fishermen, that walk upon the beach,/Appear like mice …'

How far this cliff has been correctly identified is uncertain; and the famous description can hardly have been designed as a strict copy from nature.

WILLIAM SHAKESPEARE
(1564–1616)

CAPTAIN WEBB'S HEROIC CHANNEL SWIM

Captain Matthew Webb was the son of a country surgeon. He swam the Channel at his second attempt in 1875, when he was just 26, starting at St Margaret's Bay.

Early on in his swim the sea was calm, and there was not a breath of wind. He was accompanied by two small rowing-boats. At 9pm he complained of being stung by a jelly-fish. Owing to the phosphorescent state of the sea, he was sometimes almost surrounded with a glow of light. At 2am next morning he was showing signs of fatigue, and a life-line was tied round him in case of accident. By 9am he was within a mile of the shore at Calais, but two hours previously a strong breeze had risen, and the sea, which had hitherto been like a sheet of glass, was running high, with crested waves. Webb was evidently fearfully exhausted. The tide was running strongly away from the shore, and he was battling against double odds when he was least fit for it. By 9.45 he was only half a mile from the beach. Would he ever reach it?

Just as the now utterly exhausted swimmer was beginning bitterly to think that failure even at this point was possible, a steamboat put off from Calais, and her commander placed her in such a position that she acted as a kind of breakwater - the sea was running so high that it nearly swamped the boats accompanying him. One last struggling exertion and he touched ground, so weak that he could not stand. A couple of men instantly went to his assistance, and he was able to walk slowly ashore. He had been in the water for twenty-one and three-quarter hours.

'I can only say', said Captain Webb, 'that the moment when I touched the Calais sands, and felt the French soil beneath my feet, is one which I shall never forget, were I to live for a hundred years. I was terribly exhausted at the time, and during the last two or three hours I began to think that, after all, I should fail. On the following day, after I had had a good night's rest, I did not feel very much the worse for what I had undergone. I had a peculiar sensation in my limbs, somewhat similar to that which is often felt after the first week of the cricket season; and it was a week before I could wear a shirt-collar, owing to a red raw rim at the back of my neck, caused by being obliged to keep my head back for so long a period; for, it must be remembered, I was in the water for very nearly twenty-two hours'.

ST MARGARET'S BAY

THIS white-painted Victorian lighthouse (44901, below), standing 300ft above the sea below, housed a two-ton turntable operating the revolving light. The lighthouse was built in 1843, and for a further 90 years after this photograph was taken, it offered both a warning and guidance for ships passing north along the white cliffs, and for those heading for Dover harbour to the south, to avoid the Goodwin Sands.

A small community developed both as a bathing resort and as a residential quarter in the closing years of the 19th century at the foot of the white cliffs at St Margaret's Bay. The adjoining sandy beach has been the starting point for generations of Channel swimmers since the days of Captain Matthew Webb's successful feat in 1875. The popular composer Noel Coward later owned one of the small houses here.

Top: **ST MARGARET'S BAY, THE BEACH 1924** 76102

Above: **ST MARGARET'S BAY, LOW LIGHT 1900** 44901

❛ *Time has only mouldered the several parts, if not into beauty, yet into such masses of quaint and harmonious colouring as may well delight the visitor.* VICTORIAN GUIDEBOOK

SANDWICH

SANDWICH, now lying inland, was once a thriving port on the River Stour. In medieval times it was a key member of the Cinque Ports; it vied with Hastings as the most illustrious of the five coastal towns. It became England's chief naval and military port, and King Henry VII was once able to call on Sandwich for 95 ships and 1500 sailors. In later centuries the port declined, but before the advent of the railway, ships still carried coal, salt, timber, cement and other bulk commodities. These days the river scene is quieter and more tranquil, the haunt of yachts and dinghies.

The Barbican (34212, above left) was one of a chain of blockhouses built in 1539 by Henry VIII as part of his coastal defences. Fine flint and stone chequers decorate the base. Once known as Daveysgate, it later became the residence of the keepers of the toll bridge. From 1290 this was the site of a ferry across the Stour. In 1757 a wooden drawbridge was built, which became unsafe; it was replaced in 1839 by a swing bridge to permit river-borne traffic to proceed up river. This in turn was replaced by the existing bridge in 1891.

Top: **SANDWICH, THE BARBICAN AND THE BRIDGE 1894** 34212

Above: **SANDWICH, THE RIVER 1924** 76227

HARSH JUSTICE OF THE OLD CUSTUMAL

Female criminals were drowned in the Guestling, a brook which falls into the Stour above the town. Stouter thieves were buried alive in the 'thief downs', or 'dunes', near the same stream. These are provisions of the old Custumal of Sandwich, first written down in 1301. The Cinque Ports were essentially towns of sailors, who fought not only with the king's enemies, but between themselves. Yet their fierce and daring character is said to have been barely subdued by these severe ordinances.

PEGWELL BAY

The sky was without a cloud; there were flower-pots and turf before them; the sea, from the foot of the cliff, stretching away as far as the eye could discern anything at all; vessels in the distance with sails as white, and as small, as nicely-got-up cambric handkerchiefs. The shrimps were delightful, the ale better, and the captain even more pleasant than either ... And then they went down the steep wooden steps a little further on, which led to the bottom of the cliff; and looked at the crabs, and the seaweed, and the eels, till it was more than fully time to go back to Ramsgate again.

CHARLES DICKENS, 'SKETCHES BY BOZ' 1836

Above right: **PEGWELL, THE DANISH VIKING SHIP 'HUGIN' c1955** P20023

Above left: **CAVES AT PEGWELL**

SITUATED at the southernmost part of the Isle of Thanet, Pegwell Bay is surrounded by cliffs on the north and marshes to the south. They make pleasant walking, though they have become more built-up in recent years. The bay itself, an expanse of salt marsh and sand, has become the domain of ornithologists and bait diggers. The coastline of cliff, estuary, dune and marsh is now a nature reserve. In 1968 Pegwell Bay became a hoverport with a cross-channel service. With the demise of the hovercraft service, a noisy go-kart circuit was established.

The replica Viking ship, the 'Hugin' (P20023, above), was built in Denmark in 1949; in that year 50 Danish men sailed her from Denmark to commemorate the 1500th anniversary of the arrival of the legendary Hengist and his brother Horsa, Saxon chiefs, who with a band of warriors landed at nearby Ebbsfleet. Hengist was to become the first Saxon king of Kent.

The coast near Pegwell has seen some history – if legend is to be believed! It is said that in AD 449 Hengist and Horsa brought the first Saxon settlers to nearby Ebbsfleet. They came to fight for the British king Vortigern against the marauding Picts. A couple of decades later, according to Geoffrey of Monmouth (who was writing in 1136), King Arthur fought his adversary Modred on this shore. Then in 597 St Augustine came, sent by the Pope to convert the pagans of Kent. A stone memorial to the arrival of St Augustine was erected in 1884 slightly inland from the bay.

RAMSGATE was once a small fishing port, but it came into prominence with the building of the great stone harbour in 1749 as a refuge for shipping from the dangers of the Goodwin Sands. In Tudor times Ramsgate had developed links with Ostend and the Baltic, and in the 19th century it became a 'Royal Harbour'. Recently its passenger ferries have faced competition from Dover and the Channel Tunnel, but it still runs freight services.

By the beginning of the 20th century, steam-powered drifters and trawlers were well-established in the UK fishing fleets. However, as we can see here (58287p), sail would linger on in some areas for some time to come. In 1903 there were still 138 sailing smacks registered at Ramsgate.

RAMSGATE

The safe haven of the harbour at Ramsgate, whch we see in the peaceful photograph above, was one that seafarers often longed to see as they headed down the Channel. They dreaded the onslaught of bad weather and the danger to their lives caused by the treacherous Goodwin sands, just a few miles out to sea from Ramsgate. Frederick Whymper describes the sailor's nightmare:

These sands, so feared by mariners, are ten miles in length. When the tide recedes the sand is firm and safe, but when the sea permeates it, the mass becomes pulpy, treacherous, and constantly shifting. Three light vessels mark the most dangerous points ... It was a terrible sight to see a ship of 80 guns and 600 men [running aground]. She had cut away her masts, she had neither anchor nor cable ... The cries of the crew terrified us in such a manner, that I think we were half dead with the horror of it. And they knew, as well as we that saw her, that they drove by the tempest directly for the Goodwin, where they could expect nothing but destruction.

FREDERICK WHYMPER, 'THE SEA' c1885

BROADSTAIRS

BROADSTAIRS, THE HARBOUR 1897 39591

THE KENT resorts were subject to the class distinctions of the Victorian age. Margate had developed a rather vulgar, working-class image. This allowed Broadstairs to cater predominantly for an affluent middle class. In 39591 (left), rows of bathing machines along the shoreline and in front of the low white cliffs demonstrate the popularity, and prevailing prudery, of immersion in sea-water among the Victorian visitors. The shallow-draught Thames sailing barge aground on the sands dominates this photograph, taken from the foot of the Elizabethan stone jetty. The cumbersome leeboards, which helped the vessel to maintain a course, are clearly visible amidships.

The 'rare good sands', as Charles Dickens described them, still form the focal point of this old-fashioned watering place where 'Nicholas Nickleby', 'David Copperfield', 'The Old Curiosity Shop', and 'Barnaby Rudge' were all written by him in houses overlooking the beach. A fishing hamlet in 1837 when he first visited, it quickly expanded into the quiet family resort it remains today.

Upon the shore – the fishing-boats in the tiny harbour are all stranded in the mud – our two colliers (our watering-place has a maritime trade employing that amount of shipping) have not an inch of water within a quarter of a mile of them, and turn, exhausted, on their sides, like faint fish of an antediluvian species. Rusty cables and chains, ropes and rings, undermost parts of posts and piles and confused timber defences against the waves, lie strewn about, in a brown litter of tangled seaweed and fallen cliff which looks as if a family of giants had been making tea here for ages, and had observed an untidy custom of throwing their tea-leaves on the shore … In truth, our watering-place itself has been left somewhat high and dry by the tide of years. Concerned as we are for its honour, we must reluctantly admit that the time when this pretty little semicircular sweep of houses, tapering off at the end of the wooden pier into a point in the sea, was a gay place, and when the lighthouse overlooking it shone at daybreak on company dispersing from public balls, is but dimly traditional now.

CHARLES DICKENS, 'OUR WATERING PLACE' 1851

MARGATE, NEWGATE GAP BRIDGE 1890 27442

MARGATE, THE JETTY 1908 60367

MARGATE

KENT'S earliest seaside resort was Margate, popular in the 1730s through its easy direct access by boat from London. Thanks to cheap rail and paddle-steamer fares in the 19th century, it became a magnet for Cockney day trippers, and soon acquired an image of vulgarity. Its nine miles of sandy beaches made it a mecca for holidaymakers. The fully-fledged seaside pier (60367) was known as the jetty, while the harbour wall was called the pier by locals! It is claimed that Margate had a landing jetty as far back as 1800.

Below Newgate Gap Bridge (27442, left), on the right-hand side, was Charlotte Pettman's original sea water baths; she also claimed that her bathing machines were superior to any others. Donkeys could be hired here for strolls along the sands.

EUGENIUS BIRCH'S PIONEERING IRON JETTY

Margate probably had a jetty of some kind as long ago as the end of the 18th century; the jetty we see in 60367 was the first iron pier, which opened in 1855. The jetty was also renowned for being the first to be designed by the famous pier engineer Eugenius Birch. Extensions were made between 1875 and 1878, when the octagonal pier head and pavilion were added. In 1897 the pier company recorded a profit of £1,689. Like Brighton Chain Pier, Margate Jetty once had a camera obscura. Alas, the jetty was virtually destroyed by a storm on 11 January 1978, after having closed two years earlier on safety grounds. Part of the isolated pier head still survives as a rusting tangle.

CHATHAM is famous in the annals of English seafaring history. It was first developed as a safe anchorage in Tudor times. Later, a large dockyard and arsenal were established. In the 1700s the dockyard was quite small, compared with its later size. Then, it was described as being 'on the south side of the River Medway, 15 miles from the entrance of it', where the river was 'so crooked that there is [sic] only six points of the compass for a wind with which ships of the line can sail down and 10 to sail up, and that only for a few days during the spring tides.'

Brompton Barracks (34041, right) were built in 1804–06, originally for artillerymen; they became the headquarters of the Royal Engineers when the School of Military Engineering was founded there in 1812. Although wholly in Gillingham, it was known as the Chatham School until 1962, when Queen Elizabeth II granted it the 'Royal' title. In this picture the men on parade wear the uniform of the period with the spiked helmet, and the horse-drawn vehicle standing beside the post box outside the pillared portico may await an officer leaving the building.

Charles Dickens, in 'The Pickwick Papers' (the first instalment was published in 1836), wrote that the principal productions of the Medway Towns of Strood, Rochester, Chatham and Brompton (part of Gillingham) appeared to be soldiers, sailors, chalk, shrimps, officers and dockyardmen, and that the commodities chiefly exposed for sale in the public streets were marine stores, hardbake (toffee), apples, flatfish and oysters. He wrote of the lively and animated appearance of the streets, and he made Mr Pickwick observe that 'the smell which pervades the streets must be exceedingly delicious to those who are extremely fond of smoking.'

CHATHAM

6 *I walk'd away thro' Chatham, and to the barracks, where in grief I peep'd at the East Indian recruits, poor fellows torn away from their native climate (and what to me appears all happiness), never, never to return. The Marines and their barracks appear'd to be in excellent order.*

At the dockyard gate my name being ask'd, and permission granted, I made the full survey of all the cable houses, anchorage, timber yards etc., etc., etc. Nor should I have return'd so soon, had not languor and ill feels sent me back.

JOHN BYNG, 'RIDES ROUND BRITAIN' 1790
(EDITED D ADAMSON, FOLIO SOCIETY)

Above: **BROMPTON, THE RE BARRACKS 1894** 34041

Left: **CHATHAM DOCKYARD IN THE LATE 1700s**

Founded by the Romans where Watling Street bridged the Medway, Rochester has been important for nearly 2,000 years. The cathedral, founded in AD 604, is second only to Canterbury in age. It was rebuilt by the Normans, who also built the castle (59883, below). The town retains its ancient High Street, with many fine buildings including College Gate. Charles Dickens knew the city well.

The River Medway traditionally separates the Men of Kent on its east side from the Kentish Men on the west, but bridges unite the two. There has been a bridge at Rochester since Roman times, connecting Rochester and Chatham with cross-Medway Strood, but in 1914 a new road-rail bridge was built on top of the one built in 1856 (we see the 1856 bridge in 22190, left), which was then removed. That bridge was joined in the late 1960s by the dual carriageway box-girder road bridge and footway alongside, built with money from the Bridge Trust of 1391.

ROCHESTER

ROCHESTER, THE VIEW FROM THE CASTLE 1889 22190

ROCHESTER, THE CASTLE GROUNDS 1908 59883p

In 59883 (left) we see the massive Norman keep of Rochester Castle. This fine example of a Norman castle was built by William the Conqueror (1080–1126) in a strategic position to control the crossing point over the Medway. The castle has walls 20ft thick; the stone keep was added in 1127, the highest in the country. After several sieges the castle declined in importance, and only narrowly escaped total demolition in the 18th century.

GRAVESEND, THE WESTERN PROMENADE 1902 49042

GRAVESEND

NOW GREATLY expanded inland, the core of this ancient port, the gateway to the English Channel and the North Sea, is still recognisable around the two piers and the Georgian parish church. In 49042 (above) the photographer looks east towards the town piers and jetties – this view is much changed today.

At Gravesend Reach, the River Thames narrows on its way from the North Sea to London Bridge, another 26 miles upstream. Its situation opposite the Essex port of Tilbury led to its becoming the pilot station for the Port of London – at the time of this photograph still the world's busiest port. The Thames barges moored on the left, and the local bawley boats which trawled for shrimps in the estuary, competed with the uninterrupted views of the ships of all nationalities passing on the river as a source of immense interest for visitors when Gravesend became a popular resort during the Victorian era.

GRAYS

The steamers, which are constantly smoking their pipes up and down the Thames, offer much the most agreeable mode of getting to London. At least, it might be exceedingly agreeable, except for the myriad floating particles of soot from the stove-pipe, and the heavy heat of midsummer sunshine on the unsheltered deck, or the chill, misty air draught of a cloudy day, and the spiteful little showers of rain that may spatter down upon you at any moment, whatever the promise of the sky; besides which there is some slight inconvenience from the inexhaustible throng of passengers, who scarcely allow you standing-room.

NATHANIEL HAWTHORNE,
'OUR OLD HOME' c1860

ALONG the Thames estuary there were several industrial developments which increased in importance as the years went by. Long before Grays was an industrial town, it was a port, used by coastal traffic from London. Pepys, for instance, says that he once took a wherry to Grays and 'bought a great deal of fine fish'. Brick making, employing the fine brick earth around Grays, was an important industry that helped build Victorian London, but recently has been unable to compete with mass-produced products.

The lightship (G85034, below) is the 'Gull'. Built of sturdy oak timbers in 1860, she did sterling service as a warning and navigation-mark until 1946. She is over 90ft long and 21ft broad. She was bought by the Thurrock Essex & Grays Yacht Club and used as a club house for a while; she was then sold, but the Port of London Authority would not allow her to be moved, and she now lies derelict. However, there are moves afoot in Thurrock for her to be restored.

Below: **GRAYS, THE LIGHTSHIP c1955** G85034

CANVEY ISLAND, THORNEY BAY BEACH CAMP c1955 C237304

CANVEY ISLAND

THORNEY BAY has a surprisingly sandy beach. The holiday village started life as a campsite. By the 1950s its amenities included a café, an open-air theatre, and a reception building. There was also a boating-pool, popular with locals and visitors, and a number of kiosks selling ice-cream and buckets and spades.

'A week in Canvey will do you more good than a fortnight elsewhere', ran an early slogan. By the 1920s, up to 50,000 day trippers were visiting the island on a bank holiday, and it was still a popular destination when photograph C237304 was taken. Canvey had initially been marketed as a holiday-haven for East Londoners.

CANVEY ISLAND, THE BEACH c1955 C237064

SOUTHEND-ON-SEA

SOUTHEND-ON-SEA, THE PIER 1898 41377

The longest seaside pier in the world (41377), Southend's first pier lasted from 1830 to 1887. A new pier opened on 24 August 1890. Extensions were opened eight years later which took its length to a record-breaking 7,080 feet; an electric railway took people to the pier head. Southend Pier had become so popular that the rail track was doubled in 1929, and the Prince George steamer extension was built. After the war a new electric train was installed, but by 1960, visitor numbers had halved from the 6 million of the pier's post-war peak. Twenty years later, local councillors planned closure, but a last-minute rescue ensured its future. A new pier railway was opened in 1986 by Princess Anne. Southend was the favourite pier of Sir John Betjeman, first President of the National Piers Society.

SHOEBURYNESS

SOUTHEND'S initial aim had been to attract 'persons of the first rank and fashion' and 'the genteelest company'. However, it was opened up once and for all by the railway, and Southend became the favourite resort of holidaymakers from London's east end. In 41382 we see pleasure boats lined up to collect trippers for the obligatory sail down the estuary – the picture was taken from the pier. The seafront architecture has changed little, but the shop blinds have vanished to make way for amusement arcades.

THE PIER AT WAR

At the beginning of the Second World War the Royal Navy requisitioned Southend's pier and renamed it HMS 'Leigh'. They installed pill boxes and anti-aircraft guns, and the forces based there were equipped to drop depth charges on to marauding enemy submarines. However, there was only a single attack of any significance - a strafing by the Luftwaffe. Convoys embarked from the pier head, and the pier railway was used to transport injured and wounded soldiers from ships to hospitals inland.

❛ This popular resort can be heartily commended to all, but especially to Londoners. It is reached in little more than an hour by the excellent trains of the Great Eastern Railway. It is quite remarkable to see the crowds of Londoners poured into Southend by steamboat and excursion train on a fine summer's day. The coast here is very shallow, and the tide retires nearly a mile from the shore at low water. The old town stretches along the shore eastwards from the pier in a line of shops and small houses inhabited by the boatmen and fishermen.

VICTORIAN GUIDEBOOK

Above: **SOUTHEND-ON-SEA, MARINE PARADE 1898** 41382

SHOEBURYNESS, SHOEBURY HALL FARM CAMP c1955 S275026

THE NAME 'Shoeburyness' means 'encampment on the shoe-shaped piece of land'. The earthwork in question was thrown up in 894 by Haesten, a 'lusty and terrifying' Danish chieftain who had just been routed at Benfleet by King Alfred. The sea and the barracks have obliterated most of it, though Rampart Street marks its north-east side.

The cornerstones here are brickworks, railways, farming, and the military. The Royal Artillery Garrison and School of Gunnery first came here in the mid 19th century, and although the last regiment served here in 1975, a limited presence was maintained until 1998.

During the depression of the 1930s, efforts were made to turn Shoeburyness into a tourist resort in order to combat local unemployment. It was 'one of the healthiest resorts in England'. Holidaymakers are still welcomed here today: there are still beach-huts and a café, though other features such as a putting-green and a boating-lake have gone. The concept of the caravan-park was born in the post-war years. This particular one (S275026) was especially popular with Londoners. When it closed in 1974, there were 375 caravans and a shop on the site. The camp was known for its 'select' standards and friendly atmosphere. There is housing here now.

BURNHAM-ON-CROUCH

MALDON, THE SHORE 1921 70276p

BURNHAM-ON-CROUCH, THE RIVER c1965 B325129

ALTHOUGH much of Burnham's revenue came from oysters, boat building, and sail making, it was also an important wool port in the heyday of East Anglia's wool trade. Corn and coal were transported via the quay. The buildings along the quay still have a stateliness about them, and are painted in sunny colours - reds, yellows, and whites. The town is now a major yachting centre, too, and the home of the Royal Corinthian Yacht Club. In photograph B325129 we see a club race, with dinghies beating down wind in a fair breeze.

A GREAT battle took place in Maldon in 991: the Vikings invaded the mainland after crossing a causeway that can still be seen at low tide.

It is true that the county's waterfront was not suited to large ports, because, with the exception of Harwich, there are no natural harbours. Yet Maldon – its estuary connected to Chelmsford by a canal – was once full of flourmills, maltings, ropewalks and boatyards. It was a significant port, too, handling corn, coal, chalk and hay.

SPRITTIES AND STUMPIES – TRADITIONAL WORK HORSES OF THE THAMES

The rich Essex farmland, famed for its wheat, along with the many rivers, creeks and tidal inlets, combined to make ideal locations for big corn mills. These were no local mills, catering for the immediate community, but industrial-scale mills; some were ordinary water mills, and many were tide mills. The grain and flour were transported, as were other Essex commodities – bricks, hay, lime, to name but three – by the Thames sailing barges. There are several types of these superb flat-bottomed boats with their big tan sails (the 'spritty' – a spritsail barge – and the 'stumpie', for example), but all were excellent workhorses generally worked along the creeks and rivers and along the coast to the Thames estuary. They were extremely seaworthy, and many made regular North Sea or Channel crossings. Part of the fleet has been converted to pleasure use and is based at Maldon. Races are keenly contested, just as they were in the barges' working days.

MALDON

MALDON, THE PROMENADE 1909 62098

Here we see Maldon's famous promenade – now Promenade Park – with a fine array of fishing boats and the tower of St Mary's church, with its landmark little white spire, in the background, which doubled as a seamark for the mariners. Today, the adjacent leisure area has been developed. A thin veil of mist shrouds the skyline buildings. A fishing ketch, having travelled the 15 or so miles along the River Blackwater from the sea, gently eases to port to take a yacht safely astern, down her starboard side.

ST OSYTH

ST OSYTH, THE CREEK 1912 64261

Lovers of sport … often return with an Essex ague on their backs

In this inlet of the sea is Osey, or Osyth Island, commonly called Oosy Island, so well known by our London men of pleasure for the infinite number of wild fowl, that is to say, duck, mallard, teal, and widgeon, of which there are such vast flights, that they tell us the island, namely the creek, seems covered with them at certain times of the year, and they go from London on purpose for the pleasure of shooting; and, indeed, often come home very well laden with game. But it must be remembered too that those gentlemen who are such lovers of the sport, and go so far for it, often return with an Essex ague on their backs, which they find a heavier load than the fowls they have shot.

DANIEL DEFOE, 'JOURNEY THROUGH THE EASTERN COUNTIES OF ENGLAND' 1722

PREVIOUSLY known as Chich, the village of St Osyth (generally pronounced 'Toosey') is built close to St Osyth's creek, and takes its name from an East Anglian princess. She established a nunnery here; in 653 it was sacked by the Danes, and Osyth was beheaded. It is said that a holy well gushed forth where her head hit the ground. St Osyth Priory, founded in 1118, supposedly occupies the nunnery's site.

St Osyth once had thriving lime-kilns and maltings, as well as wharves and a tide-mill. There was already a corn-mill here in 1413. Its successor, pictured in 64261 (opposite), was built c1730, but was damaged by the weather and by a mine during the Second World War. It finally collapsed in the 1960s. The boat is a 'stackie' – a Thames barge – loaded up with hay for the London market.

Above: **ST OSYTH, THE FERRY, POINT CLEAR BAY c1955** S38055p

AGAINST THE THREAT OF INVASION

ST OSYTH, THE MARTELLO TOWER AT POINT CLEAR BAY c1960 S38050

Martello towers were built in the time of Napoleon to guard the coast. The Martello tower in photograph S38050 has been converted into a shop – how are the mighty fallen! The Ferry Boat Inn opposite is named after the ferry boat we see in S38055.

The towers … were from about 35 feet to 40 feet high: the entrance to them was by a low door-way, about seven feet and a half from the ground; and admission was gained by means of a ladder, which was afterwards withdrawn into the interior. A high step of two feet led to the first floor of the tower, a room of about thirteen feet diameter, and with the walls about five feet thick. Round this room were loopholes in the walls, at such an elevation, that the men would be obliged to stand on benches in the event of their being required to oppose an attack of musketry. Those benches were also used as the sleeping-places of the garrison. On this floor there was a fire-place, and from the centre was a trap-door leading downwards to the ammunition and provision rooms. The second floor was ascended by similar means.

THE ILLUSTRATED LONDON NEWS 1851

JAYWICK

Holiday chalets and bungalows on the three-horse Essex plotlands

JAYWICK is divided from Clacton by a golf course and a Martello tower. This became a popular holiday area after Jaywick Farm was sold following the farming recession of the late 1920s. The land was sold in small plots, and chalets and bungalows – intended as holiday homes only – were built on them. Colin Ward, in his paper 'The Hidden History of Housing' (published on the website History and Policy), explains that the Essex plotlands were on the heavy clay known to farmers as 'three-horse land', which was the first to go out of cultivation in the agricultural depression; other plotlands grew up on vulnerable coastal sites like Jaywick Sands and Canvey Island. In J4026 (below left) we see a typical bungalow: it looks flimsy, and it has no foundations, but the child is obviously anticipating a happy holiday. In J4036, three girls relax in the typical full skirts and ballet pumps of the 1950s; behind them rather basic buildings offer table tennis and fish and chips.

Left: **JAYWICK, A 'B' TYPE BUNGALOW c1955** J4026

Above: **JAYWICK, THE SEA WALL c1955** J4036

THE JAYWICK COMMUNITY'S DESIRE FOR PERMANENT HOMES

The local council felt that the Jaywick area was unsuited to permanent development, but by the 1950s Jaywick was well established. By that time, the plotlanders wanted their holiday homes to stay in the family and eventually to become their retirement home. These bungalows might appear small and jerry-built, but to their owners they were full of happy holiday memories. Colin Ward, author of 'The Hidden History of Housing', adds that 'the plotlands tended to be upgraded over time. Extensions, the addition of bathrooms, partial or total rebuilding, the provision of mains services and the making-up of roads are part of the continuous improvement process in any old settlement'. Also, the original settlers were remarkable for their 'defensive independence and their strong community bonds. The residents of Jaywick Sands, for example, had for decades organised a service for emptying Elsan closets, known locally as the 'Bisto Kids', until, after fifty years, a sewer was built.'

PHOTOGRAPH COURTESY OF KARL BENSON

CLACTON-ON-SEA

UNTIL 1864, Clacton had simply been a row of cliffs. What is now the centre of the town was a lonely desolate part of the Essex coast known as Clacton Beach after the village of Great Clacton situated about a mile or so inland. It was Peter Bruff, a railway engineer, who bought the land and started to develop a resort here. By the years just before the Second World War, it had become a thriving town attracting many holiday visitors.

In 64254 (right), we see a mixture of industry and leisure. Two Thames sailing barges discharge cargo at low water on the beach, whilst drawn higher up are some bathing machines. Horse-drawn carts, visible beside the barges, were used to transport the cargo – probably coal from the north – from the barges. Many of these magnificent flat-bottomed craft were built in Essex. The cargoes were mostly bricks, sand, cement, slate, timber and flint, and were unloaded between high tides. While straightforward in mild weather it could be hazardous if the weather turned rough. The three horses used for pulling the carts up the beach can be seen in the picture. They took the cargoes as far as Wash Lane from where they were distributed to the various builders' yards around Clacton.

Dating from 1899, Clacton's bandstand (66847, previous page) had recently been relocated to this new sunken pavilion as part of a 'general beautifying programme'. This photograph was probably taken at the time of the opening ceremony of the Band Pavilion performed on 27 May 1914 by the Sheriff of the City of London. The bandstand was completely rebuilt again in 1936, when the old structure was done away with and a new stage built inside the Pavilion. After the Second World War the Pavilion became a very popular entertainment venue and attracted some of the leading big bands in the world, including Ray Conniff, Ted Heath and Mantovani. It was also the home of resident bandmaster Ronnie Mills, one of the most popular entertainers in Clacton during the 1950s and 60s. The Pavilion played host to events such as the Ideal Holiday Girl Contest and the Evening Standard Fashion Show. It could accommodate audiences of up to 3,000.

Above: **CLACTON-ON-SEA, WEST BEACH 1912** 64254
Previous page: **CLACTON-ON-SEA, THE BAND PAVILION 1914** 66847

❛For cleanliness, firmness, and extent, the sands of Clacton-on-Sea cannot be excelled. Bathing is safe at all times, the sands sloping gently out to deep water.
VICTORIAN GUIDEBOOK

CLACTON-ON-SEA, THE BEACH AND THE YORKSHIRE PIERROTS 1912 64237Ap

CLACTON'S THOROUGHLY REFINED PIERROTS

The origin of the pierrot is said to be a legend of a sad little boy excluded from heaven. Italian commedia dell'arte troupes of the 17th century popularised the character, who was always dressed in his distinctive white costume with black pom-poms. By the 19th century the pierrot show was all the rage in France, and in 1891 the performance of the mime 'L'Enfant Prodigue' in London brought pierrots to Britain. Was it the association of the name with 'pier' that made pierrots a popular seaside entertainment? At any rate, the first troupe was formed by Clifford Essex, and they performed in Ireland and then in Cowes, where they were watched by the Prince of Wales, thus ensuring their popularity. A pierrot troupe worked hard, usually performing at least twice a day with a change of programme twice a week, which meant having to master many routines and songs. Fred Pullan's Yorkshire troupe (64237Ap) opened in Clacton in 1901. An early handbill described them as 'Up to Date - Thoroughly Refined'.

Originally they made their money by 'bottling' - while they were performing on stage one of their number would go round collecting money in a bottle. Eventually they roped off part of the beach and charged admission to the enclosure, for which privilege they had to pay Clacton Council £4 rent per week, in advance. The Yorkshire Pierrots appeared every season from 1901 until 1912, when on 6 August an unusually high tide washed their stage out to sea. After that experience, they moved to an inland site!

CLACTON-ON-SEA, THE PIER 1907 58929

IPSWICH

IPSWICH, at the head of the Orwell Estuary, has been a major port for centuries. When photograph 32208t (opposite top) was taken, the port was recovering from a long period of decline. At the end of the 18th century, large ships were unable to berth. The river was silting up, and even at high tide it was impossible to get upstream. The solution was to construct the Wet Dock by isolating a bend in the river and diverting the river itself into the New Cut. The Wet Dock provided the means for ships to be able to dock at any state of the tide – at the time, it was the largest wet dock in Europe.

In 70411 (above) we see spritsail sailing barges tied up in the Wet Dock. Adjacent to the dock are large warehouses, many of which owned their own large fleets of barges. Spritsails were the last working barges in northern Europe, continuing until the early 1960s.

By the end of the First World War, the port had expanded beyond the Wet Dock – the river was dredged, and quays were built to accommodate large ships. Increasingly today the Wet Dock is being taken over by pleasure boats, while the cargo vessels unload at the riverside quays – the oil and grain terminals are on the east bank, and the container and roll-on roll-off berths on the west.

In the town of Ipswich the masters of these ships generally dwelt, and there were, as they then told me, above a hundred sail of them, belonging to the town at one time, the least of which carried fifteen score, as they compute it, that is, 300 chaldron of coals; this was about the year 1668 (when I first knew the place). This made the town be at that time so populous, for those masters, as they had good ships at sea, so they had large families who lived plentifully, and in very good houses in the town, and several streets were chiefly inhabited by such. The loss or decay of this trade accounts for the present pretended decay of the town of Ipswich, of which I shall speak more presently. The ships wore out, the masters died off, the trade took a new turn; Dutch flyboats taken in the war, and made free ships by Act of Parliament, thrust themselves into the coal-trade for the interest of the captors, such as the Yarmouth and London merchants, and others; and the Ipswich men dropped gradually out of it, being discouraged by those Dutch flyboats. These Dutch vessels, which cost nothing but the caption, were bought cheap, carried great burthens, and the Ipswich building fell off for want of price, and so the trade decayed, and the town with it. I believe this will be owned for the true beginning of their decay, if I must allow it to be called a decay.

DANIEL DEFOE, 'JOURNEY THROUGH THE EASTERN COUNTIES
OF ENGLAND' 1722

Opposite: **IPSWICH, ST PETER'S DOCK 1921** 70411

Above: **IPSWICH, THE DOCKS 1893** 32208t

WOODBRIDGE

WOODBRIDGE'S most famous building is undoubtedly its old Tide Mill (centre of 78747, below), seen here from the banks of the Deben. The first mill was built on the site as early as 1170, but the one seen here (now restored into working condition, open to the public in 1972 and painted a dazzling white) was constructed in the east coast style of weatherboarding in the 1790s. It had remained in operation, the last of its kind, using the tidal flow of the Deben for its power, until 1957. The mill operated for about two hours each low tide as the water, which had been trapped in the mill pond on the high tide, was released. Today, fifteen thousand visitors annually admire the technology of an earlier age.

WOODBRIDGE, THE QUAYSIDE AND THE TIDE MILL 1925 78747

Orford was once a good town, but is decayed, and as it stands on the land side of the river the sea daily throws up more land to it, and falls off itself from it, as if it was resolved to disown the place, and that it should be a seaport no longer.'

DANIEL DEFOE, 'JOURNEY THROUGH THE EASTERN COUNTIES OF ENGLAND' 1722

ORFORD

ORFORD CASTLE (62018), the most impressive medieval building on the Suffolk coast, was built by Henry II in 1165, and shows the importance of the port to the realm at the time. Although now only the great circular keep remains today, this view shows the remains of the other earthworks and walls which once protected it. Orford Castle's 90ft-high keep was of a revolutionary circular construction, buttressed by three projecting square turrets which are equally spaced around it. The keep has three floors, a basement and two halls, and is constructed from the local flint with dressed sandstone quoins and windows.

HENRY II

The quay (O20036, above) is all that remains of the once-prosperous seaport of Orford, cut off now from the North Sea by the growth of Orford Ness. Some trade must have been still going on at this time, as is witnessed by the crane derrick.

Left: **ORFORD, THE CASTLE 1909** 62018
Above: **ORFORD, THE QUAY c1950** O20036

ALDEBURGH

Above: **ALDEBURGH, THE CHILDREN'S BOATING POOL AND MOOT HALL c1955** A28062p

Below right: **ALDEBURGH, THE MOOT HALL 1906** 56822

THE EAST ANGLIAN COAST – GRAVEYARD OF SMALL BOATS BATTERED BY STORMS

The East Anglian coast has always been treacherous to mariners. In 1779 the poet George Crabbe, who was born in the Suffolk town of Aldeburgh, reported on a severe storm that battered the front, writing that 'the breakers dash over the roofs, curl round the walls and crush all to ruins'. Eleven houses were claimed by the sea, and Crabbe's own house was deluged in water four feet deep, forcing the family to retreat to the first floor. The lot of the fisherman's family could be a tragic one. The East Anglian fishermen ventured out in modest-sized beach yawls open to the waves, and were often obliged to row against rough seas. In his poem 'The Borough' Crabbe tells of the dreadful forebodings of those left on shore:

'Hark! To those sounds! They're from distress at sea:
How quick they come! What terrors may there be!
Yes, 'tis a driven vessel: I discern
Lights, signs of terror, gleaming from the stern ...
In various parties seamen hurry down;
Their wives pursue, and damsels urged by dread ...'

In George Crabbe's era there were no lifeboats; the service was only established in 1824. Barques and brigs were continually driven ashore off the town, or forced aground and wrecked on the many sandbanks offshore.

ALDEBURGH'S fortunes were built on fishing and boat building, and by the 16th century it was a thriving town, as the Moot Hall testifies (56822, below right). Built in 1540, this red brick and half-timbered building would have been a hotbed of commercial and legal activity during the town's most prosperous era. It has served as a police station and a jail, and today it is a museum. Only a shingle beach protects the Moot Hall from the sea. Once it was centrally placed in the town, but the sea has carried away some streets, finally pausing here.

The Regency fashion for sea bathing was the start of Aldeburgh's more recent source of income: tourism. When the railway reached the town, it brought more visitors, who helped to sustain the economy. There were still nearly 200 licensed fishing vessels in Aldeburgh at this time, catching herrings and sprats and sole. With both working boats and bathing huts sprawled on the shingle (to the right of A28062, above), the two trades still live peacefully together.

Today Aldeburgh is most well-known for its celebrated festival, drawing in performers and visitors from all over the world to play and enjoy music of the highest quality, a wonderful tribute to the co-founder of the festival, Benjamin Britten, whose music is so evocative of the Suffolk shore.

SIZEWELL

THORPENESS

THORPENESS, THE BENTHILLS 1929   82979

SIZEWELL was once notorious for its smuggling activities. In one night here during the 18th century, a staggering 8,000 gallons of contraband gin were landed.

In the 1950s, a nuclear power station was commissioned, a Magnox reactor of formidable potential, photographed here soon after its construction. Later came Sizewell B, the PWR reactor, proudly state-of-the-art; a two-year planning enquiry was held at the Snape Maltings to prepare for it. Sizewell has been part of Suffolk life for half a century now, and the grey concrete bulk of the controversial water-cooled station still dominates the coastal landscape, visible for miles up and down the shore. These modern power generators bring massive employment to the area, including 40,000 visitors annually. They produce enough electricity into the National Grid to supply a city the size of Bristol. Today the giant building stands rather incongruously where smugglers once plied a profitable trade.

Above:
SIZEWELL, THE NUCLEAR POWER STATION c1960
S582041

Left:
SIZEWELL, THE NUCLEAR POWER STATION 2006

COURTESY OF LES POWELL

THORPENESS, a purpose-built seaside village in the tiny hamlet of Thorpe in Aldringham, was built between 1910 and 1928 as a 'Garden Village and model holiday hamlet by the sea' by Glencairn Stuart Ogilvie, a Scottish landowner, playwright and barrister. The village was built round an artificial lake, the Meare, and had a Peter Pan theme. Around the Meare were imitation lath and plaster houses (actually made of concrete), and cottages that looked like a medieval gatehouse. In 82979 (above) we are looking along the Benthills road towards Aldeburgh. A variety of impressive cars have parked, possibly marking the advent of day-trippers, which Ogilvie did not really want. At one stage the residents of Benthills enjoyed exclusive use of the beach area in front of their houses – 'The Benthills Enclosure'.

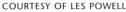

THORPENESS, THE HOUSE IN THE CLOUDS AND THE WINDMILL c1955   T38012

THE ENCHANTED HOUSE IN THE CLOUDS

When Thorpeness was built there was no mains water, so a water tower was needed. Ogilvie, the founder of the village, built a five-storey house with a 30,000-gallon water tank on the top (T38012) – the tank was disguised with a pitched roof, chimneys and mock windows. Mr and Mrs Malcolm Mason moved into the house below the tank, and Mrs Mason loved it. She wrote poems for children, and one, inspired by her house, was called 'The House in the Clouds': 'The fairies really own this house – or so the children say. In fact, they all of them moved in upon the self same day'. When she recited this to Ogilvie, he was enchanted, and exclaimed: 'The name must be changed to The House in the Clouds!'. The elegant post mill, originally a corn grinding mill, used to stand in nearby Aldringham. It was moved in 1923 to serve a different purpose – to pump water to the huge tank.

DUNWICH

> *This Dunwich is a curious little place, but interesting. All along at the base of the sandy cliff (striped with layers of rolled pebbles) you come upon human bones that have dropped from the shallow alluvial soil at the top. The land is sinking all along this coast, and a great city that flourished in Saxon times and was decaying at the Norman Conquest lies miles under the sea. There is one ruined church left just at the edge of the cliff. I believe 'the oldest inhabitant' can just remember when it was used for service, but its only congregation now is the owls and bats! Some of the cliff has fallen away lately and disclosed the shaft of a well. The bricks look to me Roman, but nothing has been found. There is a good lot of it, and it looks likely to fall, so one gives it a wide berth. The green marches at the back of the place are dotted with the fine cows and sorrel horses that this county is famous for.*

CHARLES KEENE, LETTER TO THE ARTIST JOSEPH CRAWHALL 1877

DUNWICH, THE BEACH 1909 62044

WALBERSWICK once enjoyed very prosperous times, but the work of nature and of man have left the village a quiet backwater. The bitter east winds have for centuries whipped up tides to attack the friable and fragile cliffs hereabouts, carrying away much that was constructed and cherished by man, homes and churches, even whole settlements. Sand and silt deposits have choked harbours and destroyed livelihoods. Today the village is quiet and picturesque, the haunt of artists, birdwatchers and holidaymakers.

There has been a ferry across the River Blyth for over 800 years, and between 1885 and 1942 it was the rather primitive steam operated chain ferry which we see here carrying a horse and cart across to the Southwold side (69126, right). Today, as in the 13th century, a rowing boat provides the service for a modest fee. So, in this case, times do not change!

Photograph 69128 (below) shows Walberswick's picture-book side. The pub and the tea-room point to the village's new role. A trader is about to make a sale – but he will not make a fortune from this cart unless all of Walberswick turns out.

All around Walberswick are tidal flats, the haunt of seabirds. The wind was prone to whip itself up on the bleak shores around and about, perfect conditions for the corn-grinding post mill that was once here, owned by a Mr Mallett. He relished the solitary atmosphere, not for poetic reasons, but because he feared that the building of houses nearby would keep the wind from the mill's sails.

WALBERSWICK

Above right: : **WALBERSWICK, THE FERRY 1919** 69126

Below right: **WALBERSWICK, THE VILLAGE 1919** 69128p

❝ *Hereabouts, they begin to talk of herrings ...*

DANIEL DEFOE, 'JOURNEY THROUGH THE EASTERN COUNTIES OF ENGLAND' 1722

SOUTHWOLD

SOUTHWOLD, EAST GREEN AND THE LIGHTHOUSE 1900   45137

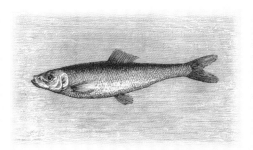

SOUTHWOLD is a town of character and characters; its history, so closely tied to the sea, abounds with glorious adventures and some extremely fishy tales. 'Hereabouts, they begin to talk of herrings ... and here also they cure sprats in the same manner as they do herrings in Yarmouth,' noted the very observant Defoe on his famous perambulation in the early 18th century. Southwold invested furiously in this trade and herring 'busses', 70ft square-rigged sailing drifters, brought wealth to the town, but only temporarily. Southwold was incapable of the kind of expansion which would rank it with Lowestoft or Great Yarmouth. Now Buss Creek embraces the town on the landward side, a nod to the vessels of old, or perhaps a hint of what might have been.

The lighthouse dominates many of the street vistas, not the least of which is East Green (45137, left). Local tradition claims that the many greens that grace the town were deliberately planned after the great fire of 1659; the townspeople decided that to prevent its happening again, they would group the houses around these open spaces. The Wesleyan chapel (left) is an intimation of the strong non-conformist tradition in Southwold. It was opened in 1890; it stands just over 100ft tall, and its light can be seen up to 20 miles out to sea – 'the light is of 800 candle power and occulates twice every 20 seconds'.

LOWESTOFT

❝ *The very pink of propriety ... no confusion, no touting, no harassing.*

CLEMENT SCOTT 1886

THE SANDLINGS, the low-lying coastal belt between Felixstowe and Lowestoft and the rivers Orwell and Waveney, contain some of the last great lowland heaths in Britain, sweeping down to reed-fringed creeks and extensive salt marshes which are the home of many rare birds. Lowestoft was developed by Sir Samuel Morton Peto in the 1840s and 1850s. He built houses for residents and visitors; built a railway to bring in trade and tourists; and created docks and harbours to bring trade and employment. Lowestoft was described in 1886 as 'the very pink of propriety'.

LOWESTOFT, THE VIEW FROM PAKEFIELD 1890
24022

Praise indeed!

❝ I shall always look on Lowestoft as the very pink of propriety. It is certainly the cleanest, neatest, and the most orderly seaside resort at which I have ever cast anchor. There is an air of respectability at the very railway station – no confusion, no touting, no harassing, and no fuss. I do not think I ever saw so neat a place out of Holland.

CLEMENT SCOTT 1886

East Anglia once had a thriving fishing industry. At Lowestoft, a few miles down the coast from Gorleston and Great Yarmouth, up to 1,500 men and boys were employed in fishing for herring and mackerel, and in related trades such as twine and rope making and ship-building. The ports along the coast here retained their importance as centres for fishing, although latter years have seen a decline due to European fishing quotas.

GORLESTON

GORLESTON has always been its own town, independent of Great Yarmouth. It is a journey of almost three miles from Gorleston harbour to the centre of Yarmouth, a journey that throughout history has been best taken by river. The long road route through Southtown has always been regarded as dangerous: the road was the haunt of footpads and cut-throats. In the 13th century it was ordered that all bushes and trees within 200 yards of the road be cut down so that no-one could hide behind them. The road was haunted in a literal sense too – the Devil appeared here in the form of an enormous black dog known as Old Scarfe. In 60662 (top) we see holidaymakers relaxing on Gorleston's pier. The sheltered niches in between the protruding timbers, which date from Gorleston's original harbour south pier in the 16th century, were known as 'the cosies' – popular sheltered spots for holidaymakers to take the sea air, watch the comings and goings of boats in and out of the harbour, or just to sit and read. They were also a popular place at night for courting couples! Sadly the cosies disappeared when the breakwater was rebuilt in 1964. Not so cosy is the scene in G35504 (above right) showing a fishing boat struggling to enter the harbour in high seas, a reminder of the harsh life in the herring fishing fleet.

Above: **GORLESTON, THE PIER 1908** 60662   Above right: **GORLESTON, A FISHING BOAT c1900** G35504

CAISTER-ON-SEA, THE 'CAMP SPECIAL' ARRIVING AT CAISTER HOLIDAY CAMP c1955
C450004p

CAISTER-ON-SEA

IN 1906 Fletcher Dodd began to provide holidays for groups of socialists from the east end of London in the grounds of his house on Ormesby Road. The potential of a holiday camp soon became apparent, and Dodd acquired nearby land which became the first holiday camp in England. Although the original 1906 site has been built on, the expanded camp site was bought by Ladbrokes in 1973 and is still going today.

The railway first passed through Caister in 1877. In 1937 this halt (C450004) was built at the holiday camp to cater for the Holiday Camp Expresses which ran from London to Caister (and to the other Norfolk holiday camps at California, Scratby and Hemsby) every Saturday in summer from 1934 to 1938, and again from 1948 to 1958. The new arrivals all look as if they are looking forward to their holiday. Note the caps, the trilbys, the sensible shoes, and the cropped and brilliantined head of the boy to the right. The line was closed in March 1959 and the tracks were taken up shortly afterwards.

GREAT YARMOUTH

YARMOUTH'S prosperity was founded on herring fishing. In medieval times, herring was an important foodstuff: it was nutritious, and it kept well if smoked. From here the fish was exported all over Europe, and by the middle of the 13th century, the town was prospering. The first 40-day-long Great Yarmouth Herring Fair was held in 1270; it would carry on annually for another 500 years.

The fishing industry reached its height in the 19th century, with better equipped boats, and the arrival of the railways, which ensured better distribution. In the 1860s fishermen from Scotland introduced a method for pickling the fish in brine, rather than the traditional smoking which produced the Yarmouth bloater. So popular was it that pickled herring overtook smoked herring in popularity.

At the time of photograph G56503 (below), Great Yarmouth was the leading herring port in the world. During the season, which lasted about ten weeks from the end of September, the town's population would be swelled by thousands – fishermen, the women who gutted and pickled the fish, and the coopers to make the barrels. But after the First World War, markets had dwindled. By the mid 1950s it was clear that fish stocks were seriously depleted, and in the early 1960s, Yarmouth's huge fleet of fishing boats had dwindled to six.

GREAT YARMOUTH, THE FISH MARKET c1900 G56503

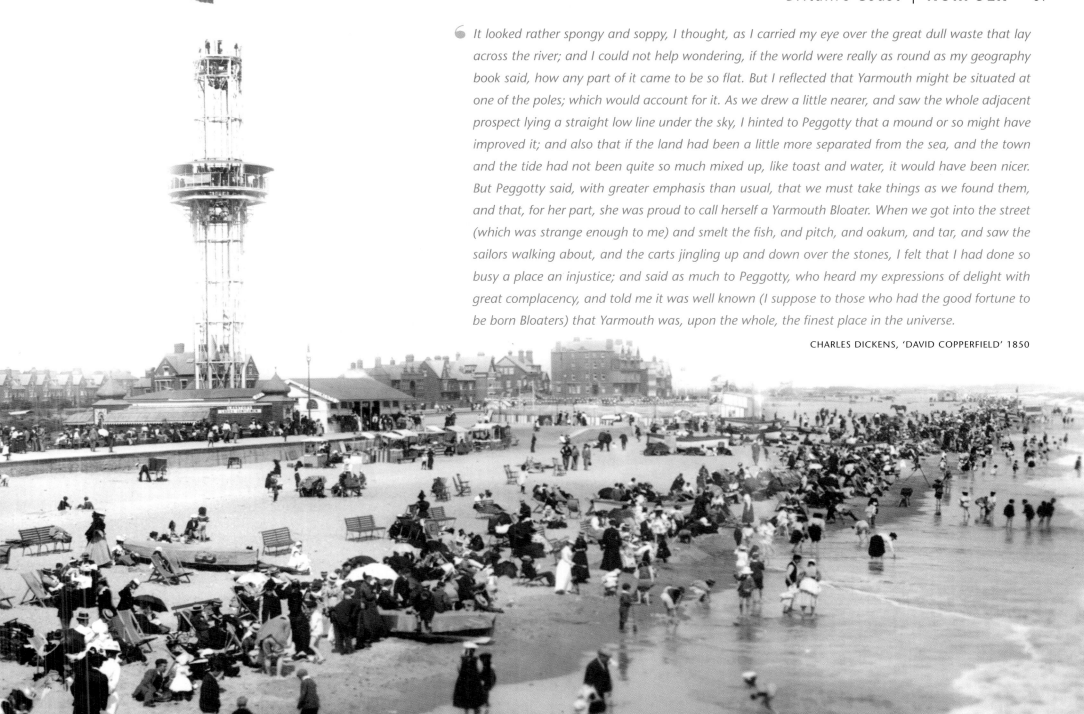

> It looked rather spongy and soppy, I thought, as I carried my eye over the great dull waste that lay across the river; and I could not help wondering, if the world were really as round as my geography book said, how any part of it came to be so flat. But I reflected that Yarmouth might be situated at one of the poles; which would account for it. As we drew a little nearer, and saw the whole adjacent prospect lying a straight low line under the sky, I hinted to Peggotty that a mound or so might have improved it; and also that if the land had been a little more separated from the sea, and the town and the tide had not been quite so much mixed up, like toast and water, it would have been nicer. But Peggotty said, with greater emphasis than usual, that we must take things as we found them, and that, for her part, she was proud to call herself a Yarmouth Bloater. When we got into the street (which was strange enough to me) and smelt the fish, and pitch, and oakum, and tar, and saw the sailors walking about, and the carts jingling up and down over the stones, I felt that I had done so busy a place an injustice; and said as much to Peggotty, who heard my expressions of delight with great complacency, and told me it was well known (I suppose to those who had the good fortune to be born Bloaters) that Yarmouth was, upon the whole, the finest place in the universe.

CHARLES DICKENS, 'DAVID COPPERFIELD' 1850

GREAT YARMOUTH, THE BEACH 1899 44496

The delights of height! By the 19th century, tourism vied with herring as the basis of Yarmouth's economy. People flocked to enjoy the delights of the Revolving Tower (44496, above), in which they could take a trip up and down in the revolving platform, or stay at the top for a while to soak up the views. There was a refreshment bar at the base of the tower for anyone in need of a mug of hot cocoa after braving the breezes up on top!

FOR THOSE IN PERIL:

THE STORY OF THE EAST ANGLIAN LIFEBOATS

THE EAST Anglian coast has always been treacherous to mariners, and the East Anglian fishermen ventured out in small beach yawls open to the rough seas.

The lifeboat service was only established in 1824, and it was not until 1851 that Aldeburgh was given its own lifeboat. Barques and brigs were continually driven ashore off Aldeburgh, or forced aground and wrecked on the many sandbanks a short distance offshore. The Aldeburgh crew had to put out in all weathers, battling against mountainous surf to row their vessel out into open water. Their courage and persistence saved many lives.

Right: **CROMER, THE LIFEBOAT 1922** 72651

Look! A flash is seen. Listen, in a few seconds, yes, there is the throb and boom of a distant gun, a rocket cleaves the darkness. And now the cry – 'Man the lifeboat! Seaward ho!' Storm warriors to the rescue.

FREDERICK WHYMPER, 'THE SEA' c1885

Photograph 72651 (above) shows the crew of the Cromer lifeboat 'Louisa Heartwell'. Like the Aldeburgh men, the 14-man crew holding aloft the oars were volunteers, who in addition to working as builders, shopkeepers, fishermen and the like, were ready to drop what they were doing to exchange leisure, comfort and sleep for cold, wet, fatigue and whatever horrors the North Sea could throw at them.

Henry Blogg, the most decorated lifeboat-man in the history of the service, was the coxswain of the 'Louisa Heartwell' from 1909 to 1947, earning three gold medals, four silver, the George Cross and the British Empire Medal. During his 53 years as a lifeboat-man the Cromer boat saved 873 lives. In 1941 Blogg was washed out of the lifeboat with five of his crew while rescuing the crew of the 'English Trader' – he was 65, an age when most of us are feeling it is time for a well-earned rest.

ALDEBURGH, THE LIFEBOAT 'CITY OF WINCHESTER' 1903 50426

The Aldeburgh lifeboat 'City of Winchester' (50426, above) was launched in 1902; she was a Norfolk and Suffolk type boat, and funded by public subscription in Winchester. She looks sturdy, but was not self-righting. The crew had to row her through the heavy surf until they could manage to raise the sails, and then still find the strength to carry out the rescue. The 'Winchester' saved many lives, and was finally taken out of service in 1928.

CROMER, THE RETURN OF THE LIFEBOAT 1921 70959

SOME NOTABLE RESCUES

Rescue calls were not always brief affairs: in 1881 the Aldeburgh boat stayed at sea in a dreadful snowstorm for almost 30 hours, having sailed a total of 120 miles. On 7 December 1899 the lifeboat was called to the aid of a stricken vessel that had run aground on the sands; she was suddenly struck broadside by two huge waves, causing twelve lifeboatmen to be flung overboard. Six of them perished, and the whole country was shocked by the disaster. In 1917, William Davie and Stewart Holmes of the Cromer lifeboat gained silver medals along with Henry Blogg in going to the assistance of the Swedish steamer 'Fernebo', which was blown in half after striking a mine in a terrific gale. The Cromer crew, having only just returned from saving another vessel, immediately turned their boat around and without a word of complaint headed straight back into the mountainous seas.

SHERINGHAM

CLEY-NEXT-THE-SEA

CLEY-NEXT-THE-SEA, THE OLD WINDMILL 1933 85836

THE RAILWAY reached the fishing hamlet of Sheringham ten years later than it did at its close neighbour, Cromer. Even then the trains arrived only from the Midlands and the North. It was not until 1906 that the line from Cromer was extended to Sheringham. Less disturbed by the outside world, the fishing community lasted a little longer, and commercial development was more restrained. Sheringham fishermen caught crabs and lobsters and also herring, cod and whiting. They were the traditional enemies of Cromer men, who referred to them disparagingly as 'shaddocks'. Nets were regularly cut, and battles fought. However, with their hats set at a rakish angle, these Sheringham fishermen (33313, opposite) look formidable adversaries.

The three fishermen in the centre of 56879 (above) rejoiced in the names of 'Red Eye' West, 'Lotion Tar' Bishop and 'Bumshee' West. Keeping their pots in good order was an essential job for the fishermen when not at sea. The pots were made of local oak and hazel, and were kept stable on the sea bed with a cast iron weight. The fishermen of East Anglia were proud and independent, looking to each other in danger and adversity, sharing not just their perilous profession but their religion – most were devout Salvationists.

Opposite: **SHERINGHAM, FISHERMEN 1893** 33313

Above: **SHERINGHAM, FISHERMEN MENDING CRAB POTS 1906** 56879p

THIS picturesque flint village was once the most significant of the Glaven estuary ports, and its old Custom House bears testimony to its prestigious past. The silting up of the waterway presaged the decline of Cley's importance, and coastal vessels now pass it by.

The fine old windmill (85836, above) dates from 1712, and guards the town from the open marshlands. It continued to operate until 1921, when it and the maltings were converted into an unusual home. Like other interesting buildings in the area, it joined the holiday industry and became a guest house. Its image can be found on many calendars throughout the country.

A REFUGE FOR BIRDS

This north Norfolk coast was a popular haunt of wildfowlers seeking tasty birds and unusual specimens for the taxidermist. However, 400 acres here were purchased by Dr Sydney Long in 1926; he believed that birds could be best appreciated alive and in their own habitat. He went on to found the Norfolk Wildlife Trust, which became the first County Nature Reserve in the country.

WELLS-NEXT-THE-SEA, THE QUAY 1929 81998t

FROM Wells to Blakeney a great sand barrier holds back all but the most vicious tides. The quay at Wells (81996, opposite right) is now stranded a mile from the open sea. It was originally constructed in stone by the Great Eastern Railway Company in 1853 as a working quayside for vessels trading in barley, linseed cake, corn, timber, salt, malt, and manure, rather than for holidaymakers. Wells quay is made unmistakable by the granary and gantry built for F & G Smith, maltsters, in 1906. Today this building has become exclusive apartments and flats.

The Wells whelkers (82003, opposite left) were renowned along this coast. It was not a comfortable trade to work in. Dropping pots from clinker-built open boats in pitch darkness and foul weather meant that the whelkers could often find themselves stranded for hours on the wrong side of the sandbar waiting for the tide. These heavily laden fishermen, paddling out of the shallows from their open boats, the 'Nell' and the 'Armistice', use shoulder yokes to carry their shellfish, much as a milkmaid carries her buckets.

WELLS-NEXT-THE-SEA

WELLS-NEXT-THE-SEA, THE QUAY 1929 81996

Above: **WELLS-NEXT-THE-SEA, BRINGING IN THE WHELKS 1929** 82003

FIGUIER'S WARNING!

While commending the mussel as an important article of food, we must not conceal the fact that it has produced in certain persons very grave effects, showing that for them its flesh has the effects of poison. The symptoms are weakness or torpor, constriction of the throat and swelling of the head, accompanied by great thirst, nausea, frequent vomitings and eruptions of the skin.

LOUIS FIGUIER (1819–1894)

BURNHAM OVERY STAITHE, PACKING MUSSELS c1955 O80011

BURNHAM OVERY STAITHE

THE WORD 'staithe' is derived from Old English, and means a bank, or a landing stage. At Burnham the Burn winds its way through sea lavender-covered salt marshes, home to thousands of geese in winter. On the shore, sand dunes stretch away to Holkham to the east and Scolt Head Island to the west. A number of the boats here were clinker-built open working boats (O80011, left) that took fishermen out to the mussel beds, which were renowned for the size and quality of their shellfish.

Ferries take passengers to Scolt Head Island from Burnham Overy Staithe in season and according to the tides, it is a fantastic place for picnics, beachcombing or bird watching on its golden sands.

HUNSTANTON

MANY OF Norfolk's ancient ports have long since silted up and have discovered new roles as popular resort towns. Cromer, Sheringham, Wells and Hunstanton are now thronged with visitors in the summer months. Behind their crumbling cliffs are wide, solitary marshes, some now drained and cultivated, and rich in bird life.

The popular seaside town of Hunstanton (58901, left) was built around a mill and an old village. It is unique for north Norfolk resort towns in that it looks west across the sea and not east. The cliffs here rise to about 70ft, and are the seaward end of the chalk ridge which stretches right across Norfolk. These cliffs are distinctive and unique along the Norfolk coast (38410, opposite). The base is carrstone, a dark brown tint below and yellow above. On this rests a band of bright red chalk, topped by the white chalk which forms the upper part of the cliff face.

Hunstanton had been described in the 1860s as 'a compact little watering place with everything on a miniature scale'.

❝ *The little town is perched upon a hill 60ft above sea-level, the top of which is a chalk down, while the western side forms a picturesque sea-cliff, overlooking a pleasant and safe beach which extends far seaward at low water, and at the base of which the sea (except in very stormy weather) permits a safe passage for the wayfarer.*

VICTORIAN GUIDEBOOK

HUNSTANTON, THE CLIFFS 1907 58901

TEA BY THE BEACH WITH PRINCESS ALEXANDRA

This bungalow (61116, right) was situated on the beach for the convenience of Princess Alexandra. She often visited on summer days with her entourage of servants and guests. Sadly it became storm damaged and fell into disrepair; it was eventually demolished.

Nearby Sandringham has been a royal residence since 1861, when Prince Albert purchased the estate to give his son the Prince of Wales a country estate with good shooting, well away from the temptations of London. On the Sandringham estate, another cottage was built for Princess Alexandra; it is a similar design to the Swiss Cottage at Osborne House. The princess loved to entertain her friends here with tea and cakes, and butter and cheese made in the dairy from Danish cows which she had brought over from her homeland.

SNETTISHAM, PRINCESS ALEXANDRA'S BUNGALOW 1908 61116

HUNSTANTON, THE CLIFFS FROM THE SOUTH 1896 38410

The sea has claimed much of the old coastline of Norfolk. Whole towns and villages have steadily fallen beneath the waves as year by year more of the cliffs are nibbled away or the occasional high seas and storms bite a chunk off. Towns like Eccles and Whimpwell have been reduced to a scattering of houses built years after the original settlement disappeared. Nothing is left of Shipden, the town that once stood the seaward side of Cromer, although old fishermen claimed they would not go to sea if they heard the submerged bells of Shipden church booming beneath the waves – there would be a bad storm brewing!

KING'S LYNN, THE QUAY 1898 40893p

KING'S LYNN, THE CUSTOM HOUSE 1898 40878

KING'S LYNN

LOCATED on the south-east corner of the Wash, King's Lynn was built on the edge of the sea, probably with help from the Romans, and much later from the Dutch. From ancient times it was always a populous and flourishing seaport, borough and market town. In its heyday you could walk right across the river on the decks of over 300 ships.

The jetties (40893p, above left) forced the river current eastwards, and since the 13th century they have provided a safe landing stage. The deep anchorage is difficult because of the oozy silt on the riverbed, so mooring posts and blocks are deeply embedded in the quay so that ships can be tied up with strong ropes and chains. Steam-driven tugs (left) made a good living for their skippers by towing vessels in high winds and strong tides.

Built in Ketton stone and opened in 1685, King's Lynn's famous custom house building (by Sir William Turner, based on a design by Bell) was shared by merchants on the lower floor and HM Customs on the first floor (40878, above right). Outside the entrance, a strict-looking customs official is keeping his eagle eye on the photographer as well as on the fishing boats, which were often used for smuggling tobacco, wines and spirits.

❝ It is a beautiful, well built, and well situated town, at the mouth of the River Ouse, and has this particular attending it, which gives it a vast advantage in trade; namely, that there is the greatest extent of inland navigation here of any port in England, London excepted. The reason whereof is this, that there are more navigable rivers emptying themselves here into the sea, including the washes, which are branches of the same port, than at any one mouth of waters in England, except the Thames and the Humber. By these navigable rivers, the merchants of Lynn supply about six counties wholly, and three counties in part, with their goods, especially wine and coals.

DANIEL DEFOE, 'JOURNEY THROUGH THE EASTERN COUNTIES OF ENGLAND' 1722

THE DANGER OF SILT

Silt has always been a problem at King's Lynn, and in November 1889 a 193-ton bulk maize cargo ship went aground, breaking her back. Local fishermen did well by removing much of her cargo. After several unsuccessful salvage attempts she was abandoned, creating worry that this would affect the silting-up even more. It is not recorded whether the ship was being piloted at the time; it was the Pilot Master's job to place the buoys and beacons at his own expense out of his excellent wage of £350.

BOSTON

BOSTON, THE DOCKS 1893 32078

BOSTON was laid out along the River Witham around 1100, and rapidly became a great port. It acquired town walls in 1285, and in 1353 it wrested away Lincoln's wool staple. It was the wool trade that built the town, with its seething market and vast numbers of ships. Boston declined in Tudor times: the wool trade upon which the town had waxed fat faded away, and the river silted up – it was not until the 18th century that the town recovered. The railway arrived in 1848. A new dock was authorised by Act of Parliament in 1881 and was opened in 1882, partly paid for by the Great Northern Railway, who extended a branch line to it. Built south of the town, the new docks were 825ft long by 450ft wide, and are still busy.

Boston's High Street ends at the river, the buildings terminating in an elegant early 19th-century five-storey warehouse with a hipped roof (26066t, previous page): it is more like a very tall villa. The warehouses of Boston have suffered recently; the ones on the right bank have been converted into flats, but the distant one has been demolished, like so many of its companions.

❝ ... I took a ramble by myself about the town; and chance led me towards the riverside, at that part where the port is situated. Here were large buildings of an old-fashioned aspect, apparently warehouses, with high roofs, and windows in them. The Custom House seemed to be accommodated within an ordinary dwelling-house. Two or three large schooners were moored along the river's brink, which had a stone margin; another large and handsome schooner was evidently just finished, rigged, and equipped for her first voyage; the rudiments of another were on the stocks, in a shipyard bordering the river. Another, while I was looking on, came up the stream, and lowered her mainsail, from a foreign voyage. An old man on the bank hailed her and inquired what her cargo was; but the Lincolnshire people have a queer accent, and I could not understand the reply. Still another vessel – a good-sized brig – was further down the river, but approaching rapidly under sail. The whole scene made an odd impression of bustle, and sluggishness, and decay. NATHANIEL HAWTHORNE 1883

THE BOSTON STUMP

The town centre is visually overwhelmed by the mighty church steeple (visible in the distance on the left of 26066), built in 1460 and universally known as the Boston Stump. Crowned by an octagonal lantern, it soars 272 feet above the town and can be seen from miles around, even from Lincoln. It served as a daymark for shipping, and as a lighthouse – the lantern used to have a beacon lit in it at night.

DETAIL FROM BOSTON 1890 26071

SKEGNESS

Above: **SKEGNESS, GRAND PARADE AND THE CLOCK TOWER 1899** 44195

Opposite above: **SKEGNESS, THE BEACH 1910** 62867

Opposite below: **SKEGNESS, FIGURE OF EIGHT 1910** 62862

SKEGNESS was developed with genteel excursions in mind – trippers used the railway, with influxes from the Midlands, particularly Nottingham. A new town was laid out from 1876 by the Earl of Scarborough; in 1881 it acquired a splendid pier (just visible on the left in 62867, below). It was not until 1921, when the council bought the sea-front and foreshore from the earl, that the town assumed its brasher kiss-me-quick character.

The acres of superb sand are what make these Lincolnshire coastal resorts such a pleasure. There was the inevitable licensed donkey ride man, a tall helter-skelter, and a beach fun fair. Trips round the bay in open sailing boats were highly popular (62867). Skegness's most famous fairground ride was the Figure of Eight (62862, below), which was regarded as a worthy rival to Coney Island! No doubt it looks tame to the present generation reared on the terrors of Alton Towers, but at this date it was quite scary enough. It is now replaced by a more testing version.

A vital landmark is the Jubilee Clock Tower (44195, above), erected at the junction of Lumley Road with Grand Parade and South Parade. It was built to commemorate Queen Victoria's Diamond Jubilee: this photograph was taken on 11 August 1899, and shows its formal opening by the Countess of Scarborough.

LINCOLNSHIRE'S sandy beaches beyond the sand dunes were seen to have potential for seaside resort development; the arrival of the railways from the Midlands in the second half of the 19th century led to their rapid, some might say under-regulated, development and their flooding with Midland day-trippers arriving by railway. A whole string of seaside resorts grew up, from Cleethorpes in the north to Skegness via Mablethorpe.

Donkey rides on the beach (M1053p,right) are a vital childhood rite of passage. Haven't we all clambered up and dug our heels into the flank of a beast that seemed as high as an elephant? Nothing could have been more exciting than the peculiar rocking motion of the donkeys as they trotted over the sands, continually turning their heads and baring their teeth as they tried to bite our ankles. Nowadays, according to the Horses (Protective Headgear for Young Riders) Act 1990, a donkey is a horse, so riding one without a protective helmet is an offence. Each donkey must have a veterinary certificate, an identifying hoof brand and a designated rest day a week. All very proper, too. There are still around 850 donkeys working on Britain's beaches today.

Right: **MABLETHORPE, DONKEY RIDES c1955** M1053p

MABLETHORPE

CAMPERS! ARE WE HAPPY? YES WE ARE!

INGOLDMELLS, BUTLIN'S HOLIDAY CAMP c1955 I47026

FOR A long time, the motto inscribed all along the front of the large roadside buildings of Butlin's was 'Our True Intent is All for your Delight' – a quotation from 'A Midsummer Night's Dream'. However, the motto and these really quite impressive Art Deco buildings have disappeared in a virtual rebuild of the camp. Built in 1936, it was the first holiday camp in Britain. Locals were most surprised when it was claimed in a broadcast by Lord Haw Haw, Hitler's propagandist, to have been sunk during the war; at that time it was a Royal Navy training camp known as HMS 'Royal Arthur'.

Today, the idea of spending a holiday at a post-war Butlin's is not as attractive as it was – indeed, the original appeal had started to lose its charm as early as the 1960s. The chalets were arranged in straight lines, as if in a military camp, and there were barbed-wire fences and communal bathrooms. Constant instruction blared out from the tannoy system: get up; queue for breakfast; go to the lido; buy an ice cream; don't forget the three-legged race – and so on, right through until bed time. But everyone loved it, and had an unforgettable time.

ANDERBY CREEK, FISHING c1955 A210016

ANDERBY CREEK

ANDERBY CREEK is located between Chapel St Leonards and Sutton-on-Sea. It was the perfect place for family holidays in the years before cheap foreign holidays, with glorious beaches and dunes. In A210011 (right), we see a classic example of the caravan sites that sprang up all over Britain after the war. One problem in the early days of caravanning was that the few sites were so packed that they resembled holiday camps, hardly reflecting the freedom and spontaneity that caravanning was meant to be all about. Donald Chidson, of the Caravan Club, had a successful campaign to establish smaller, more intimate caravan sites like the one in this photograph.

Fishing had long been the most popular sport in the country, even as early as the 1950s. Many people, like these young men lining the creek (A210016, above), would take their ease on a sunny afternoon. There might be a roach, a dace, a perch or a gudgeon, or even a bream – but that wasn't the point. As the old saying goes, 'There's a lot more to fishing than catching fish.' Even if you were not successful, there was warming consolation from within a thermos – or even a hip flask.

ANDERBY CREEK, ROSE'S CARAVAN CAMP c1955 A210011

THE CALL OF THE OPEN ROAD

For some, the crowds and regimentation of a holiday camp were anathema, as was the hustle and bustle of a seaside resort. They preferred to take to the open road, to travel at their own pace and choose their own stops and destinations. Before the war, caravanning had been associated with the well-to-do, the only people who could afford cars. However, as car ownership spread through society in the 1940s, a caravan holiday became a practical possibility for many more. Caravans became more affordable, too, particularly as the first post-war models, such as the 1946 Eccles 'Enterprise', were built on strictly utilitarian lines. Later, caravans became more sleek and almost luxurious – for example the popular 'Sprite' of 1954.

ATLAS
CARAVANS & TRAILERS
REGISTERED DESIGNS
£75

COLLAPSE OF CLEETHORPES' OYSTER INDUSTRY

In the early 19th century Cleethorpes oysters became famous, and were shipped by rail to places such as Leeds and Sheffield. However, in 1903 there was a typhoid epidemic in Sheffield. The sewage outfall at Cleethorpes was blamed, and the oyster industry collapsed.

On the right is a somewhat unlikely Victorian explanation as to the origins of eating oysters!

PHOTOGRAPH COURTESY
OF NEIL GOULD

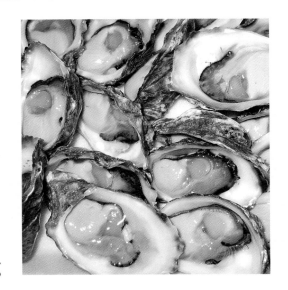

An old adage tells us that 'He was a 'bold man who first ate an oyster'.' A Mr. Bertram tells us how the discovery was made. 'Once upon a time a man was walking by the shores of a picturesque estuary ... when he espied a very old and ugly oyster-shell, coated over with parasites and weeds. Its appearance was so unprepossessing that he kicked it aside with his foot; whereupon the mollusc, astonished at receiving such rude treatment, gaped wide with indignation ... Seeing the beautiful cream-coloured layers that shone within the shelly covering, and fancying that the interior of the shell was probably curious or beautiful, he lifted it up for further examination, inserting his finger and thumb within the valves. The irate mollusc, thinking, no doubt, that this was intended as a further insult, snapped its nacreous portcullis close down upon his finger, causing him considerable pain. After relieving his wounded digit, our inquisitive gentleman very naturally put it in his mouth. 'Delightful!' he exclaimed, opening wide his eyes; 'what is this ?' and again he sucked his finger. Then flashed upon him the great truth that he had discovered a new pleasure – had, in fact, opened up to his fellows a source of immeasurable delight. With a stone he opened the oyster's threshold, and warily ventured on a piece of the mollusc itself. 'Delicious!' he exclaimed; and there and then, with no other condiment than its own juice, without the usual accompaniment, as we now take it, of 'foaming brown stout' or a pale Chablis to wash it down – and, sooth to say, it requires neither – did that solitary, nameless man indulge in the first oyster-banquet!

JAMES BERTRAM, 'THE HARVEST OF THE SEA' 1873

CLEETHORPES

CLEETHORPES began as a resort in 1863, when a single railway line was opened from Grimsby, although earlier in 1844 it had already been predicted that the town would become busy thanks to the network of the new railways. In 1884 a multi-track railway came into being, and the town became a bustling resort. The pier was built in the early 1880s, and in 1902 improvements to the sea defences and the foreshore were carried out on land reclaimed beyond Brighton slipway. Cleethorpes remains a popular tourist spot today.

The pleasure beach, otherwise known as 'Wonderland', and the flying machine dominating the sky-line of photograph 55736p (right), were rivalled only by Blackpool. For safety reasons the flying machine was removed during the Second World War – how sad that it was never replaced.

Right: **CLEETHORPES, THE BEACH AND THE FLYING MACHINE 1906** 55736p

GRIMSBY

IN ITS day, Grimsby was the biggest fishing port in the world. Sited at the confluence of the river Haven and the Humber, it rapidly prospered as a fishing and commercial centre. In view 55750p (below) the local fish merchants wait alongside creels of freshly landed cod to start bidding for the best fish – see the line drawing below which shows a typical cod.

The Dock Tower (33272, left) was a unique and original engineering achievement. It was built in 1854 as a hydraulic accumulator to control the water pressure which enabled the dock gates to be opened and closed; it also supplied power to the 15 cranes. Queen Victoria and Prince Albert opened the Dock Tower in 1855, and Albert rode by lift the 309 feet to the top. The tower's design was influenced by the Palazzo Publico in Sienna. At the time of its construction it was the tallest brick-built building in the country, and its cast iron spiral staircase of 350 steps was once the longest in the world.

Above:
GRIMSBY, THE DOCKS
1893 33272

Right:
GRIMSBY, THE FISH
PONTOON 1906 55750p

TRUE OR FALSE?
THREE MYSTERIES

Grimsby's Dock Tower has for 150 years been a source of mystery through three bizarre claims. The first is that the foundations are built upon large bales of cotton to absorb water seepage from the river. Secondly, it is claimed that one million bricks were necessary to complete the construction. Thirdly, perhaps most bizarre is the claim that the millionth brick is enclosed in a glass case. The tower is now deservedly a Grade One listed building, so we will not see it demolished – thus these mysteries can remain a part of Grimsby folklore.

THE LEGEND OF GRIM

A 13th-century poem, 'The Lay of Havelock the Dane', tells the story of Grim and Havelock:

After the death of King Athelwold of England, the new king, Godrich Earl of Cornwall, took care of Goldborough, Athelwold's baby daughter, and promised to marry Goldborough to the strongest man in England when she was of age. Meanwhile, when King Birkabeyn of Denmark died, Earl Godard was supposed to care for the baby Havelock and his two sisters. But Godard, wishing to rule, killed the king's daughters and instructed a local warrior and fisherman, Grim, to drown Havelock; but Grim and his wife decided to bring the baby up as one of their own.

They saw light shining out of the baby's mouth and a royal birthmark on his shoulder. Realising the baby's royal heritage, and the danger they were in, Grim and his family set sail for England; where they landed, they founded the town of Grimsby. As Havelock grew up, he gained the reputation of being the strongest man in England. Havelock's fame reached Godrich, Earl of Cornwall, and accordingly Goldborough and Havelock married. Goldborough too saw light shining from his mouth; Grim confirmed Havelock's birthright, and Havelock returned to Denmark to claim his throne. He returned victorious, and he and Goldborough become king and queen of Denmark and England. They had 15 children, and reigned happily together for 60 years.

HULL

> ❝ *A port of extreme bustle and activity.*

VICTORIAN GUIDEBOOK

HULL (officially, Kingston upon Hull) is situated where the river Hull flows into the Humber. It has always been a far-sighted place, overtaking Liverpool to become the third largest port in the country after London and Southampton. In the 19th century Hull was the biggest whaling port in Britain, processing whale oil, seal skins, and whalebone (see the line illustration of a whaling ship). Recently it foresaw the coming of roll-on roll-off freight traffic, and via the building of Queen Elizabeth dock in 1971 was able to capitalise on the growth of exports to Europe.

Originally intended as another coal dock, the success of Alexandra Dock (49825, above and H133045, opposite above) was guaranteed from the start, as the newer steam vessels were turned around more quickly. It soon became used for all manner of commodities, including timber, fruit and vegetables, and grain and oil seeds. Ships from Vera Cruz, Rosario, Pernambuco, Karachi or Havana were a common sight following the establishment of trade routes to Australia, South America and Asia. The dock closed in 1982, but owing to increased demand it re-opened in 1991.

The whole area shown in 49807t (right) is now a pedestrian precinct – Queen Victoria (far left) has a more peaceful view today. The Dock Offices are now a whaling and maritime museum. The towering monument topped by the statue of the anti-slavery MP William Wilberforce was moved to the grounds of Hull College.

Opposite: **HULL, ALEXANDRA DOCK 1903** 49825

Above: **HULL, ALEXANDRA DOCK c1955** H133045

Right: **HULL, THE DOCK OFFICES 1903** 49807t

WITHERNSEA, THE LIGHTHOUSE 1955 W177010

WITHERNSEA

The mariners' lamp that looms over the town roofs

THE VILLAGE developed into a holiday resort after the opening of the railway line from nearby Hull. During the latter part of the 19th century, ship owners petitioned Trinity House for a light which would cover the area between Spurn Point and Flamborough Head. For many years, this area of water had become a graveyard for shipping – for instance, in 1888 seven ships had been lost close to Withernsea during a single storm. A year later, four more coasters had run aground during heavy weather. Trinity House agreed to establish a light at Withernsea. Yet there were objections, especially from the local people, who were concerned about the tower having to be built in the town. It took nearly two years before Trinity House could begin to erect the 127ft-high octagonal Withernsea lighthouse. Its light was set at a majestic 138ft above sea level. The light was lit for the first time on 22 September 1892, with its beam visible to shipping from 20 nautical miles away.

MEMORIES OF THE LIGHT – AND OF A STAR

Withernsea lighthouse was discontinued in 1976. In the late 1980s the people of Withernsea restored the tower and converted it into a museum. It contains memorabilia of local fishing history, and displays many exhibits relating to lighthouses and HM Coastguard, including ships' bells, models, and old photographs recording the history of shipwrecks. There is also a special display that commemorates the Withernsea lifeboats and their crews, who saved 87 lives between 1862 and 1913. The lighthouse also contains a tribute to the late Kay Kendall, the actress - indeed, it is called the Kay Kendall Memorial Museum. Born in Withernsea, Kay (a famous film star during the 1950s) and her family were very much involved with maritime life in the town. Her grandfather, Robert Drewery, worked on the construction of the lighthouse from 1891 to 1893, and he was also the coxswain on the last off-shore rowing lifeboat from 1911 to 1913.

BARMSTON, SOUTH CLIFF BUNGALOWS c1955 B850037

BARMSTON

Clifftop bungalows ruthlessly claimed by Neptune

BARMSTON is a popular holiday retreat to be found on the rough road that leads off the main A165. Along with the village amenities there is a post office, a village store, and a lively pub called the Black Bull. The views both north and south along the coastline here are magnificent, and on a clear day one can see for miles in both directions and out to sea. As one might guess from photograph B850037 (left), coastal erosion is the big problem here – it is believed that the sea has claimed a stretch of land two and a half miles wide since Roman times. On a fine summer's day, these bungalows must have looked ideal to the prospective buyer, with clean sea air all round and a beautiful view. Sad to say, Neptune claimed them one by one in the 1970s.

SPURN HEAD

THE SPURN lighthouse is situated on the south-eastern tip of the Holderness plain on a narrow, sandy promontory, known as the spit, on the north bank of the Humber estuary – this is one of the largest river estuaries in England. The spit has been used for centuries as a strategic point for lighthouses and beacons to guide shipping. It is about 5 km long, and because it is made up of sand and silt, it is unstable and thus only keeps its shape for a relatively short time. Every 250 years or so, it is reconstructed at a slightly different location to the west of its present position – there have been at least five Spurn Points. The area is a haven for naturalists: it is teeming with bird life, and it also has many plants that are unique to this strange part of England. It is now a National Nature Reserve.

The lighthouse was erected in 1895. It is now just an empty shell; it was closed down and the light went out at dawn on 31 October 1986. The only light on Spurn today is a flashing green starboard light on the very tip of the point.

Left:
SPURN HEAD, THE LIGHTHOUSE 1899 44754

BRIDLINGTON

The 138-ton paddle tug 'Frenchman' (to the right of 50022, above) was built at South Shields in 1892 as the 'Coquet'; she was owned by T Gray & Company of Hull. In 1920, she was integrated into the United Towing Company of Hull, later to become the most powerful towing fleet in the United Kingdom. Around 1930, she was employed at Staithes as a coal hulk, and was eventually scrapped in New Holland as late as 1963.

BRIDLINGTON used to be the most genteel of the Yorkshire seaside resorts. However, the arrival of the railway made it possible for the working people of West Yorkshire to enjoy the breezy prospects of this coast, and our photographs show a paddle steamer packed to the gunnels with trippers.

In photograph 50022 (opposite), the paddle tug 'Frenchman' is landing the gangway after loading a full complement of passengers, whilst many more people remain watching on the quay. These craft were quite difficult to manoeuvre; instead of being employed as tugs, they were therefore frequently used on the more lucrative passenger trade between Hull and Bridlington, especially during the summer months.

A bracing north-easterly catches flags and furls the lugsails of three packed boats entering harbour (66246, above). Although apparently safe, the inner of the three sailing craft could well find herself on a collision course, unless due caution is exercised. The paddle tug 'Frenchman' continues her passenger trade in the background.

Opposite:
BRIDLINGTON, THE HARBOUR
1903 50022

Above:
BRIDLINGTON, THE HARBOUR
1913 66246

BEMPTON

JUST NORTH of Bridlington is the Bempton Cliffs RSPB reserve. Because these forbidding, almost vertical cliffs are chalk, erosion through time from the sea and wind has left little 'pockets' in the cliff face, which make it an ideal situation for birds: indeed, it is the largest bird breeding ground in Britain. An estimated 200,000 birds of many different species nest here. The reserve consists of a narrow strip of clifftop grassland and the magnificent chalk cliffs themselves. These are the highest chalk cliffs in the country, dropping 400 feet into the sea.

In addition to the thousands of other birds, the cliffs and bay are of international importance because of the colony of over a thousand pairs of gannets (see photograph right). There are also fifteen 'new' species of butterfly, twelve recorded types of bee, and two new day-flying moths – the Narrow-Bordered Burnet and the Chimney Sweeper.

Above: **GANNET** (COURTESY HSICHEN HSIEH)

Below: **BEMPTON, SILEX BAY** 1908 59913

FLAMBOROUGH HEAD

THE LANDSCAPE here is unlike anywhere else in Britain, and truly a walker's paradise. Rich and fertile farmland swells gently from the flat meadows of Holderness, gradually rising and rolling over the chalky uplands of the Yorkshire Wolds to end with a flourish at the great chalk cliffs plunging down into the North Sea at the dramatic site – and sight – of Flamborough Head. This region has been populated since the earliest times. Remains of rhinoceros, hippopotamus and straight-tusked elephants have been excavated at Sewerby, suggesting a warmer climate in the past, possibly before the last Ice Age, 10,000 years ago.

These atmospheric photographs (18001, opposite) and 18009, below) show how important fishing was to the local economy. In 18001 men watch as the fishing boats are hauled up the beach; baskets wait to be laden with the catch. In 18009, we see the boats pulled well up on shore away from the rough waves. These fishing boats are the local craft known as cobles.

❝ The Head is the termination of the chalky Yorkshire Wolds, and it is surrounded by islands of chalk, showing plainly that the sea has cut them off from their former connection with the land. The cliffs around Flamborough Head are riddled and tunnelled by the sea waves, and there are many arches and caverns … Crowds of sea birds startle the visitor, who is doubtless regarded as an intruder, as they flock out from all the crevices of the cliffs filled with their eggs, and cover both land and sea in their circling flight. The somewhat giddy feat of descending the face of the cliff with the aid of ropes, for the sake of the eggs, is one by which the Flamborough men gain their living in the summer. A more familiar hazard is run by the bold fishers of this coast, who, in their little cobles, set forth from the north or the south landing to visit, perhaps, the Dogger Bank, possibly to return no more. 'The sea gat him,' is too often the reply to your enquiry for some honest fisherman who may have been your boatman round the promontory.

FREDERICK WHYMPER, 'THE SEA' c1885

Above: **FLAMBOROUGH HEAD, THE SOUTH LANDING c1885** 18009
Opposite: **FLAMBOROUGH HEAD, THE NORTH LANDING 1886** 18001p

Flamborough's name is probably derived from the flame or light placed on the head to help mariners in the navigation of these treacherous waters. Ships have foundered here for centuries. However, in the words of a guidebook of the early 19th century, 'on the 1st of December, 1806, the revolving light which has ever since flamed by night from the Head, burst forth for the first time. The utility of this erection cannot be more strikingly illustrated than by the following fact, quoted from the Notes to Coates's Descriptive Poem, on Bridlington Quay – 'From June, 1770, to the end of the year 1806, not fewer than 174 ships were wrecked or lost on Flamborough Head and its environs, but since the erection of the lights, to March, 1813, not one vessel had been lost on that station when the lights could be seen.''

EAST COAST CLINKER-BUILT COBLES

Cobles (pronounced 'cobbles') are the traditional fishing boats of the north-east coast (see 18001, opposite). Open sailing boats, they are designed to be launched and landed bow first on the beach, often in rough seas, so they are sturdy vessels, clinker-built to give maximum strength with minimum weight. The shallow aft section and flat, raked stern help the waves lift the boat off or up onto the shore. A conventional keel would dig into the sand or pebbles of the beach, so from amidships to the stern cobles have two 'drafts', which act like sledge runners. This is why cobles need an extra long rudder to keep the boat stable in the absence of a full-length keel.

THORNWICK BAY, THE ROCKS c1950 T169008

THORNWICK BAY

THESE wind and wave-sculptured cliffs, 300 to 400 feet high here, are really a continuation of Flamborough Head. They are the best and largest breeding ground for sea birds in England, with numbers at their peak in the first half of July.

The only mainland colony of gannets is increasing, and so are the numbers of kittiwakes, guillemots,

COURTESY OF ELKE ROHN

razorbills and puffins. This part of the rocks was a favourite place for the 'climmers' or climbers to risk their necks to plunder the nests to sell eggs to the spectators. This trade was stopped by Act of Parliament in 1954 - for the safety of all.

FILEY BRIGG

STRETCHING down from the north side of town towards the coble landing, Filey is still a mixture of a fishing village and a Victorian resort. From the coble landing there is a splendid walk out to sea on the mile-long rock promontory, Filey Brigg. At low tide the Brigg was a favourite spot for Victorian holidaymakers, amateur geologists, and fossil-hunters alike (23488, left). They could explore ledges around the cliff, caves, caverns and pools. The Brigg forms a natural breakwater for Filey and shelters its sandy beach from the worst of the gales – certainly the holidaymakers in 80163 (below) had a calm sea for their trip.

Far left:
FILEY, FILEY BRIGG 1890
23489

Near left:
FILEY, FILEY BRIGG 1890
23488

Below:
FILEY, THE BOAT CART 1927 80163

❝ *Along the great slabs of Oolitic rock, where-in are entombed by hundreds the relics of creatures that tenanted the Jurassic sea – ammonites and belemnites, sea-urchins and spiral univalves – one can clamber till the waves dash up their spray – sometimes in too close proximity – on either hand, or explore the rock-pools with their tiny forests of coral-line and seaweed, and watch, sometimes a little enviously, the lazy life of the anemones and limpets. But not for its marine aquaria only, or for its sea-breezes – rich in iodine, or ozone, or whatever is therapeutic in air – is the Brigg dear to all visitors at Filey. It commands a magnificent view of the coast backwards to Scarborough, and forwards to the white cliffs of Speeton and Flamborough; and it would not be easy to find a nobler bay than Filey along all the northern shore of England.*

VICTORIAN GUIDEBOOK

SCARBOROUGH

SCARBOROUGH has long been important as a fishing port, and photograph 39463 (below) reminds us that the harbour was essential not only to the pleasure boats. Victorian holidaymakers, attracted by the glorious beaches, brought continued prosperity to Scarborough, and it became known as 'the queen of watering places'. Many of the large, dignified 19th-century buildings survive, giving the town an air of grandeur; but the sea front is now packed with amusement arcades, bingo halls and cafes, rather than the genteel entertainments that the Victorians enjoyed.

This delightful study (23476Ap, right) shows a group of people taking the sea air and enjoying the view over South Bay. It provides detailed information about both clothing and baby carriages of the period. This spot is at the end of St Nicholas Cliff looking south over the Valley Road footbridge towards the Spa.

SCARBOROUGH, NORTH BAY 1897 39463

SCARBOROUGH, BELMONT 1890 23476Ap

A band concert attracts a sizeable crowd in Clarence Gardens (39463, left). Approaching our cameraman are two soldiers dressed in their walking-out uniforms. It is unusual at this period to find pictures of soldiers walking out in public with an arm around a lady; such conduct was forbidden under Queen's Regulations. On the other hand, sailors belonging to the Royal Navy were under no such restrictions.

❛ *Romantic from its situation along a cliff that over-hangs the sea.*
TOBIAS SMOLLETT

Scarborough, though a paltry town, is romantic from its situation along a cliff that over-hangs the sea. The harbour is formed by a small elbow of land that runs out as a natural mole, directly opposite to the town; and on that side is the castle, which stands very high, of considerable extent, and, before the invention of gun-powder, was counted impregnable. At the other end of Scarborough are two public rooms for the use of the company, who resort to this place in the summer to drink the waters and bathe in the sea; and the diversions are pretty much on the same footing here as at Bath. The

Spa is a little way beyond the town, on this side, under a cliff, within a few paces of the sea, and thither the drinkers go every morning in dishabille; but the descent is by a great number of steps, which invalids find very inconvenient.

Betwixt the well and the harbour, the bathing machines are ranged along the beach, with all their proper utensils and attendants. You have never seen one of these machines – image to yourself a small, snug, wooden chamber, fixed upon a wheel-carriage, having a door at each end, and on each side a little window above, a bench below – the bather, ascending into this apartment by wooden steps, shuts himself in, and begins to undress, while the attendant yokes a horse to the end next the sea, and draws the carriage forwards, till the surface of the water is on a level with the floor of the dressing-room, then he moves and fixes the horse to the other end – the person within being stripped, opens the door to the sea-ward, where he finds the guide ready, and plunges headlong into the water.

TOBIAS SMOLLETT, 'HUMPHREY CLINKER' 1771

SCARBOROUGH, THE PIERHEAD AND LIGHTHOUSE 1890 23471t

RAVENSCAR

RAVENSCAR, THE CLIFFS 1901 46801

RAVENSCAR was once a tiny village known as Peak, with the lord of the manor's house (now the Raven Hall Hotel) on the headland. The estate was sold to a development company in 1895, and the intention was to build a large resort. Roads were built (their traces can still be seen), and sewers were laid, but the company was assailed by financial difficulties in 1913, and very few houses were ever completed, as we see in 46802 (below). Billboards on the side of the Station Square shop advertise land for sale. Sad to say, investors were unimpressed, even though the railway threaded a path along the coast from Scarborough (the railway line and the station were immediately behind the photographer).

MADNESS, LEECHES AND WOODLICE

It is said that George III was treated for his bouts of insanity at what is now the Raven Hall Hotel in Ravenscar. Peak House, as it was then known, was the home of the Reverend Doctor Frank Willis, who owned an asylum in Lincolnshire. The treatments consisted of bleeding with leeches and immersion in cold water, amongst other rather barbaric medical practices – not much in the way of a cure by modern standards! Doctor Willis was said to have later lost his house in a gamble over a race between two woodlice running over a saucer.

RAVENSCAR, NEAR THE STATION 1901 46802

Today, this is a stunningly beautiful coast (46801, above left). It is hard to believe that Ravenscar was a vast industrial site of world-class importance from the 17th to the mid 19th century: the local shale was the source of alum (used to fix dyes and cure leather). The extraction process was complicated and rather unpleasant - the shale had to be burnt and then soaked in human urine, which was imported here by the boatload. We can see part of the old alum works in the colour photograph above.

ROBIN HOOD'S BAY

ROBIN HOOD'S BAY, THE TOWN 1901 46794

ROBIN HOOD'S Bay was a mainly fishing community six miles south of Whitby, though a number of sail colliers and coastal trading vessels worked from here. It was also home to some serious smuggling; by 1800 the revenue believed that every household was involved in the trade in one way or another. Houses in Robin Hood's Bay were built close together, and were often intertwined with connecting cellars; in fact in Robin Hood's Bay, or Baytown as it was known, it was said that 'a bale of silk could pass from the bottom of the village to the top without seeing daylight'. Sad to say, owing to erosion hundreds of houses have been lost in Robin Hood's Bay and the other coastal villages that were built near the shoreline or on the sides of the cliffs over the centuries.

The rocky shoreline (80187, left) with its distorted and upturned strata is a popular place with fossil hunters, although one has to take great care when digging under the cliffs – they are notoriously unstable, and a prolonged rainstorm can set off mini landslides.

Left: **ROBIN HOOD'S BAY, THE SHORE 1927** 80187

WHITBY

WHITBY owes much to Queen Victoria. She it was who went spectacularly into permanent mourning, and black became highly fashionable. The town's jet industry came into its own, and jet craftsmen toiled in workshops all over Whitby working on this fossilised monkey puzzle tree. Local men were not slow to start digging up the black gold all along the coast.

For centuries the people of Whitby earned their living from the sea; some still do. The town was once a whaling port, and there were blubber houses along the inner harbour. Between 1766 and 1816 the local whaling fleet caught 2,761 whales and about 25,000 seals. When whaling declined, herring became important to the town's prosperity; but the herring fishery is now all but gone, and the town relies mainly on tourism.

In view 74310 (below) we are looking towards the East Cliff, where the parish church of St Mary and the ruins of Whitby Abbey stand. St Mary's was made famous by Bram Stoker in his Gothic novel 'Dracula' as the place where the count sought refuge in the grave of a suicide. The lighthouse on the right was designed in 1831 by Francis Pickernell, Engineer to the Harbour Trustees; the lighthouse on the East Pier was erected in 1854.

WHITBY, 'GEMINI' 1891 28862p

GEMINI

The two charming (and rather sulky) children in 28862p (above) have provoked much speculation in Whitby. Are they girls or boys? Are they actually twins, as the title of the photograph implies? After this picture was recently published in the Whitby Gazette, information came in from local people: we now know that these children are boys and indeed twins, Matthew Peart (left) and his brother Robert, three years old at the time of this photograph. Robert's life was tragically short – he was swept overboard and drowned near St Petersburg at the age of 20 on 19 July 1908.

Opposite: **WHITBY, FROM THE AIR 1965** AFA152957
Above: **WHITBY, EAST CLIFF 1923** 74310

❛ *The next turn of the road showed them the red peaked roofs of the closely packed houses lying almost directly below the hill on which they were. The full autumn sun brought out the ruddy colour of the tiled gables, and deepened the shadows in the narrow streets. The narrow harbour at the mouth of the river was crowded with small vessels of all descriptions, making an intricate forest of masts. Beyond lay the sea, like a flat pavement of sapphire, scarcely a ripple varying its sunny surface, that stretched out leagues away till it blended with the softened azure of the sky. On this blue trackless water floated scores of white-sailed fishing boats, apparently motionless, unless you measured their progress by some land-mark; but still, and silent, and distant as they seemed, the consciousness that there were men on board, each going forth into the great deep, added unspeakably to the interest felt in watching them. Close to the bar of the river Dee a larger vessel lay to. Sylvia, who had only recently come into the neighbourhood, looked at this with the same quiet interest as she did at all the others; but Molly, as soon as her eye caught the build of it, cried out aloud: 'She's a whaler! She's a whaler home from t' Greenland seas! T' first this season! God bless her!' and she turned round and shook both Sylvia's hands in the fullness of her excitement. Sylvia's colour rose, and her eyes sparkled out of sympathy.*

MRS GASKELL, 'SYLVIA'S LOVERS' 1863 (Whitby was renamed Monkshaven in the novel, and the River Dee is the Esk)

STAITHES

STAITHES, FISHWIVES c1960 S176105p

THE INTRIGUING fishing village of Staithes lies between two prominent headlands, Penny Nab and Cowbar Nab (18209, opposite left). Here the past is along every alleyway. Red-tiled cottages are squeezed into narrow passages that rise dramatically from seashore to cliff top. Staithes was an important fishing port, landing sufficient cod, mackerel and haddock for the North Eastern Railway to run three or four special fish trains a week. In 18209 we see nets hung out to dry along the bridge. Lining was one method by which the fish were caught. It would be the women who baited the lines, usually with mussels, or sometimes limpets. In S176105p (above) four women show off the crabs caught by the local boats.

STAITHES' FAMOUS SON

The young James Cook was sent by his father to Staithes from Great Ayton to serve an apprenticeship to a grocer and haberdasher, Mr Sanderson. The call of the sea must have been too much for him, for within a year he had left to go to Whitby and embark on what became a famous career of seafaring and exploration. He started as an apprentice on a collier, and next entered the Royal Navy. Having impressed the Royal Society with charts he drew up of the Newfoundland coast, he was given command of an expedition to the Pacific, to make an observation of the transit of Venus. This was the first of his three great voyages, during which he re-discovered New Zealand, made landfall for the first time at Australia, and proved that New Guinea was a separate island. He died on Hawaii in a tragic accident, as a result of a blow to the head from some angry villagers, who believed his men had killed one of their chiefs.

Above: **RUNSWICK, FROM THE BEACH c1885** 18200

Above: **STAITHES, THE BRIDGE 1886** 18209

RUNSWICK BAY

THE SMALLER villages along the cliffs hereabouts, such as Staithes, Runswick and Robin Hood's Bay, had (and still have) plenty of visitors who liked nothing better than to poke around the narrow lanes that wove between the jumble of little houses, looking into gardens full of lobster pots and old bits of fishing net – and there were the stories of smugglers and excise men to feed their imagination.

In 1682, two hundred years before this photograph (18200, above), the old Runswick collapsed into the sea during a violent storm. Every dwelling except one was destroyed. No lives were lost, as the village was evacuated in time. Another landslide in 1858 demolished an iron smelting works. Undaunted, each time the villagers rebuilt their cottages further up the cliff, where they seem to hang precariously. Their view of the turbulent and cruel North Sea is a potent reminder of their vulnerable location. The villagers once relied almost solely on fishing; note the cobles pulled up high and dry on the shore.

SALTBURN-BY-THE-SEA

SALTBURN, originally a tiny fishing village, is a breezy cliff-top resort, purpose-built in the 19th century, and much more sedate than its neighbours. From here, the scenic Heritage Coast runs south-east to Cowbar and into North Yorkshire. Many little becks and streams meander down the hills and through the valleys around Saltburn.

This part of the coast was notorious for the smuggling trade. The ravines that ran for miles gave perfect cover for the smugglers to take their goods inland and dispose of them. One well known rogue was John Andrews, who was the landlord of the Ship. In 1827 he was caught by the revenue men and imprisoned. Most of the villagers would have been involved in the illegal trade in some way, either in hiding or buying illicit rum, tea, gin and tobacco.

Built in 1884 to save the villagers and visitors the long climb up and down from the village to the lower promenade, Saltburn's cliff lift is the oldest remaining working water balance cliff lift in Britain (66354, left); every year it still carries 70,000 people down to the beach and back up again.

UP AND DOWN BY WATER POWER

Saltburn's cliff lift (66354) was designed and engineered by local man John Anderson in 1884. The height of the lift is 120ft, and the length of the track is 207ft. The smart carriages had red plush seating and stained glass windows - these have recently been renewed. The carriages are connected by cables running round pulley wheels, and each carriage has a water tank beneath it. When water is run into the tank of the top carriage, the carriage moves down thanks to the weight of the water, and the carriage at the bottom is pulled up. When the first carriage reaches the bottom, it releases the water from its tank so that the process can start again.

THE FIRM, sandy beaches of Cleveland stretch to South Gare, passing Marske-by-the-Sea and Redcar in their seemingly never-ending length. In 1908 a 60hp Napier Mercury recorded 102 miles per hour along this stretch near Marske. Thousands of people lined the beach to watch. In later years, Malcolm Campbell used the sands to practice for the world land speed record.

MARSKE-BY-THE-SEA

Above: **SALTBURN-BY-THE-SEA, THE PIER ENTRANCE 1913** 66354

Right: **MARSKE-BY-THE-SEA, THE SANDS 1923** 74148t

Above: **REDCAR, THE ESPLANADE 1886** 18131

Previous page: **REDCAR, THE BOATS 1924** 75681

❛ *The sands of Redcar can nowhere be surpassed in extent, being ten miles in length and a mile broad at low water; they stretch from the Tees mouth to Saltburn, and have been characterised as 'smooth as velvet, yet so firm that neither horse nor man leave their imprint on them as they tread the strand' … The town is old-fashioned, and consists of one long, and in places, wide street, parallel with, and at some distance from the shore.*

VICTORIAN GUIDEBOOK

REDCAR'S motto is 'Mare et Ferro', 'by sea and by iron', and indeed it is thanks to the sea and iron that Redcar has flourished. Since medieval times a trading and fishing port, Redcar became a holiday resort in the 19th century thanks to its beautiful beach. Iron ore was mined in the Cleveland Hills to the south, and since the 19th century Redcar has housed and employed iron workers and their families. Today Redcar is the home of Corus (British Steel).

The photographs all focus on Redcar's role as a place for a seaside holiday. Work started on the pier in 1870 (37594, left); when completed, it was over 1,000 feet long. The two entrance pavilions were a toll collector's office and a shop selling buckets and spades. The pier is also visible in 18131 (above left), where a woman pedals her three-wheeled cycle along the Esplanade. She has probably hired it from the two men sitting talking in the sun while waiting for customers. The pleasure boat in the centre of 75681 was the 'Mayflower'. The children are certainly enjoying themselves – there will have been a few pairs of wet knickerbockers when they arrived home!

Left: **REDCAR, THE PIER 1896** 37594

MIDDLESBROUGH

HARTLEPOOL, ELEPHANT ROCK 1886 18845

🙶*Middlesbrough is bristling with chimney-stacks, on a dead flat, and redolent of smoke. It is the capital of the Cleveland steel and iron district. It has a fine Town hall and public buildings.*

BADDELEY'S 'GUIDE TO YORKSHIRE' 1902

Above: **MIDDLESBROUGH, THE TRANSPORTER BRIDGE 1913** 66412

Right: **MIDDLESBROUGH, THE TRANSPORTER BRIDGE c1965** M71055

HARTLEPOOL

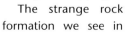

TEN THOUSAND years ago this landscape was emerging from the ice, and what is now the North Sea was once low-lying fenland. Around this coast, usually in January or February, certain low tides reveal an ancient forest, which once stretched to Scandinavia. Parts of trees and even acorns are clearly discernible, preserved forever in their petrified state. Hartlepool has one of the largest areas of this landscape still visible. The Longscar rocks between Seaton Carew and Hartlepool were notorious for damage to shipping.

TO THE south-east of the Tees is Middlesbrough; the town, built on industry, is very diverse, with people of many cultures, and the buildings are a mixture of very old and modern. The existence of the town was due to the Stockton & Darlington Railway, which needed deep water coal staithes (wharves); from then on, industry very quickly moved in. In 1818 the population was just 40, but by 1920 it was well over 1,000,000.

Middlesbrough's famous transporter bridge (66412, above) is an amazing feat of engineering skill fashioned in iron and steel and a monument to the ingenuity and inventiveness of Middlesbrough's industrial heritage. The bridge opened in 1911. Pedestrians and vehicles cross by means of a suspended platform which can carry 600 people at a time; it moves to and fro across the Tees 160ft above the river, and each trip takes just two and a half minutes. Whether it is worth the cost of the upkeep has long been a matter of debate – the bridge is often closed for repair, or because high winds make it dangerous to use. On the other hand, it is a vibrant symbol of Middlesbrough's industrial past.

The strange rock formation we see in 18845 (above), which stood near the lighthouse, no longer exists, apart from its 'feet', which can sometimes be seen at low tide; unfortunately, it eroded away, and finally collapsed in May 1891. The story goes that the day this elephant disappeared, the inhabitants of Hartlepool saw their first real elephant: a circus came to town.

EASINGTON

NOT ALL the Durham coastal fringe was a pleasing mixture of summer skies and golden sand. Some areas were polluted with spoil dumped directly into the sea from nearby collieries. Enterprising locals discovered that wave action separated coal from stone, so there was no need to buy coal when it could be picked for free from the beach; some even turned it into a business. At least one local authority tried to put a stop to the practice, but deservedly fell foul of the common law right to pick sea coals for nothing.

At this time, Easington was one of the pits situated along the coast of County Durham (E71027, below left); others were Wearmouth, Vane Tempest, Dawdon, Seaham and Horden. Between them they employed over 10,000 men and extracted over 4 million tonnes of coal a year from seams stretching out under the North Sea. Easington opened in 1899 and closed in 1993, and at its peak in the 1930s employed over 3,000 people.

Above left:
BLACKHALL ROCKS, BLACKHALL COLLIERY c1965 B327010

Below left:
EASINGTON COLLIERY c1955 E71027

TRAGEDY AND BRAVERY AT EASINGTON

Coal mining has always been an arduous and dangerous occupation, and the history of mining is scarred by tragedy. An example chosen at random of one disaster at Easington is an explosion that happened on 29 May 1951, killing 83 men. The long, thorough and painstaking report on the accident by the Chief Inspector of Mines found that the accident was caused by fire damp propagated by coal dust ignited by sparks from picks striking pyrites. One reason why so many died was that 'by a tragic trick of fate this was a time when there were two shifts of men in the district ... Only one of these men was rescued alive, and he died of his injuries a few hours later ... all the others, mercifully, died almost immediately.' The rescue lasted 257 hours and over 350 men took part. This was a highly dangerous operation - at one point 'the air was so foul with afterdamp that the canaries carried by the party were overcome almost immediately' – and two of the rescue workers died. The Chief Inspector paid tribute to the rescue workers: 'The work was prolonged, the distances travelled considerable and the atmosphere so lethal that anyone making a mistake or taking a liberty was likely to pay for it with his life. Nevertheless, and in spite of the death of two of their comrades, these men never faltered and their morale throughout was maintained at a level that reflected the greatest credit on them as individuals and on the system in which they had been trained.'

SEAHAM

IN 1819 Charles Stewart (later the third Marquis of Londonderry) married Frances Anne Vane-Tempest, heiress to an extensive property and coal-owning empire. Pretty soon, Stewart was in dispute with the port authorities at Sunderland over handling charges for coal from his Rain collieries. He resolved the matter by buying the small fishing port of Seaham, with the intention of turning it into a coal exporting facility, and ever since the town has grown and flourished.

In S287008 (below left), colliers await their turn alongside the coal staithes (wharves). Nearest the camera is the paddle tug 'Hardback', which was built in 1901 for the Hodbarrow Mining Company of Whitehaven, and sold to Seaham Harbour in 1925. Her livery was black hull with a yellow line and red boot-topping, buff paddleboxes and superstructure, and black funnel with a yellow band.

In S287007A (above left) we are looking across the old inner harbour to the coal staithes. Partially hidden by one of the staithes is the paddle tug 'Seaham'. Built for the Seaham Harbour Dock Company in 1909, she spent her entire working life at Seaham before being scrapped in 1962. She was designed so that she could enter the lock and work in the small north basin.

Above: **SEAHAM, THE HARBOUR c1955** S287007A   Left: **SEAHAM, THE HARBOUR c1955** S287008

NOT POPULAR WITH A POET

In 1815 Lord Byron married Anne Isabella Milbanke at Seaham Hall; the marriage is recorded in the church register at St Mary's. Byron hated Seaham, and the marriage was not made in heaven. Of Seaham, Byron wrote: 'Upon this dreary coast we have nothing but county meetings and shipwrecks; and I have this day dined upon fish, which probably dined upon the crews of several colliers lost in the recent gales'.

SUNDERLAND

SUNDERLAND on the river Wear has a long cultural history along with its industrial heritage. The monastery of St Peter and St Paul was founded here in Anglo-Saxon times, and here the Venerable Bede wrote the first history of England. Sunderland was also a prosperous industrial and trading town by 1500. But it was in the 18th and 19th centuries that Sunderland grew spectacularly. The vast amount of coal mined on Wearside needed ships to transport it, and so Sunderland became an important shipbuilding town. Over 600 years of shipbuilding on the Wear came to an end with the closure of North East Shipbuilder's Southwick yard in 1989.

The photographs above and on the opposite page show Sunderland in its thriving heyday. A tram rattles across the old road bridge bound for Grangetown in S263003p (above); the 236ft single span cast-iron bridge was designed by Thomas Paine, author of 'The Rights of Man'. Built between 1793 and 1796, it was an engineering masterpiece. It was replaced by a new Wearmouth Bridge in 1929. Just beyond is the North Eastern Railway's bridge over the Wear. In photograph S263004 (above, opposite) we see the old bridge, and the dredger 'Titan'. Beyond are several tugs, one of which belongs to Lambton Collieries, whose coal staithes can also be seen in the background.

AT THIS time Tynemouth was still a major industrial area, and there were dozens of coal mines in operation. Shipyards still lined the banks of the Tyne and the Wear, and railway locomotives were being built at Gateshead, turbines at Heaton, and armoured vehicles at Elswick. Townships often depended upon one large employer to provide most of the local jobs which in turn fuelled the local economy.

At the beginning of the 20th century, British shipyards were at the forefront of world shipbuilding and the ship repair industry. In those days British yards could build a battleship twice as fast as any American yard, and five times faster than those of the embryonic Japanese shipbuilding industry. Thousands found work in the yards on the Tyne and Wear. In 1903 Swan, Hunter & Wigham Richardson was formed at Wallsend from the amalgamation of the yards of Charles Swan & Hunter and Wigham Richardson & Co. The new shipbuilding giant also purchased the intervening yard of the Tyne Ship & Pontoon Co to give a continuous river frontage, and took a majority holding in the marine engine building firm Wallsend Slipway and Engineering.

Left: **SUNDERLAND, THE BRIDGES c1900** S263004

TYNEMOUTH

❝ I never saw anything less inviting or more discouraging for a bather than the appearance of everything around ... The general character of all the three places is that of ugliness – Tynemouth itself, perhaps, being the worst, and with the aspect of poverty to boot. Yet here upon these sands ... do the Newcastle people and others from the neighbourhood repair, for the luxury of washing off with muddy salt water the sooty layers deposited on their skin during the lengthened winter season.

DR GRANVILLE, 'SPAS OF ENGLAND AND PRINCIPAL SEA-BATHING PLACES' 1841

Left: **TYNEMOUTH, ACROSS THE BAY c1955** T142065

Above: **TYNEMOUTH, THE RIVER TYNE c1955** T142067

CULLERCOATS

IT WAS not all collieries and shipyards around Tyneside; much of the landscape was developed for agriculture during the late 18th to the mid 19th centuries, and remains so to this day. Fishing, too, was once an important contribution to the economies of places like Craster, Alnmouth, Cullercoats, and North Shields.

A coal port in the 17th century, and a seaside retreat for the well-heeled of Newcastle from the late 19th century onwards, Cullercoats was also a noted fishing community. From the doors of these cottages (C283006, left) fishwives in their distinctive costume sold fish.

Cottages like the ones in C283006 are typical of the fishing communities of the north-east. The tiny houses were often built in rows or in squares round a courtyard. Like these ones, the cottages usually consisted of one room, with one door and one window. Inside, the flagstone or cement floor might be covered with linoleum; a hooky (rag) rug, made by the fisherman's wife, would only be brought out for special occasions. As we see here from the large chimneys, each cottage had an open fire, which as well as providing heat was often used for cooking as well. A large pot was kept beside the fire for storing hot water. Note the pebbledash on the walls, a very necessary protection from the harsh weather.

Left: **CULLERCOATS, FISHERMEN'S COTTAGES c1955** C283006

FISHING BOAT REGISTRATION LETTERS AND NUMBERS

All fishing boats must display a port of registration, and this is shown by letters and a number, painted on the bows.

AB: Aberystwyth	CT: Castletown	J: Jersey	PH: Plymouth	SS: St Ives	AD: Ardrossan	IE: Irvine
BE: Barnstaple	DH: Dartmouth	LA: Llanelli	PL: Peel	SSS: South Shields	AR: Ayr	K: Kirkwall
BW: Barrow	DO: Douglas	LI: Littlehampton	PN: Preston	ST: Stockton	BA: Ballantrae	KY: Kirkcaldy
BS: Beaumaris	DR: Dover	LL: Liverpool	PT: Port Talbot	SU: Southampton	BF: Banff	LH: Leith
BK: Berwick on Tweed	E: Exeter	LN: Kings Lynn	PW: Padstow	TH: Teignmouth	BO: Bo'ness	LK: Lerwick
BD: Bideford	F: Faversham	LO: London	PZ: Penzance	TO: Truro	BRD: Broadford	ML: Methil
BH: Blyth	FD: Fleetwood	LR: Lancaster	R: Ramsgate	WA: Whitehaven	BCK: Buckie	OB: Oban
BN: Boston	FE: Folkestone	LT: Lowestoft	RN: Runcorn	WH: Weymouth	BU: Burntisland	ME: Montrose
BR: Bridgewater	FH: Falmouth	M: Milford Haven	RR: Rochester	WI: Wisbech	CN: Campbeltown	PD: Peterhead
BL: Bristol	FY: Fowey	MH: Middlesborough	RX: Rye	WO: Workington	CY: Castlebay	RO: Rothesay
BM: Brixham	GE: Goole	MN: Maldon	RY: Ramsey	WT: Westport	DE: Dundee	SR: Stranraer
CA: Cardigan	GR: Gloucester	MR: Manchester	SA: Swansea	WY: Whitby	DS: Dumfries	SY: Stornoway
CF: Cardiff	GU: Guernsey	MT: Maryport	SC: Scilly		FR: Fraserburgh	TN: Troon
CH: Chester	GY: Grimsby	NE: Newcastle	SD: Sunderland	SCOTLAND	GH: Grangemouth	TT: Tarbert
CK: Colchester	H: Hull	NN: Newhaven	SE: Salcombe		GN: Granton	UL: Ullapool
CL: Carlisle	HH: Harwich	NT: Newport, Gwent	SH: Scarborough	A: Aberdeen	GW: Glasgow	WK: Wick
CO: Caernarfon	HL: Hartlepool	P: Portsmouth	SM: Shoreham	AA: Alloa	GK: Greenock	WN: Wigtown
CS: Cowes	IH: Ipswich	PE: Poole	SN: North Shields	AH: Arbroath	INS: Inverness	

NEWBIGGIN-BY-THE-SEA

AT THE turn of the century Newbiggin was a popular resort, with visitors arriving daily in the summer by train. Many families, mainly from Newcastle, had holiday homes overlooking the beautiful bay. Over the years some of the bay has collapsed, possibly owing to the lead mine workings. In recent years much has been done to restore the town.

Sad to say, industry is a blot on many otherwise beautiful landscapes, and here the power station at Blyth is no exception (N76067, above left). Of course, the up side to this is that industry supplies our modern-day conveniences and employment. The caravan park in N76067 still caters for visitors in the summer months. In N76062 (below left) an old red phone box stands outside the post office to the left. Two children are enjoying ice cream, while the older generation sit on the benches or lean on the wall to look out at the sea. A rather flashy Art Deco café contrasts with the fishing boat in front of it.

CRASTER

CRASTER, DUNSTANBURGH CASTLE c1960 C352065

Top: **NEWBIGGIN-BY-THE-SEA, SANDY BAY CARAVAN SITE c1960** N76067
Above: **NEWBIGGIN-BY-THE-SEA, THE PROMENADE c1960** N76062

DUNSTANBURGH Castle (C352065) was built in the 14th century; the largest castle in the county, this once magnificent building occupied 11 acres of land. It was well protected by nature on three sides; to the north were sheer cliffs, which made this an ideal site to build a fortress. The castle had a barbican, a gatehouse and three towers. However, it was only lived in for 150 years. Badly damaged during the Wars of the Roses, it was never repaired, and is now a magnificent ruin atop 100ft-high cliffs overlooking Embleton Bay. Dunstanburgh is haunted by a knight, Sir Guy. His anguished cries are said to be heard as he tries to find a way to enter the castle in pursuit of a lovely lady who lives there.

BEADNELL

BEADNELL, THE HARBOUR c1955 B550050

THE EARLIEST record of the village dates from 1161. Agriculture was once the mainstay of the economy, with corn being taken to the harbour to be shipped out. Limestone quarrying was also an industry carried out here in the 18th and 19th centuries – lime kilns stand by the harbour in B550050 (above).

Above left: **FARNE ISLAND, PUFFINS c1935** F152005

Above right: **GULL** (COURTESY RUI RODRIGUEZ)

Below left: **FARNE ISLAND, HERRING GULL STEALING A GANNET'S EGG c1960** F152024

FARNE ISLAND

LIME KILNS

Lime is an important commodity, used since prehistoric times to make mortar, and for limewash to paint houses; since the 17th century it has been used as a fertiliser. Limestone is not suitable for spreading on the land unless it is finely ground, and in earlier times the easiest way to break it down was to burn it in lime kilns (see B550050, above left). Lime burning must have been an exhausting and unpleasant job. First, the limestone had to be unloaded from ships onto the wharf, and the large boulders broken up with 28lb sledgehammers. Then a fire was lit in the kilns: layers of logs and coal were topped with a layer of stone, then more coal, and so on. The fire would have to be fed and tended for days, giving off noxious fumes in the process. Barry Hughes, a local historian from Devon, has written vividly of the lime kiln workers: 'In cold wet weather, it was probably a relief to leave the task of stone breaking on the smoky kiln top and go down into the hot, dark arches between the kilns to rake out the burnt lime. Swathed in sacking and bent almost double under the low arches leading to the fire grates, the workers had to pull the red-hot stones and cinders from beneath the fire bars. Scarves or head cloths covered all but their eyes, as quicklime dust reacts violently with moisture, producing instant heat and burning. After drawing out the lime, they would emerge red-eyed and choking from the fume-filled arches.'

THE GREAT Whin Sill was formed by a kind of basalt being forced underground between layers of rock during the volcanic era. This dramatic natural formation stretches from Upper Teesdale in the west to the Farne Islands in the east. The islands are home to around 4,000 grey seals, a protected species here; they breed at the rate of about one thousand seal pups a year. Guillemots, terns, razorbills, puffins (F152005, opposite) and eider ducks are some of the wild species of birds that use the Farne Islands as their breeding grounds from mid May to mid July. In F152024 (opposite) we see the mother gannet has left the nest unattended, so the cheeky seagull has sneaked onto the nest to steal its dinner. Gulls are scavengers - and where better to scavenge than these islands in the breeding season.

This distinctive lighthouse (F152002, below) was built in 1826. It was manned for 160 years before giving way to modern technology and becoming disused. It was the home of Grace Darling and her family at the time when they carried out the famous rescue of crew of the steamer the 'Forfarshire' on the evening of 5 September 1838. The stricken vessel struck a rock off Farne in complete darkness, and the sea broke over her hull in huge waves, drowning the shrieks of the terrified passengers. Eight of the crew managed to launch a boat, and could only watch as the many passengers were swept away into an ocean grave. The lighthouse stands silent guard over the wild terrain and its inhabitants.

Grace Darling's brave and heroic errand of mercy

❝ *The weather was so bad that the lighthouse keeper, Mr Darling, doubted the possibility of rendering assistance. But his daughter Grace entreated her father to go at all risks, and offered herself to take one oar … Mother and daughter aided him in launching the boat. After a hard pull through the boiling foam they reached the rock, where they found nine persons shivering and trembling for their lives. The joy of the rescued people may well be imagined, and their amazement at finding that one of their deliverers was a young girl.*

FREDERICK WHYMPER, 'THE SEA' c1885

St Cuthbert's Chapel (F152004p overleaf) on Inner Farne was built in about 1370 on top of an earlier building – there are traces of 12th-century masonry in the north wall. Outside the west wall are the foundations of what may be a galilee, or porch chapel, a typical feature of churches dedicated to St Cuthbert. This chapel was built and dedicated to him here because he spent a large part of  his life in his beloved Farne Islands, first as Prior of Lindisfarne from 664. In 676 he retired to live the life of a holy hermit, some say on an islet near Lindisfarne. In 685 he was consecrated Bishop of Lindisfarne, but a year later he returned to his hermitage, where he died in 687. He was buried at Lindisfarne, where many miracles were reported – Cuthbert was known as 'the wonder-worker of England'. Today his bones lie in Durham Cathedral.

Left: **FARNE ISLAND, THE LONGSTONE LIGHTHOUSE** c1960
F152002

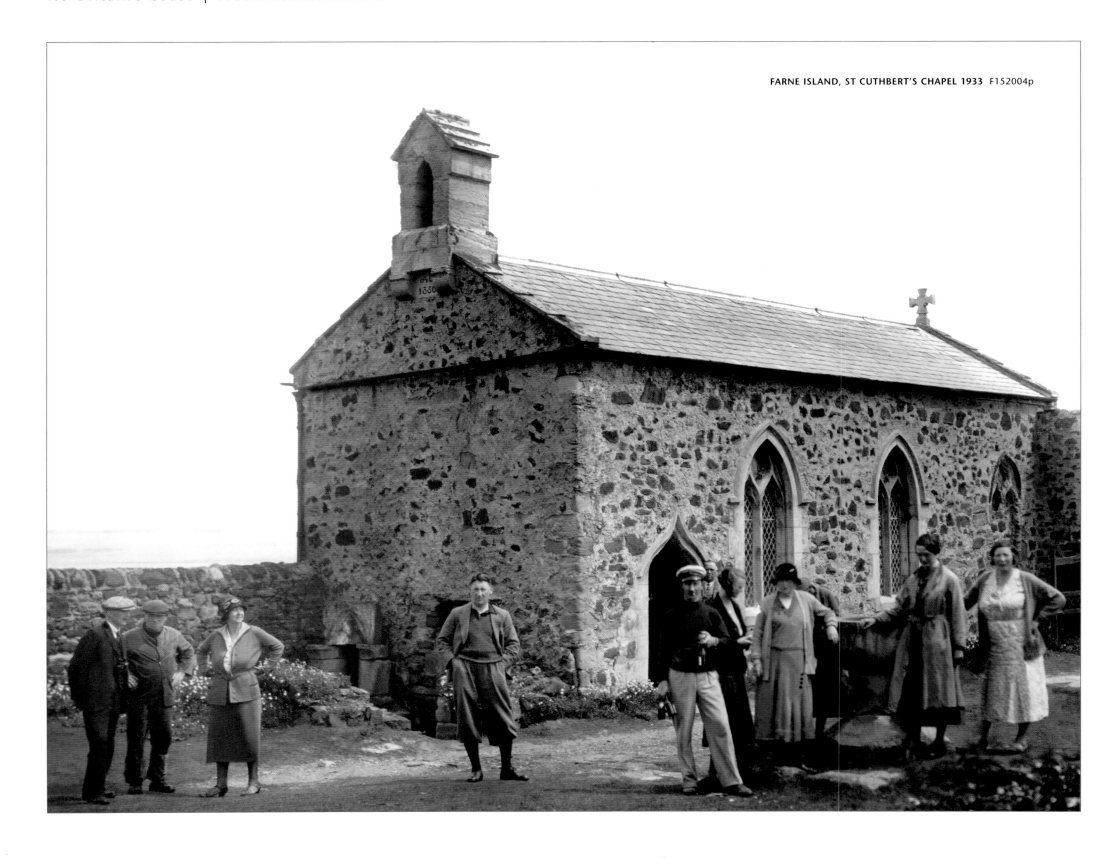

FARNE ISLAND, ST CUTHBERT'S CHAPEL 1933 F152004p

Above: **SEAHOUSES, THE HARBOUR c1936** S521027t

SEAHOUSES

THIS village grew up in 1889, when the harbour was built to improve the fishing industry in the area. Steam drifters took over from the smaller fishing boats at the end of the 19th and beginning of the 20th century in most of the coastal towns and villages. Seahouses managed to hang on to their sailing boats until the 1920s, when motor-driven drifters began to be used. We can see the signs of the industry in S521027t (left) – crab and lobster pots are stacked on the pier. The fishing industry still carries on in some of the coastal towns and villages, but on a much smaller scale than 100 years ago. Now many of them are quiet resorts used by tourists as a base from which to visit other places nearby. Others treble their population in the summer months – at Seahouses trips can be made to the Farne Islands.

THIS has been a fortified site since the 6th century – from here Anglo-Saxon kings once ruled Northumbria. The Norman castle at Bamburgh dates from the 11th century. It was besieged in 1095 by William II. Unable to take the fortress from Robert de Mowbray, third Earl of Northumberland, William headed south, leaving the prosecution of the siege to others. Mowbray attempted to escape, but was captured. His wife only surrendered Bamburgh after her husband had been paraded before the walls under threat of being blinded. Bamburgh holds the distinction of being the first castle to be breached by gunfire, when forces loyal to Edward IV deployed two large cannon. However, the garrison was already on the point of surrendering, having eaten the last of their horses. During the Wars of the Roses the castle was damaged and went into decline. Restoration was carried out in the 18th century, and then again in the 19th century by Lord Armstrong, a Victorian engineer and industrialist.

BAMBURGH CASTLE

Right: **BAMBURGH, THE CASTLE c1950** B547027

LINDISFARNE'S TREASURE

Lindisfarne's beautiful Gospel book is justly famous. It was created in the early 8th century for ceremonial use at Lindisfarne monastery. Its text, which was written out by a single scribe, is a Latin version of Saint Jerome's Vulgate, which was popular in the western world at this period. The Gospels contain fifteen elaborately decorated pages.

Far left: **HOLY ISLAND, THE CASTLE c1935** H348112

Below: **HOLY ISLAND, A PLEASURE BOAT c1935** H348133

HOLY ISLAND

FROM just north of Berwick-on-Tweed to Tynemouth stretch miles of virtually unspoilt coastline. The waves of the unpredictable North Sea pound against rugged cliffs, wash gently onto the sandy beaches of the sheltered bays, and lap against the moored boats of the coastal villages.

Out of every 24 hours there are up to 11 when Holy Island (Lindisfarne) is cut off from the mainland. At low tide the island is surrounded by a vast expanse of sand on which thousands of wild birds feed. Sited atop Beblowe Craig (once a volcano), picturesque Lindisfarne Castle (H348112, above) can be seen for many miles around. It was built after the Dissolution of the Monasteries from the stones of the priory. In 1901 it was bought by Edward Hudson, editor of Country Life, and he commissioned the eminent architect Edwin Lutyens to convert it into a home. Today the castle is owned by the National Trust.

The boatman in H348133 (right) stands in the centre with his boathook, while his passengers pose for the camera. They certainly look as though they are all enjoying themselves. On the stern of the boat a small flagpole displays a Red Ensign.

NORTH BERWICK

TANTALLON was a stronghold of the Douglases, a powerful family who were wardens of the Border Marches, lords of Galloway, and by the end of the 15th century masters of much of Lothian, Stirlingshire and Clydesdale. Even in its ruined sate Tantallon still looks formidable. The great curtain wall with its central gatehouse and flanked at either end by massive round towers dates from the last quarter of the 14th century. The gatehouse incorporated the castellan's quarters, and represents a shift away from the keep or donjon to the keep-gatehouse. Other gatehouse castles include Kildrummy, Dundonald, and Doune. Linlithgow was remodelled with a keep-gatehouse in 1304, designed by Edward I's brilliant castle builder Master James of St George.

James V resented the Douglases and besieged Tantallon in 1528. Red Douglas held out for three months before surrendering. He was lucky he was allowed to go into exile, his estates forfeited to the Crown. Another victim of James's vendetta, Lady Glamis, was burnt at the stake for alleged witchcraft.

NORTH BERWICK, TANTALLON CASTLE 1897 39186

NEWHAVEN

A LITTLE more than one mile to the west of Leith is the small fishing village of Newhaven. It was here that James IV founded a royal dockyard where he could build his navy. The first ship to be launched was the 'Great Michael', a huge warship capable of carrying 420 gunners and 1,000 soldiers.

The original population of Newhaven probably came from across the North Sea. For generations, the people rarely moved out of their own community, keeping their traditions and customs alive. The fishermen's wives were noted for their dresses, which probably reflected their Dutch and Scandinavian origins.

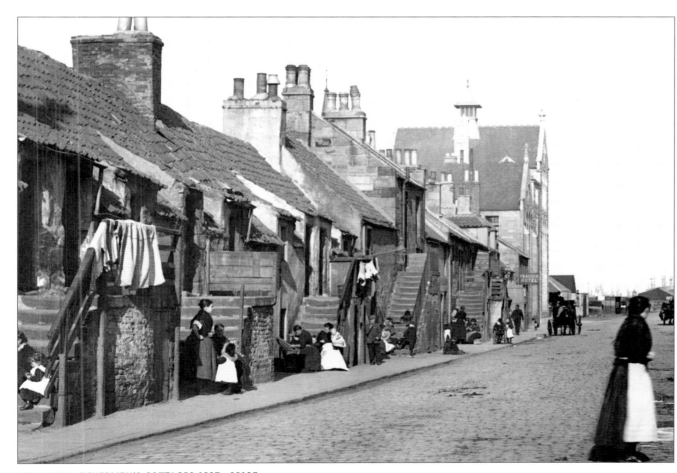

NEWHAVEN, FISHERMEN'S COTTAGES 1897 39137

QUEENSFERRY

SOUTH Queensferry on the south shore of the Firth of Forth and its counterpart North Queensferry are said have been so named because Queen Margaret crossed the Forth at this point on her way to Dunfermline.

Designed by Sir John Fowler and Sir Benjamin Baker, the Forth Bridge cost over £3 million to build (£235 million in today's money). Of the workforce of 4,500 men, 57 were killed in work-related accidents, despite rescue boats stationed under the bridge which did save eight lives. Construction of the bridge began in November 1882. The first test trains ran from January 1890, and the official opening took place on 4 March 1890. The bridge is over 2,760 yards long, including the approach viaducts, and gives a clear headway at high water of 150ft. The lofty steel cantilevers are supported on granite piers. The deepest foundations are 88ft below high water. The bridge is Scotland's largest listed structure, and it remains a vital part of the railway system, carrying up to 200 train movements a day.

FORTH RAIL BRIDGE FACTS AND FIGURES

The bridge was built using the balanced cantilever principle. Three double-cantilevers constructed with tubular struts and lattice-girder ties are connected by girder spans resting on the cantilever ends and secured by man-sized pins. The shoreward ends of the cantilevers carry weights of about 1,000 tonnes to counter-balance half the weight of the suspended span and the bridge's load. The bridge's construction used 54,000 tonnes of steel and 6,500,000 rivets. As for the legendary painting that never stops - today a new painting regime is being instituted that is hoped to give protection to the bridge to last 20 years!

QUEENSFERRY, THE FORTH BRIDGE 1897 39145

ABERDOUR, THE PIER 1900 45912

ABERDOUR

ABERDOUR in the Kingdom of Fife, lying between Burntisland and Dalgety Bay, is described in the 1906 Baedeker as 'a favourite little sea-bathing place, with an old castle and the ruins of a Norman church'.

In 45912 (left), a packed steamer from Leith is kept firmly alongside the pier as the master on the bridge plots her progress carefully – he is either about to put warps ashore or to take them aboard. The length of the boat is fairly substantial compared to the head of the jetty and requires delicate and careful manoeuvering if she is to be handled safely. A rapidly moving tide sets boats awash as they shelter in the lee of the stone wall. This part of the harbour dries completely at low water.

DUNNOTTAR CASTLE

Below: **DUNNOTTAR CASTLE c1900** D80401

THE CASTLE stands to the south of Stonehaven on a rocky headland overlooking the North Sea. It was Sir William Keith, Marischal of Scotland, who built a tower house at Dunnottar in the late 14th century; he is said to have been excommunicated for his trouble by the Bishop of St Andrews for building on sacred ground – the site had been occupied by the parish church of Dunthoyr since the 1270s. After Charles II was crowned at Scone, the Scottish crown and royal regalia (the Honours of Scotland) could not be returned to Edinburgh Castle because it had been taken by Cromwell. Therefore Charles ordered the Earl Marischal to hold the Honours and his private papers at Dunnottar. In May 1652 Dunnottar was besieged by General Lambert in an attempt to seize the Honours and the king's private papers. The regalia were lowered down to the beach and then kept in her bed by the minister of Kinneff's wife, and the papers were smuggled out under the skirts of a brave young woman, Anne Lindsey.

SCOTTISH FISHING

6 *Buy my caller herrin', they're bonnie fish and halesome farin' ... Ye little ken their worth!*

Top: **FRASERBURGH, HERRING BOATS c1900** F63003

Above: **ABERDEEN, THE FISH MARKET c1900** A90316

Opposite: **FRASERBURGH, HERRING BOATS c1900** F63002p

IN 1881, a converted tug called 'Toiler' arrived in Aberdeen with a new style of fishing. She used her powerful engines to drag a conical net, held open by a heavy wooden beam, across the sea bottom, sweeping up all the fish in its path. This was the trawl net, and it brought large quantities of fish ashore. Soon, purpose-built trawlers were fishing off Aberdeen.

So great were the catches that an open quayside was insufficient to handle them. The Council and the Harbour Board had the foresight to build a covered fish market in 1886. Here, fish were displayed while being auctioned; in A90316 (below left) we see the fish being set out before the auction – and note the trawler to the left with her Aberdeen Fishery Registration (A 69) on her funnel. The trawlers came to Aberdeen in increasing numbers. The trawlers made it the biggest fishing port in the world up until the First World War.

The fishwives were known for their cries when selling fish: 'Caller Herrin' (fresh herrings) and 'Caller Ou' (fresh oysters) – see the verses below by Lady Nairn.

6 *... Buy my caller herrin',*
They 're bonnie fish and halesome farin';
Buy my caller herrin',
New drawn frae the Forth.
An' when the creel o' herrin' passes,
Ladies, clad in silks and laces,
Gather in their braw pelisses,
Toss their heads and screw their faces;

Buy my caller herrin',
They 're bonnie fish and halesome farin';
Buy my caller herrin',
New drawn frae the Forth.
Wha'll buy my caller herrin'?
They 're no brought here without brave darin',
Buy my caller herrin',
Ye little ken their worth ...

In the 1960s, Aberdeen was to see something new and completely unexpected. Strange vessels started to appear in the harbour. Some seemed to have huge pylons, like those for carrying the National Grid electric cables, amidships. They were drilling for oil in the North Sea, from structures called 'rigs', most of which were too big to enter the harbour here. In 1971 the large Forties Field was 'proved'. Now the oil started to flow ashore. Scotland found herself in the company of Persia and Saudi Arabia as a producer of the most valuable commodity in the world's economy.

ZULU FACTS AND FIGURES

There are several stories as to how the zulu fishing boat got its name, but the first of the type does appear to have been built around 1879 at the time of the Zulu War. It was as a direct result of changing to carvel building (the planks do not overlap, unlike clinker-built craft) that the overall length of zulus increased. The masts had no standing rigging, being supported by the sail halyard and burton stay tackle. Note the mast on PF114 (on the right in F63003, top left): at deck level it appears to be at least two feet thick. The zulu beam to length ratio was in the order of 1:4. In later variants the tiller was replaced by steering wheels; steam capstans, which were used to work both rigging and the trawl, came as standard.

THE BUSTLING activity of fishermen at Fraserburgh, preparing a multitude of boats for immediate departure, provides us with a uniquely picturesque photograph (F63002p, above) that contrasts strongly with many of our more placid shots. A century later, this fishing port continues to thrive in the face of considerable European Community legislation.

The fishing boats in F63002 and F63003 (opposite above) are the type known as Zulus. The zulu is considered to have been one of the finest fore- and mizzen-rigged lugger designs of the late 19th century. The craft was a hybrid, incorporating features of the scaffie and fifie, and ranging in size from 60ft to 80ft in length, though a number of 120-footers were eventually built. Zulus carried a large amount of canvas, and the bigger boats had holds capable of taking 70 to 80 tons of herring. The zulu in the foreground of F63002p mounts a double flywheel hand capstan.

ST KILDA

THE ARCHIPELAGO of St Kilda is the remotest part of the British Isles: it lies 41 miles west of the Outer Hebrides. It is also one of the most important seabird breeding sites in Europe. It was occupied from prehistoric times until 1930, a remarkable survival of a hard way of life. The small, isolated population was almost self-sufficient – grain, fish, meat, and wool came from each family's plot, and the islanders risked their lives on the cliffs to kill gannets, fulmars and puffins for meat, oil and feathers. Photograph S250001 (left) was taken on the main island, Hirta, looking across the landing bay. A boat is approaching the jetty; near the shore were the church, the manse, the Factor's house, and a store.

By the time of the photograph, the St Kildans were not as cut off as they had been. From the 1850s, steamships made summer cruises to the islands, and fishing fleets brought supplies, heralding a gradual loss of self-sufficiency – the islanders began to rely more on imported goods, and learnt to dislike their isolation. Some of the islanders emigrated to Australia, and the younger men began to leave the island. In 1930 there were just 36 islanders left. They decided to request evacuation to the mainland. Today the islands are cared for by the National Trust for Scotland.

Left: **ST KILDA, THE BAY 1890** S250001

THE FEARLESS BIRD CATCHERS OF ST KILDA

❛ *In St Kilda, a small speck of an island, a few people, who from infancy [are] accustomed to precipices, drop from crag to crag as fearlessly as the birds themselves. Their great dependence is upon ropes of two sorts; one made of hides, – the other of hair of cow's tails, all of the same thickness. The former are the most ancient, and still continue in the greatest esteem, as being stronger, and less liable to wear away, or be cut by rubbing against the sharp edges of rocks. These ropes are of various lengths, from ninety to a hundred and twenty and nearly two hundred feet in length, and about three inches in circumference. Those of hide are made of cows' and sheep's hides mixed together ... It is indeed astonishing to what a degree habit and practice, with steady nerves, may remove danger. From the island of the South Stack above mentioned, boys may be seen frequently scrambling by themselves; or, held on by an urchin or two of their own age, letting themselves down the picturesque precipice opposite the island, by a piece of rope, so slender and apparently rotten, that the wonder is why it does not snap at the first strain. Yet, without a particle of fear, heedless of consequences, they will swing themselves to a ledge barely wide enough to admit the foot of a goat, and thence pick their way with or without the rope, to pillage the nest of a Gull, which, if aware of its own powers, might flap them headlong to the bottom.*

EDWARD STANLEY, 'A FAMILIAR HISTORY OF BIRDS' 1851

ST KILDAN HOUSES

In the foreground of S250001 (opposite page) we can see the remains of early stone corbelled structures with turf roofs; Martin Martin wrote in 1697 that the houses were 'low-built, of Stone, and a Cement of dry Earth; they have Couples and Ribs of Wood cover'd with thin earthen Turff, thatch'd over these with Straw and the Roof secur'd on each side with double Ropes of Straw or Heath, pois'd at the end with many Stones: their Beds are commonly made in the Wall of their Houses ... to make room for their Cows which they take in during the Winter and Spring.' The main village street is just visible nearer the sea, with more modern two-roomed houses built in the 1860s.

TYPICAL HOUSES OF THE WESTERN ISLES

NORTH UIST

NORTH UIST, NEWTON FERRY c1960 N110301

NORTH Uist, one of the Outer Hebrides, is a beautiful island 18 miles long and 13 miles wide, two hours by sea from the Isle of Skye. Its coast is punctuated by beaches of white sand, where the turquoise waters lap the shore, and by sea lochs, including Loch Maddy and Loch Eport. As we can see from photograph N110301 (above), the island is mostly flat, and inland is a network of small lochs, bogs, and machair land – this is fertile land composed of seashells ground up by the restless waves. Most of the inhabitants of North Uist are crofters, and the photograph shows typical crofters' cottages. A fishing fleet is based at Lochmaddy, the main settlement.

Newton Ferry (or Port nan Long) used to be the departure point for the ferry to the island of Berneray. Today causeways connect North Uist to Berneray and to the islands of Benbecula and Baleshare, and a ferry goes to Skye.

STORNOWAY

'GOD'S providence is our inheritance' is Stornoway's motto, and its inheritance is the prosperity brought by the sea. Stornoway's harbour is the best natural harbour on the north-west coast, and by the 1850s ship building and repair were being carried out here. In photograph S249001 (right) we see part of the huge herring fleet that sailed out of Stornoway – during the 19th century the fleet was 1000 boats strong, and Stornoway was the major herring port of Europe. During the season an extra 6000 people – fishermen, gutters, packers, curers and coopers – swelled the population. Barrels of salted herring were exported to Germany, Russia and the Baltic, while boxes of kippers went down to Billingsgate. The two world wars hastened the decline of the herring fishery, however, and today the fishing fleet catches shellfish and white fish.

STORNOWAY, THE HERRING FLEET 1890 S249001

IONA

Above left: **IONA, THE ABBEY 1903** 50889

SAMUEL Johnson, greatly impressed by Iona, wrote, 'That man is little to be envied, whose patriotism would not gain force upon the plain of Marathon, or whose piety would not grow warmer among the ruins of Iona.'

Iona of my heart, Iona of my love,
Instead of monks' voices there shall be
*   lowing of cattle:*
But before the world comes to an end
Iona shall be as it was.

So said St Columba (who founded a Christian community in Iona, just off the extreme south-west of Mull, in 563) shortly before he died. Indeed, although the monks endured here from the 6th to the 16th century (the Benedictines founded a monastery here in 1203), after the Reformation their voices were silent for a long time, and the abbey fell into ruin. At last, at the beginning of the 20th century, the Duke of Argyll gave the abbey church to the Iona Cathedral Trust in the hope that restoration work might be undertaken; the building was eventually re-roofed, and used for worship again in 1910. In 1938, George Macleod founded the Iona Community and began the restoration of the buildings. Today, modern pilgrims come in their thousands, and the Community lives, worships and teaches here, just as Columba's community and the Benedictine monks did in the past - Columba's words have proved true.

The fascinating photograph 50889 shows the ruins as they were before restoration began - these are the ruins of the Benedictine monastery; little remains today of Columba's community. Nearer the camera is St Oran's chapel, dating from the 11th century; in the graveyard beside it, the oldest burial ground in Scotland, are the graves of 48 Scottish kings and chieftains, and the graves of kings of Ireland, France and Norway.

❝ *Prince Albert, the Prince of Leinengen, the Duke of Norfolk, Earl Grey and Sir James Clark landed on the island in August, 1847, while the Queen herself was contiguous on the royal yacht, at the time of the progress northward to Ardverikie; and they had a reception from the people so primitive and decorous as was probably given anywhere to any ancient Lord of the Isles. A few plainly dressed is-landers stood on the shore, carrying tufted willow-wands, and prepared to act as an escort; the body of the people, for the most part decently dressed, stood behind, looking eagerly on as spectators, yet all maintaining a respectful distance; only a few children, in the usual fashion of the island, offered pebbles and shells for sale; and when the august visitors, after quietly surveying the curiosities of the place, returned to the barge, all the population gave loud voice in a hearty farewell cheer.*

THE IMPERIAL GAZETTE

IONA, THE BEACH AND THE VILLAGE 1903 50887

STAFFA, FINGAL'S CAVE 1903 50897

ST COLUMBA

St Columba was a member of the O'Neill clan; he left Ireland after the battle of Cuil-dremne. It is said that it was Columba himself who caused the battle: he was accused by the High King of taking a psalter without permission, so Columba appealed to his clan for help in clearing his name, and the matter was settled by sword and axe. On his arrival in Scotland, St Columba chose Iona as the site for a religious house from where he could carry out his missionary work.

STAFFA

Like the inside of an immense organ, black and resounding, and absolutely without purpose

THE INTERNATIONALLY famous rock formations of Fingal's Cave on the Isle of Staffa were first publicised to the outside world in 1772 by Joseph Banks. 'Compared to this what are the cathedrals or the palaces built by men!' Felix Mendelssohn visited Staffa in 1829 and was inspired to compose 'Fingal's Cave', as a tribute to the beauty and atmosphere he found in these rocks. JMW Turner was soon to follow, and produced an impressively brooding painting of the mouth of the cave. More and more people were growing aware of the charms of the area.

Sir Walter Scott visited Staffa and said that Fingal's Cave was 'one of the most extraordinary places I ever beheld. It exceeded, in my mind, every description I had heard of it ... Composed entirely of basaltic pillars as high as the roof of a cathedral, and running deep into the rock, eternally swept by a deep and swelling sea, and paved, as it were, with ruddy marble, it baffles all description'.

We were put out into boats and lifted by the hissing sea up the pillar stumps to the celebrated Fingal's Cave. A greener roar of waves surely never rushed into a stranger cavern – its many pillars making it look like the inside of an immense organ, black and resounding, and absolutely without purpose, and quite alone, the wide grey sea within and without.

FELIX MENDELSSOHN 1829

OBAN

OBAN is the port for the islands on the west coast of Scotland, and the importance of the part that these islands have played in the establishment of tourism in the area should not be underestimated. Indeed, in photograph O4001 (left) we can see many ships of varied sizes in the harbour, and also the railway which brought tourists here to embark on the ships. The route around the Isle of Mull to the isles of Iona and Staffa was particularly popular.

Boswell and Johnson passed through Oban on their way back from Iona. Johnson described as 'tolerable' the inn at which they stayed the night – high praise indeed from a man who could be so scathing of all things Scottish. In the summer of 1814, Walter Scott was invited to join Robert Stevenson, the famous lighthouse builder (the grandfather of Robert Louis Stevenson) on a voyage of inspection around the coast of Scotland. Inspired by the coast of Lorn and its islands, Scott wrote 'The Lord of the Isles'. This epic poem relates the adventures of Robert the Bruce and his battles with the MacDougalls, and proved highly popular – the first edition (in 1815) soon sold out.

Left: **OBAN, THE RAILWAY STATION AND THE NEW PIER c1900** O4001

QUEEN VICTORIA VISITS OBAN

Perhaps the single most momentous day in the history of Oban was the sunny day of 19 August 1847, when Queen Victoria and her Prince Consort, Prince Albert, sailed into Oban Bay on the royal yacht 'Victoria and Albert.' They were escorted by five other vessels, including the fearsome HMS 'Fairy'. We know from the council minutes that there was much fuss made over this visit. Plans were made for six large bonfires on the hilltops around the town. Oban itself was to be illuminated with 'variegated' lamps in welcome of Her Majesty. The council presented the queen with an address expressing their congratulations on her safe arrival and also 'the perfect enthusiasm that pervades all Ranks, at this marked expression of Your Majesty's Gracious Confidence in the loyalty and devotion of your Celtic subjects, and we hail this, Your Majesty's first Visit ... to a locality celebrated for one of the ancient seats and very interesting associations as an Auspicious Era in our County's History and another Link between Your Majesty and your Royal Family and us your most Devoted and Deeply attached subjects.'

 # ISLAND OF ARRAN

LOCH Ranza (A93001p, left) is a sea-loch that forms an inlet of the Kilbrannan Sound. This view was photographed near the northern tip of the island. Lochranza Castle dates from the late 13th century to the mid 14th century with 16th-century additions, and features one of the earliest examples of an added jamb or wing which was built on to increase the castle's defence capability. The square tower projects to cover the entrance, and is equipped with long arrow slits of an early design. The original entrance was of the heavily ribbed barrel-vaulted type.

Now owned by the National Trust for Scotland, Brodick Castle (A93002 below), once the seat of the Dukes of Hamilton, dates from the 14th century. It was from here in 1307 that Robert the Bruce launched his campaign to liberate mainland Scotland from the English. Brodick was enlarged when garrisoned by Cromwell's troops, and the tower is a mid 19th-century addition.

Left: **ARRAN, THE CASTLE AND LOCH RANZA c1890** A93001p

❝ The island of Arran is about 20 miles in length by 12 in breadth, and a large district occupying much of the northern half still remains as mountain moorland ... On the calm sea, on a fine summer evening, the whole water is covered with boats and vessels; the dark sails of the former, no less than their beautiful pyramidal outline, sprinkling the whole blue expanse in every variety of combination and of magnitude. Within the bay, the different groups are disposed nearer the eye in a thousand picturesque assemblages, varying at every moment, as they are hoisting their sails to stand out to sea, or as they run alongside the sloops where the flag is flying to receive their cargoes. On shore crowds of men, women and children surround the sail-tents, where the smoke of the fires scattered along the margin of the water is ascending to the hills, mixing with the evening mists, and contrasting with the yellow of the setting sun.

VICTORIAN GUIDEBOOK

Right: **ARRAN, BRODICK CASTLE 1890** A93002

TARBERT, FROM THE SOUTH 1890 T102001

TARBERT

TARBERT, the gateway to the Kintyre peninsula, lies south of Lochgilphead, on the isthmus between West Loch Kintyre and East Loch Tarbert, an inlet of Loch Fyne – indeed, its name is the Gaelic 'tairbeart', meaning isthmus, literally 'draw boat' – a piece of land across which a boat can be dragged. It is said that in 1093 Magnus Barefoot dragged his longship overland between the two lochs, claiming Kintyre as a Norse possession.

Kintyre has been occupied since Mesolithic times, and has probably always been important as the best route between the Western Isles and the Clyde. By the early 13th century, a castle had been built overlooking Tarbert's harbour, and it remained important militarily until the 18th century. Photograph T102001 (left) shows the town clustered around the shores of East Loch Tarbert. At this time, regular steamers to and from Glasgow were calling here. Today, Tarbert is linked by ferry to Islay, Portavadie, Lochranza, and the Isle of Gigha, and its fishing fleet catches all kinds of seafood, including prawns, herrings, scallops and mackerel – there is a seafood festival here every year. The harbour is popular with yachtsmen too.

LOCHGILPHEAD

AS ITS name suggests, Lochgilphead stands at the head of Loch Gilp, a small loch heading north west from Loch Fyne. It is unusual in that it is a completely planned town, first laid out in a grid pattern in 1790, when the road from Inverary to Campbeltown was built. Its importance grew after 1801, when the Crinan Canal was constructed to form a short cut across the Kintyre peninsula – it runs just to the west of Lochgilphead to meet Loch Fyne at Ardrishaig. Further transport links came in the 1830s (the road from Lochgilphead to Oban and also a pier, making it easier to travel by steamer to Glasgow), and the town became the administrative centre for Argyll and Bute, a role that continues today.

The Kintyre peninsula is 40 miles long but only 8 miles wide. Its north-south spine is rough and rocky, and from it streams and waterfalls flow down into the glens. The eastern coast is punctuated by many beautiful coves; one of the bays consists of flat oval stones which form a strange beach a mile long. The geology here is complex, with the different rocks having formed sands of different colours.

Right: **LOCHGILPHEAD 1890** L133001

DUNOON

SINCE the 1850s, Dunoon has always been a favourite resort for Glaswegians. The 'doon the watter' trips from the Broomielaw in Glasgow became almost an institution from then until the Second World War. Today, ferries from Gourock still ply their trade. Dunoon was also a place of residence for many American naval personnel, whose submarine base was in the Holy Loch until recently. During the last weekend of every August the Cowal Highland Gathering is held, which provides two days of highland games; on the Saturday the spectacle of pipe bands from all over the world can be seen as they march along the main street. Robert Burns's 'Highland Mary' – Mary Campbell – was born locally; a statue to her stands on the hillside above the pier. They intended to marry, and emigrate to the West Indies, but she took ill and died, and Burns in his grief decided to remain in Scotland.

During the early 1880s problems with drunken Glaswegians running amok in the coastal towns had led to the withdrawal of Sunday excursion sailings. With pubs in Glasgow being shut on the Sabbath, the only place to get a drink had been on board an excursion steamer.

Today, the buildings and the pier in 52620 (left) have been modernised to cope with holiday traffic demands. The steamers now plying between the resorts all belong to the one company, Caledonian MacBrayne, who operate all the services on the west coast of Scotland and the Western Isles.

Above: **DUNOON, THE PIER 1904** 52620   Below: **DUNOON, THE PS 'COLUMBA' 1904** 52621

THE 'COLUMBA'

Launched on 11 April 1878, the Clyde paddler 'Columba' (52621) was the last vessel built for David Hutchinson & Co; the firm changed its name to David MacBrayne the following year. Ordered for the Glasgow-Tarbert-Ardrishaig run, the 'Columba' was not only the first Clyde paddler fitted with full-width passenger saloons, but she also had a bookshop, a hairdressing saloon, a fruit stall and a post office. Her designed speed of 18 knots at 36rpm was improved upon in 1900 when she was fitted with haystack boilers, making her capable of 19 knots at 40 rpm. In September 1936 she was laid up at Greenock for the last time and sold the following March for scrap. She was broken up at Dalmuir.

ROTHESAY

ROTHESAY, THE PIER 1897 39836

ROTHESAY is the county town on the eastern side of the Island of Bute, set in an ideal location in the sheltered 'sweet Rothesay Bay', to quote the popular song. The pier has changed little from the way it looks in this photograph (39836, above): in the holiday period it is still as busy as it was a century ago. The main sailing destinations from here are to Wemyss Bay on the Ayrshire coast and, in the summer season, to the Island of Arran, as well as holiday excursions.

As one paddler loads, another leaves. It is 1897, and a golden age for the Clyde excursion steamer industry is dawning: operators sense that the ban on landings at some piers on the Sabbath will soon be broken. The paddler pulling away might be the 'Ivanhoe', photographed shortly after her sale to the Caledonian Steam Packet Company, but before her paddle-boxes were painted white and a bar installed. At 282 grt (gross registered tonnage), the 'Ivanhoe' had been built in 1880 by D & W Henderson for the Firth of Clyde Steam Packet Co as a temperance ship. Everyone said that the idea would never work, but it did; she proved very popular with families desperate to avoid having to mix with the heavy drinkers, who often made trips miserable for everyone except for themselves. The ship was always immaculately turned out, and her crew wore naval uniform. In 1894 she spent a couple of months on charter on excursion work along the newly opened Manchester Ship Canal, but returned north in time for the summer season.

ON THE Firth of Clyde, this seaside resort looks across the Firth towards Kilcreggan, Loch Long and Dunoon. It is a centre for yachting and for boating trips in the Firth and to the Kyles of Bute. On the cliff side of Gourock is a prehistoric monolith, Granny Kempock's Stone, still associated with ancient myths and superstitions. There are splendid views over the resort and estuary from Gourock Golf Club situated high above the town. As well as being a resort, Gourock was well known for its herring curing – the first recorded curing of red herrings took place here in 1688.

Photograph 45975p (above left) shows the backs of buildings along Kempock Street. Kempock Place is just in view on the extreme left of the picture. Over to the right is Seaton's Temperance Hotel, one of several in the town. At this time temperance hotels abounded throughout the UK, but there was in fact little difference between them and private hotels, as neither had liquor licences.

In 45986 (above right) we see the lighthouse at Cloch Point, between Gourock and Inverkip. Built in 1796, the lighthouse stands 76ft high and is a notable Clyde estuary landmark, looking across to the light on the Gantock rocks. During the Second World War an anti-submarine boom ran across the river from Cloch Point to the Gantocks. Additional defences were fixed gun positions at Cloch Point, Toward Point and Dunoon.

❝ *No man living has ever beheld, in my opinion, a river, the banks of which presented a greater number and a greater variety of views, or more beautiful views, than those which are presented to the eye on the banks of the Clyde.* SAMUEL JOHNSON

GOUROCK AND THE CLYDE

Top left: **GOUROCK, FROM THE PIER 1900** 45975p

Top right: **CLOCH POINT, THE LIGHTHOUSE 1900** 45986

Above: **RIVER CLYDE, YACHTS 1897** 39824

*The steamers that put from the Clyde,
And the whalers that sail from Dundee,
Go forth in their season on top of the tide
To gather the grist of the sea,
To ply in the lanes of the sea.*

*By fairway and channel and sound,
By shoal and deep water they go,
Guessing the course by the feel of the ground
Or chasing the drift of the floe,
Nor'west in the track of the floe.*

*And we steer them to harbours afar,
At hazard we win them abroad,
Where the coral is furrowed by keels on the bar
And the sea-floor is swept by the Lord,
The anchorage dredged by the Lord ...*

PERCEVAL GIBBON (1879–1926)

GREENOCK

GREENOCK was a beneficiary of the River Clyde's industrial heyday. It is sad that most of the shipbuilding and heavy industry have gone into decline. The first square-rigger ever to be built was launched here in 1760, and James Watt, the great engineer who pioneered the steam engine, was born here. However, there are still sugar refining and textile works in Greenock. Near the West Pier is the West Kirk, the first church to be built after the Reformation and relocated on this site. On a hill viewpoint just outside the town is a Cross of Lorraine with an anchor, which is a memorial to the Free French sailors who gave their lives in the Second World War during the Battle of the Atlantic.

Dense smoke from a distant inward bound steamer (just visible on the horizon of 39814, right) is caught by strong winds and blown across towards dockside shipping in this busy commercial port. The same breeze catches the starboard quarter of the paddle steamer approaching her temporary berth alongside the jetty, causing her to enter at an angle slightly more acute than perhaps would be usual, allowing the wind to assist berthing without smashing the boat alongside. Greenock Custom House was built in 1818. In the distance are Cartsdyke mill and east yards, the Gravel graving dock, and the entrance to the James Watt Dock.

❝ *I cannot ... take leave of Greenock without observing on the contrast which it formed with all the other sea-ports that I had ever seen in my life. Captain Cobb, with whom I crossed the Atlantic the last time, used to be everlastingly pestering me with his praises of Greenock; about its solidity, cleanliness, and the good manners of the people. As I was going to the church, the sight brought Cobb to my mind. All the people seemed to be in the streets; all going away to their different churches; no noise of any sort; no dirtily-dressed person; and not a soul to be seen who did not seem seriously in the business for which the day was set apart. Cobb used to say, that it was like a Connecticut sea-port; and I dare say it is; for the religion is the same, and I dare say that the manners of the people are very much alike.*

WILLIAM COBBETT (1763–1835)

GREENOCK,
CUSTOM HOUSE QUAY
1897 39814

> *The rocky height on which the castle stands, is a very striking object, bulging up out of the Clyde, with abrupt decision, to the height of five hundred feet. Its summit is cloven in twain, the cleft reaching nearly to the bottom on the side towards the river, but not coming down so deeply on the landward side. It is precipitous all around …Our path led us beneath one of these precipices, several hundred feet sheer down, and with an ivied fragment of ruined wall at the top. A soldier, who sat by the wayside, told us that this was called the Lover's Leap, because a young girl (in some love-exigency or other) had once jumped down from it and came safely to the bottom …*
>
> *When Dr Johnson visited the castle, he introduced his bulky person into a narrow doorway, and found it difficult to get out again. A gentleman who accompanied him was just stepping forward to offer his assistance, but Boswell whispered him to take no notice, lest Johnson should be offended; so they left him to get out as he could. He did finally extricate himself, else we might have seen his skeleton in the turret.*
>
> NATHANIEL HAWTHORNE 1857

DUMBARTON CASTLE

DUMBARTON CASTLE 1897 39809

DUMBARTON Castle straddles the 240ft-high basalt rock that dominates the burgh. Protected on three sides by water, the rock was the ideal location for a fortification, and for around 600 years it was the capital of the Kingdom of Strathclyde. The oldest part of what remains here today is a 12th-century gateway; most of the buildings date from the 17th and 18th centuries.

It had been from Dumbarton Castle that five-year-old Mary, Queen of Scots had left for France where she was to wed the Dauphin in return for French aid to rid Scotland of the English. Though Mary remained in England for the rest of her life, Dumbarton Castle was held in her name until it fell to Sir Thomas Crawford of Jordanhill in 1571. Only Edinburgh Castle was to hold out longer.

GLASGOW

GLASGOW, THE BROOMIELAW 1897   39799p

THE BROOMIELAW Quay has been Glasgow's harbour since the end of the 17th century. From here ships travelled down the Clyde to the sea. In 1812, Henry Bell's world-famous 'Comet' left from here, the first European commercial steamer service. The 19th century was probably the Broomielaw's busiest time, with ferry services carrying thousands of workers to and from the thriving shipyards, docks and workshops of the Clyde; but by the dawn of the 20th century, trams and Glasgow's subway catered for commuters. The Broomielaw has always been the point from which steamers left for Ireland, and from here pleasure boats and paddle steamers left for trips 'doon the watter' to the various holiday resorts of the Clyde, ever popular with workers and families.

The Glasgow & Inverary and the Loch Goil & Loch Long Steamboat Companies sported the same colour scheme, black hull and paddle boxes with white saloons and lifeboats. The funnel colour was red, with two white bands enclosing a black one. The top of the funnel was also painted black.

WILLIAM COBBETT PRAISES THE CLYDE

No man living has ever beheld, in my opinion, a river, the banks of which presented a greater number and a greater variety of views, or more beautiful views, than those which are presented to the eye on the banks of the Clyde. Some persons delight most in level pastures on the banks of rivers; some in woods of trees of various hues; some in hills rising up here and there nearer to, or more distant from, the banks, some of the hills clothed with woods and others with verdure; others (delighting more in utility than show) seek on the sides of rivers for an inter-mixture of corn-fields, pastures, and orchards; others (having a taste for the wilder works of nature) want to see deep banks, some of them three or four hundred feet high, with woods clinging to their sides down to the water's edge; while there are others … that are not satisifed unless they see the waters come foaming and tumbling down rocks thirty or forty feet high, with perpendicular sides, as if cleft by a convulsion of nature, and these side rocks crowned at the top with every variety of trees, over the tips of which you, from the opposite bank, see the verdant land covered with cattle and with sheep, or the arable land with corn or with turnips, the finest that the eyes of man ever beheld. Such are some of the various tastes of various persons: let them all come to the banks of the Clyde, and each will find that which will gratify, as far as this matter goes, every wish of his heart.

WILLIAM COBBETT (1763–1835)

LARGS, THE HARBOUR 1897 39855

LARGS

THE BATTLE of Largs, famous in Scottish history, took place in 1263; victory went to the Scots, which put paid to any attempts by Norwegian Vikings to dominate. Every year in September, Largs holds a Viking Festival, with enthusiastic participation by the Norwegians; this includes parades, bonfires and music. Largs is a popular holiday resort and sporting centre, and its sheltered waters are an attraction for yachting and other sailing sports. The town has many amenities to appeal to tourists; the resort has redesigned its seafront and provided facilities for the holiday maker and day-tripper. There is an interesting recently opened Viking museum, and Nardini's famous ice-cream parlour is eagerly enjoyed by the visitors.

Largs is an embarkation point for sailings to the various Clyde resorts, and also to Millport, just across from and within sight of Largs, on the island of Great Cumbrae. The town used to be well-served by steamers from all parts of the Clyde, and by the South Western Railway to Ardrossan.

WHITEHAVEN, THE HARBOUR AND THE TOWN 1950 W313014

WHITEHAVEN

THE MINERAL riches of the Cumbrian fells began to be exploited in medieval times. Granite from Shap, copper ore from the Coniston fells and iron and lead from the Pennines around Alston began to increase in importance. By the 18th and 19th centuries, Cumbria was probably better known for its industry than its scenery. Later, the Industrial Revolution was fired by coal and iron, and the Whitehaven and West Cumbrian coalfield had the distinct advantage of ease of transport from ready-made ports like Whitehaven and Maryport.

Whitehaven is a Georgian planned town, developed by Sir John Lowther; inspired by Wren's designs for London, Sir John laid out Whitehaven's streets in a grid pattern, and many of the fine Georgian buildings remain, including St James's Church, which Pevsner described as 'the finest Georgian church interior in the county'. The town's prosperity grew, founded on mining and shipbuilding.

BARROW-IN-FURNESS

BARROW-IN-FURNESS, WALNEY BRIDGE 1912 64407

THE AMERICANS INVADE

In April 1778, during the American War of Independence, John Paul Jones came to Whitehaven – he was hoping to destroy Britain's merchant fleet. John Paul Jones, the creator of the American navy, had previously been a Whitehaven seafarer. Now, commanding the American ship 'Ranger', he sailed up the west coast, doing what damage he could. He and his crew actually landed at Whitehaven, overpowering the harbour master so that the Americans could enter the harbour and set fire to the many ships berthed there, but the story goes that the American sailors were tempted by the rum and beer in the local pubs, and were easily routed. In 1999, Whitehaven forgave the Americans for invading by offering them the freedom of the harbour.

BARROW'S first iron works opened in Barrow in 1859; it later merged with Schneider & Hannay's iron works, which became the Barrow Haematite Steel Company. It was the area's largest employer and the biggest iron works in Europe. In 1859, Barrow had a population of around 800. From then on, thousands came to the town to find work.

The expanding population of Walney made a bridge to replace the ferry essential – in 64407 (above left) we see a stream of workers swarming across the bridge back to Walney at the end of the working day. It had to be an opening bridge to allow the passage of shipping up the channel. The bridge opened on 30 July 1908, having cost £175,000; it was a toll bridge until 1935. Barrow started to develop as a shipyard town from 1863, and in 1873 the first ship built by the Barrow Iron Ship Building Company slid down the slipway. In 1886 the shipyard was taken over by the Naval Construction and Armaments Company, starting the tradition of building naval vessels in Barrow. The crane in B26029 (below left) is still in use, and can be seen from many parts of the town. Here, it is helping in the fitting out of the 'Oronsay' in Buccleuch Dock.

ULVERSTON, CANAL FOOT 1923 74525

ULVERSTON

ACCESS to the Furness and Cartmel peninsulas has never been easy because of the surrounding terrain: behind are the Lakeland fells, and there was much marshland hereabouts. The main route to the area was across the treacherous sands of Morecambe Bay, with side routes off across the Leven and Duddon estuaries. These ways to the peninsulas, whilst shorter than the landward routes, were also hazardous, and many lives have been lost. The Ulverston Canal (74525, above) made travel easier. It was opened in 1796 to connect the town with the Leven estuary, and to enable both exports and imports to be increased.

BARROW-IN-FURNESS, THE SHIPYARDS c1960 B26029

GRANGE-OVER-SANDS

GRANGE-OVER-SANDS overlooks the broad sweep of Morecambe Bay. It was once just a small fishing village; then trippers began to come to Grange by boat from across Morecambe Bay, and spa waters were taken at Humphrey Head between Kents Bank and Flookburgh. Tourism had arrived.

Grange had two piers, Bailey Lane Pier and Clare House Pier (67426t, below left), which is said to have come from Piel. They were built for traffic across the bay from Morecambe and Arnside (the last steamer called in 1910, and very little remained of Clare House Pier by the 1930s). Here, the tide is full in to the promenade, and eight boats of varying sizes are gathered around. The two vessels in full sail have just discharged their passengers – they would not have long in Grange before having to return to Morecambe before the tide left the pier.

Left: **GRANGE-OVER-SANDS, THE MOTOR BOAT 1923** 74147

Below left: **GRANGE-OVER-SANDS, PLEASURE BOATS 1914** 67426t

In 74147 (above), the 'Silver Spray', an early motorboat registered in Grange, sets out with a party of trippers, apparently going towards Arnside. The two typical Morecambe Bay sailing boats have large cockpits so as to take more passengers on trips. Fishermen sometimes used to take out adventurous passengers to meet the tidal bore coming in, something that would not be allowed now for safety reasons.

ARNSIDE

THE RIVER Kent enters Morecambe Bay at Arnside (34128). Arnside became a popular seaside resort in the 19th century, when pleasure boats would come up from Morecambe and Fleetwood. Notice the little Victorian girl posing among the rowing boats laid up on the beach (left). Once a thriving port and Westmorland's only link to the sea, Arnside eventually lost its trade to better placed harbours.

Arnside Tower (34134) is a large, ruinous pele tower built during the 15th century as a protection against marauding Scots. It was badly damaged by fire in 1602, but still watches over the Kent Estuary beneath the limestone mass of Arnside Knott.

Left:
ARNSIDE, FROM THE BEACH 1894
34128

Below:
ARNSIDE, ARNSIDE TOWER AND ARNSIDE KNOTT 1894 34134

This charming little place is developing very rapidly

❝ *Arnside has not, perhaps, such fine views of the Bay as may be obtained from Grange. This place can be thoroughly 'done' in a very short time. The visitor to Arnside will, however, notice the substantial appearance of the neat villas, houses, and shops; the firm and excellent sands, on which the children are at play; and the delightful situation of the town on the slope and at the foot of the hill known as Arnside Knot. A little stone pier projects from the promenade, and from it the pleasure-boats put off. A notable feature of the estuary is the rapidity with which the flood tide covers the vast expanse of sands here, so that one runs some little risk in rambling over the sands too far away from the shore. This charming little place is developing very rapidly, and is already a formidable rival to its popular neighbour, Grange-over-Sands.*

VICTORIAN GUIDEBOOK

THE PRESENT Castle Rushen (C47501, right) dates from the 12th to the 14th centuries. It was here in 1265 that Magnus, the last of Man's Norse kings, died, ushering in nearly 70 years of Scottish rule. In 1312 England was on the brink of civil war. Robert the Bruce seized the advantage, reducing England's Scottish possessions to a handful of fortresses. In 1313 Robert invaded Man, besieging and almost destroying Castle Rushen in the process. The Isle of Man came under English rule when it was taken by Edward III of England.

When William Montacute, Earl of Salisbury, was appointed First Lord of Man he chose Castletown for his capital. Montacute strengthened the fortress's defences, adding a new tower on the eastern side and a twin-towered gateway. Later 14th-century improvements included a curtain wall and the heightening of the keep. The glacis was added by Cardinal Wolsey c1540 while he was serving as a trustee for the under-age Earl of Derby.

MONDAY, 15 OCTOBER: *'Steamer coming! seen crossing the bay, 9 hurry to boat, with Manx kitten in a basket ... Men pull fast, one swinging a lantern for signal –'She mayn't wait for you! –'She's brought to!' Alongside, I tumble up, boxes ditto; one of the men –'You were very near being left behind.' Saloon, chat. On deck, Ramsey light in the distance, Point of Ayr brilliant. Goodbye! Manx kitten escapes and is recovered after an exciting hunt ... I turn in, drest. In the morning some one asks, 'Steward, where are we now?' Steward (aggrieved, with an Ulster accent): 'Ah, it's a shame for you to be always asking me questions! You haven't given me a bit a' pace the whole night.'*

WILLIAM ALLINGHAM 1849

CASTLETOWN

PRELATES ARE IMPRISONED

In the early 1720s, Bishop Wilson was held prisoner in Castle Rushen for nine weeks for failing to pay a fine. Then in 1722 an ecclesiastical court found a certain Lady Horne guilty of slander. Lady Horne happened to be the wife of the Governor, who was naturally none too pleased. The Governor declared that the ecclesiastical courts were acting illegally, and that they must drop all such cases. The bishop and his vicars-general refused to do so, and finished up in jail themselves.

Above right: **CASTLETOWN, CASTLE RUSHEN c1885** C47501

Below right: **DOUGLAS, THE PROMENADE AND THE CLOCK TOWER 1895** 36724

DOUGLAS

Above: **DOUGLAS, A ROUGH SEA 1903** 50660p   Below: **DOUGLAS HEAD 1893** 33003

REGULAR steamship services between Douglas and Liverpool were begun in 1822 by the St George Steam Packet Company, and though the summer service was adequate, winter sailings appear to have been sporadic early on. By 1906 visitors could travel to the island from a number of ports. From Liverpool there were two sailings a day, with additional services on Fridays and Saturdays.

The Irish Sea can be as flat as a mill pond, but when an easterly, south-easterly or north-easterly gale blows up, this is what happens at Douglas (50660p, left). Sir William Hillary, founder of the RNLI, settled in Douglas in 1808. He became so concerned by the loss of seamen in local wrecks that he erected the Tower of Refuge in Douglas Bay.

The Jubilee Clock at the junction of Victoria Street and Loch Promenade (36724, opposite below) was presented to the people of Douglas by George Dumbell in 1887. Dumbell was a banker, a director of the Laxey mines and a Deemster (justice of the Tynwald), but the failure of his bank on Saturday 3 February 1900 ('Black Saturday') was one of the greatest financial disasters to hit the island.

A Victorian guidebook describes Douglas as 'well supplied with all ordinary requisites, excellent hotels, piers, and promenades. At Douglas, passengers can land at all states of the tide. The bay has been compared by local enthusiasts to the Bay of Naples, because at night a long crescent of lights is seen rising from the water. On the south side are the handsome stone piers, and a deep harbour cutting off most of the town from the cliffs of Douglas Head. Here lies the old town, whose narrow and crooked streets have been cloaked, so to speak, by the fine sea front spreading round to the north end. A fine broad street of handsome shops connects the shore with the upper part of the town. The latter shelters fully 200 Manx boats.'

MORECAMBE

MORECAMBE, THE PROMENADE 1899 42860

❦ *Morecambe is much frequented by trippers from the busy towns of Lancashire and Yorkshire, for whose recreation are provided abundant entertainments of a distinctly popular order. There are swimming-baths and assembly rooms – of a sort – a People's Palace, and a few other places of amusement, chiefly conducted on music-hall lines.*

VICTORIAN GUIDEBOOK

THE SEASIDE town of Morecambe, situated on Morecambe Bay, has wonderful views of the hills of the Lake District. The brine-tinged air from the bay, softened by the fresh air flowing in from across the Lake District, produced a relaxing and exhilarating environment for a break or holiday. The whole area has been designated one of Outstanding Natural Beauty, and the bay itself is one of Europe's best habitats for migrating birds.

Because of its closeness to the northern border, Morecambe always had a 'Scotch Week' when workers from Glasgow and the surrounding area would descend and 'let loose'. It was a sort of Wakes Week, Scottish style; it was always in mid-July. Was it Scotch Week when 42860 (above) was taken? The Promenade is certainly teeming with holidaymakers.

There were two piers at Morecambe in the past. The one we can see in the distance in view 42860 is the Central Pier, opened in 1869 to give visitors and holiday-makers a change – they could walk over the water and look down on the sea. Holiday-makers could purchase a weekly ticket for only a shilling (5p), and stroll over the sea for a full seven days.

HEYSHAM, FAIRY CHAPEL ROCKS 1912 64233

HEYSHAM, ST PATRICK'S CHAPEL RUINS, HEYSHAM HEAD 1888 21071p

❝ *The coast [here] becomes a little more broken, and the neighbourhood generally prettier. The picturesque village of Heysham, with its singular church and burial-place, occupies a rocky knoll of red sandstone, over-hanging the shore.* VICTORIAN GUIDEBOOK

HEYSHAM

NO HOLIDAY in Morecambe or Lancaster was complete without a day at Heysham. The rocky coast around Heysham Head provided excitement and danger for its Victorian and Edwardian visitors. Nicknames or folk names gave places added attraction to those day-trippers; here we see the rock formation known for many years as the Fairy Chapel (64233, left). Our two visitors seem impressed enough to pose for their photograph.

St Patrick himself is said to have been shipwrecked on the head; years later, monks came from his monastic foundation in Ireland and built this chapel in his memory (21071p, above). Perching above low cliffs overlooking the sea, it dates from Saxon times, the 8th century. One of the reasons it has stood so long in such an exposed spot is the mortar: it is ground-up sea shells, heated and mixed with boiling water to give a cement-like substance. It is the only example left in England of a single-cell Saxon chapel. Originally it was 24ft long by 8ft wide, with walls nearly 3ft thick. Our Victorian ladies posing by the chapel add charm to our photograph – which apart from them could have been taken today.

FLEETWOOD

FLEETWOOD was built on a salt marsh and rabbit warren for Sir Peter Hesketh-Fleetwood of Rossall Point as a port, a fishing centre and a tourist resort. The end of the Victorian era was a prosperous time for Fleetwood; it was busy as a port, sending ships all over the world from Shanghai to San Francisco. Linked by rail to Euston, Fleetwood developed as a major port, handling passengers and cargo bound for Ireland, the Isle of Man and Glasgow.

In 59940 (opposite) we see the Furness Railway paddle steamer 'Philomel' entering Fleetwood. Built in 1899 for the General Steam Navigation Company, the paddler was purchased by the Furness Railway in 1907, and entered service on the Barrow-Fleetwood run in April 1908.

❝ *The streets were marked out by the plough, and so arranged that all the principal thoroughfares, with the exception of the main road of entrance into the town, converge towards the largest 'star hill', now known as the Mount.*

VICTORIAN GUIDEBOOK

THE KNOTT END FERRY

The ferry (and some fishing boats) are shown in 47069. In the distance is the landing stage at Knott End-on-Sea. For years the service from Fleetwood to Knott End was worked by two boats, the 'Progress' and the 'Wyresdale'. The first Knott End ferry began as a family business shortly after work on Fleetwood started, but in 1894 it was taken over by the municipal council. During the resort's heyday it was a popular excursion for visitors: at one time, the boat carried almost one and a half million passengers a year.

Opposite: **FLEETWOOD, PS 'PHILOMEL' 1908** 59940p

Above: **FLEETWOOD, THE FERRY 1901** 47069

GLASSON, THE DOCK c1950 G260004

GLASSON

IN 1780 the River Lune was silting up, and so the dock that had been established at Sunderland Point was having problems getting goods into and out of Lancaster. Lancaster's solution was to build a dock near the village of Glasson.

Work began in 1783, and by 1791 it was a fully operational port. Though it solved Lancaster's problems of import and export, it did nothing to improve her communications with the growing industrial heart of Lancashire to the south. The Lancaster Canal Company solved the problem by opening the canal to Preston in 1819. In 1826 the branch to Glasson Dock was completed, and thus the river and dock were connected to the canal and Lancaster. The Glasson Dock branch, just three and a half miles with six locks, was the most important section of the Lancaster Canal as far as Lancaster merchants were concerned.

After the turn of the 19th century, Glasson Dock was used more and more by pleasure craft. Wealthy mill owners and industrialists kept their boats in the shelter of the dock or the canal basin, and leisure became more and more a source of income for Glasson Dock. Photograph G260004 (above) shows the main dock, with a sailing ship tied up.

❝ A rate was raised for the purpose of giving the town's attractions wide advertisement through the medium of handbills and flaring posters. One would hardly think that this was the best way of drawing the most satisfactory class of visitors to the finest promenade in England.

VICTORIAN GUIDEBOOK

THE COMING of the railway during the middle of the 19th century was the catalyst that sparked Blackpool's development as a holiday resort, and factory and mill workers flocked from the northern industrial towns. Photograph AFA47419 (opposite) shows strikingly how the railway delivered Blackpool's visitors right into the centre of things, next to the tower and the beach. Such were their numbers that the tradition of 'wakes weeks' was established, ensuring that the town could accommodate the thousands of visitors that arrived each summer.

The world-famous tower (B116015, right), which took over three years to construct, was inspired by Gustave Eiffel's great tower in Paris; but at 518 feet, Blackpool Tower is only a little over half the Eiffel Tower's height. However, it boasted a ballroom, a permanent circus, and an aquarium, all incorporated within the building at its base. Beyond the tower, the North Pier, built in 1863, was the first of three to be erected. Other attractions soon followed: the Winter Gardens opened in 1876, and electric trams appeared along the sea front in 1885.

ST ANNE'S

ST ANNE'S is the newest of the Fylde holiday resorts; the first major buildings were erected from 1875. Previously, it was a sandy wilderness known as Lytham Common. It was always a genteel place, a mood conveyed here by the well-dressed strollers on its 330 yards long Victorian pier that had opened in 1885 (66462, left). Ornate arbours and a Moorish-style pavilion provided seats sheltered from the wind, and a floral hall hosted shows and concerts. But crowds must have sometimes been a problem, for signs on the lamp posts direct people to 'keep to the right'. The pier's extravagant pavilions suggest something mysterious and exotic, a world away from the industry of the nearby towns. The pier was reconstructed in 1903, but the Moorish Pavilion was destroyed by fire in July 1974.

Top right: **BLACKPOOL, THE PROMENADE AND BLACKPOOL TOWER 1947** B116015

Above: **ST ANNE'S, THE PIER 1913** 66462

BLACKPOOL

Main photograph: **BLACKPOOL, FROM THE AIR 1952** AFA47419
Above: **BLACKPOOL, FROM NORTH PIER 1906** 53853t

SOUTHPORT

SOUTHPORT, THE BATHING POOL 1914 67465p

ONCE known as South Hawes, the town took its name from the South Port Hotel, which was built in 1798. By 1825, Southport was extremely busy. Of a visit that year, Ellen Weeton, a young lady who kept a diary between 1807 and 1825, wrote: 'I have seldom bathed but at Southport, and there it is sadly exposing ... and the modest complain much, gentlemen's and ladies' machines standing promiscuously in the water!' What Ellen would have made of Scarborough, where gentlemen were taken out by boat to bathe naked, we can only guess at. However, Ellen went on to complain that not enough time was allowed for getting dressed again; the owner of the machines, Peter Ball, would bang on the door for the bathers to get out so that others could get in.

Facilities had improved immensely by the early 20th century. A new attraction opened in time for the long hot summer of 1914 was the open-air bathing pool (67465, above). On Sunday 28 June, as Lancashire enjoyed the hottest day of the year, an event was taking place that would set Europe aflame. In Sarajevo, Bosnia, the heir to the throne of the Austria-Hungarian Empire, Franz Ferdinand, and his wife were assassinated.

❝ *The shore itself, the tide being then low, stretched out interminably seaward, a wide waste of glistering sands; and on the dry border, people were riding on donkeys, with the drivers whipping behind; and children were digging with their little wooden spades; and there were donkey-carriages far out on the sands, – a pleasant and breezy drive. A whole city of bathing-machines was stationed near the shore, and I saw others in the seaward distance. The sea-air was refreshing and exhilarating …*

There was, indeed, a shipwreck, a month or two ago, when a large ship came ashore within a mile from our windows; the larger portion of the crew landing safely on the hither sands, while six or seven betook themselves to the boat, and were lost in attempting to gain the shore, on the other side of the Ribble. After a lapse of several weeks, two or three of their drowned bodies were found floating in this vicinity, and brought to Southport for burial; so that it really is not at all improbable that Milton's Lycidas floated hereabouts, in the rise and lapse of the tides, and that his bones may still be whitening among the sands.

NATHANIEL HAWTHORNE (1804–1864)

❝ Here ships are loaded, unloaded and repaired. Their crowded masts appear like a leafless, winter-bound forest extending as far as the eye can see and barring the whole horizon to the north.

HIPPOLYTE TAINE, 'NOTES ON ENGLAND' 1860–70

LIVERPOOL

'GATEWAY to the British Empire', 'door to the New World' - fitting names for the city of Liverpool. From a creek in the River Mersey, to seven miles of docks full of ocean-going ships at the start of the 1900s, Liverpool had become a world-class city.

Construction of St George's Dock (14149, right) was authorised in 1761. The town's third dock, it had to be built because the Old Dock was prone to silting, while the Salthouse Dock was now too small for the larger ships then being built. St George's covered just over 20,000 square yards and its quays stretched 700 yards. It was linked to the two older docks and the graving dock, allowing vessels to move between them without having to enter the Mersey. St George's was later enlarged and linked to Prince's Dock. When it was eventually filled in, its site was occupied by the Mersey Docks & Harbour Board, the Cunard Building, and the Royal Liver Insurance Building.

At the time of Frith's earliest photographs, Liverpool would have had upwards of two hundred ships every week leaving for every corner of the great British Empire, and indeed the world. Ships went to Canada for corn, and carried iron goods to South America and Africa, and railway carriages to Brazil and South Africa.

LIVERPOOL, ST GEORGE'S DOCK c1881 14149

CHARLES DICKENS ON THE MISERIES OF TRAVELLING STEERAGE

In 1879 nearly 118,000 steerage passengers left the port of Liverpool for the United States. The woes of steerage passengers have been graphically described by Charles Dickens. He tells us that 'unquestionably any man who retained his cheerfulness among the steerage accommodations of that noble and fast-sailing packet, the Screw, was solely indebted to his own resources, and shipped his good humour like his provisions, without any contribution or assistance from the owners. A dark, low, stifling cabin, surrounded by berths filled to overflowing with men, women, and children, in various stages of sickness and misery, is not the liveliest place of assembly at any time; but when it is so crowded, as the steerage cabin of the Screw was every passage out, that mattresses and beds are heaped on the floor, to the extinction of everything like comfort, cleanliness, and decency, it is liable to operate not only as a pretty strong barrier against amiability of temper, but as a positive encourager of selfish and rough humours.' Dickens follows with a dismally correct picture of the passengers, with their shabby clothes, paltry stores of poor food and other supplies, and their wealth of family. He adds that every kind of suffering bred of poverty, illness, banishment, and tedious voyaging in bad weather was crammed into that confined space, and the picture, almost revolting in its naked truthfulness, was not overdrawn in those days.

FREDERICK WHYMPER, 'THE SEA' c1885

NEW BRIGHTON

IN 1830 a retired builder from Everton by the name of James Atherton bought 170 acres of sandhills on the northern tip of the Wirral with the express aim of creating a new seaside resort to rival Brighton - hence the new resort's name. When the town was first laid out, it was to be an exclusive place; but costs kept rising, and within a few years cheap terraced houses had been built - Atherton's vision was in tatters.

Note the photographers' tents in the foreground of 20067: trippers were delighted to have their portraits taken as a souvenir of their holiday. Fort Perch Rock (20067, background) was designed by Captain John Kitson of the Royal Engineers and built between 1826 and 1829 at a cost of £27,000. Construction of a fort to defend the seaward approach to Liverpool was first proposed during the Napoleonic Wars, but a fort was not built at that time because there were arguments over who should pay for it.

BUILT NOT ON SAND, BUT ON COTTON

Tradition says that a lighthouse was built on the beach here in the early 1700s, but it collapsed into the sand. Then a ship carrying cotton bales was shipwrecked off the Wirral, and the bales washed ashore. The parts of the ship soon sank into the sand, but the bales of cotton did not. Then grass started to grow on the cotton bales, and this held firm. As an experiment, bales of cotton were deliberately sunk into the foreshore and a wall built on them; the wall did not collapse. Therefore the two lighthouses on this coast were built on this same principle, Leasowe first, then New Brighton (20069) in 1827 at a cost of £27,000.

Top: **NEW BRIGHTON, THE LIGHTHOUSE 1887** 20069

Above: **NEW BRIGHTON, THE BEACH 1887** 20067

THE TRANSPORTER bridge, viewed in R67043 over the roofs of Runcorn (opposite), connected Runcorn with Widnes on the north shore of the river Mersey. It was built in 1905 and remained in use until 1961, when it was replaced by the road bridge on the left. The gleaming road bridge was built between 1956 and 1961 to accommodate the enormous increase in road traffic; the roadway hangs from a single steel arch 1,082ft long, the top of which is 306ft above the high watermark level. When it was first built it was the largest steel arch in Europe. Today it carries four lanes of traffic, having been widened in 1977. It was renamed the Silver Jubilee Bridge in 1977 to commemorate the Queen's Jubilee.

A RIVER NEVER WITHOUT A BREEZE

August 21st: Yesterday, at twelve o'clock, I took the steamer for Runcorn, from the pier-head. In the streets, I had noticed that it was a breezy day; but on the river there was a very stiff breeze from the northeast, right ahead, blowing directly in our face the whole way; and truly this river Mersey is never without a breeze, and generally in the direction of its course, – an evil-tempered, unkindly, blustering wind, that you cannot meet without being exasperated by it. As it came straight against us, it was impossible to find a shelter anywhere on deck, except it were behind the stove-pipe; and, besides, the day was overcast and threatening rain.

NATHANIEL HAWTHORNE (1804–1864)

RUNCORN, THE WIDNES BRIDGES c1961 R67043

RUNCORN

A bridge or a ferry? A transporter bridge (like the one in R67043, above) is in some ways more like a ferry than a bridge – passengers are carried over the river, but on a platform rather than a boat. The platform is hung by cables from a structure which travels on rails along the bridge (this one is a high latticed girder suspended from the towers on each bank). On a busy waterway like the Mersey, it is important to hinder water traffic as little as possible, and a transporter bridge allows shipping to pass under it at any time. A transporter bridge is also relatively cheap to construct.

RHYL

Rhyl is a most uninteresting place, – a collection of new lodging-houses and hotels, on a long sand-beach, which the tide leaves bare almost to the horizon. The sand is by no means a marble pavement, but sinks under the foot, and makes very heavy walking.

NATHANIEL HAWTHORNE (1804–1864)

THIS popular seaside resort sits in a wide sweep of bay on the north coast, with wooded hills behind the promenade, which fronts miles of safe sandy beach. The resort, less brash than Rhyl and its cohorts, has been well patronised since the 1860s, and prides itself on its mild climate. Wonderfully evocative of a classic seaside holiday, this picture (42375, below) shows all age-groups enjoying themselves on the famous Colwyn Bay sands, where the pier was soon to stand. Note the pram with its penny-farthing-style wheels. The building on the right, with its steeply-pitched slate roof, is the old Colwyn Bay Hotel, demolished in 1975.

COLWYN BAY

Above left: **COLWYN BAY, GENERAL VIEW c1950** C141002

Below: **COLWYN BAY, ON THE SANDS 1898** 42375

CLWYD enjoys only a short strip of the North Wales 'Riviera', with Rhyl and Prestatyn its representatives. Rhyl Sands are famous as a great windy expanse of beach facing into Liverpool Bay. They were painted with vigour by David Cox in 1854, and were the inspiration in the 1870s for Gerard Manley Hopkins's poem 'The Sea and the Skylark'. This bustling scene (65731, opposite), so typical of the glorious seaside holidays of the past, looks east to the pier pavilion. The bucket and spades, bare feet, donkeys and wickerwork basket chairs recapture a vanished era. 'The sands form an excellent bathing-ground, entirely free from danger', says a Victorian guidebook. 'Hence Rhyl has become noted for the number of children that visit it, and these little ones find an inexhaustible fund of pleasure on its beach'.

More pleasure is in store: donkeys are awaiting the arrival of the day's holidaymakers (29151p, above). The Victoria Pier behind them cost £23,000 to build in 1867; in 1891 a grand pavilion was built at the entrance, capable of seating 2,500 people, and one of the largest organs in Britain was installed behind the stage.

Opposite: **RHYL, THE BEACH 1913** 65731

Above: **RHYL, DONKEYS ON THE SANDS 1891** 29151p

LLANDUDNO

WHEN the Welsh traveller Thomas Pennant rode over the Great Orme in the 1790s and described it as 'a beautiful sheepwalk, consisting of fine turf, except where the rock appears', he could scarcely have imagined the transformation of a century later. It is still the natural beauty of the Great Orme which dominates Llandudno. The views, including the mountains of Snowdonia and along the north Wales coast, are sufficient reason to visit it.

Happy Valley (41491Ap, below) is famous for its flora and fauna; the mild climate here lets many tropical plants and palms grow alongside native trees, shrubs, herbaceous plants and alpines, laid out in grand terraces and rock gardens. Today Happy Valley is as popular as ever. From here the cable car takes passengers to the top of the Great Orme. Opened in 1969 and the longest in Britain, the Llandudno cable car system carries passengers 160 feet over the quarry to the summit.

If only we could eavesdrop on the conversations at this very popular café near Llandudno (L71613, right)! The photograph was taken at a time when marketing simply meant painting the service you offered in bold letters on your roof. Waitresses in traditional Welsh costume brought your tea and lemonade to enjoy alfresco – weather permitting.

Below: **LLANDUDNO, HAPPY VALLEY 1898** 41491Ap   Above: **LLANDUDNO, PINK FARM CAFE c1960** L71613

MINSTRELS IN HAPPY VALLEY

Happy Valley was well known in Victorian times for its minstrels - we can see the crowds watching a show in 41491Ap (left). At the height of the popularity of outdoor entertainment here, a stage area with dressing rooms was built in the valley, and thousands of visitors were able to enjoy the fun. Outdoor shows continued into the 20th century; Billy Churchill's troupe of minstrels entertained King George V and Queen Mary here in 1912. Although the outdoor theatre has been taken down in one of the many changes that Happy Valley has undergone throughout its existence, some features remain from the Victorian era. A drinking fountain was erected to celebrate the jubilee of Queen Victoria, and was one of many such patriotic gestures undertaken by towns throughout the land at that time.

CONWY, THE CASTLE AND THE BRIDGES 1906 54812

❝ I think no description, however enthusiastic, can do justice to one of the most romantic and interesting spots that exist in Europe.

JOHN HICKLIN

CONWY

SET AT the mouth of the River Conwy, this medieval walled town with its famous castle, one of Edward I's 'iron ring' around Wales, is still remarkably self-contained. The new road tunnel beneath the river diverts through traffic from its streets. The quay is busy today with pleasure craft, rather than the commercial traffic of the past. Conwy was once an important port with a major fishing fleet. There are mussel beds at the mouth of the river, while freshwater oysters found upstream were famous for their pearls. Photograph 42386 (left) shows a panoramic view of Conwy Castle and Stephenson's tubular railway bridge of 1848; just behind it is Telford's graceful suspension bridge of 1826 – the drawing (below left) gives us a closer view of it.

I think no description, however enthusiastic, can do justice to one of the most romantic and interesting spots that exist in Europe ... there is something so singular, so beautiful, and so aerial in a suspension bridge, that it can scarcely be thought out of character with the Moorish-looking towers and turrets to which it leads ... With all the legends of supernatural buildings with which Wales abounds, it would not be difficult for the imagination to conceive that the Genii threw these delicate chains over the wide space that divides the castle from the opposite rocks, and thus obtained a triumph over the giant who kept the fortress.

JOHN HICKLIN, 'EXCURSIONS IN NORTH WALES' 1847

CONWY'S HISTORIC BRIDGES

Telford's suspension bridge of 1826, designed to fit in with the medieval architecture of the castle, is 327ft long. It hangs on eight chains in two sets over two piers, with adjustment at one end into the rock under the castle, and at the other end into solid rock. It was built to carry Telford's Holyhead road, and replaced a notorious ferry across the dangerous waters of the Conwy estuary.

Stephenson's 412ft-long tubular railway bridge, a masterpiece of engineering, was built on the line of the old L & NWR Railway in 1848 just behind the suspension bridge. A 19th-century guide describes how it increases in height above high water from around 22ft at the ends to 25ft at the centre. The two tubes are each 14ft wide and weigh around 1,300 tons.

Top: **CONWY, THE CASTLE AND THE RAILWAY BRIDGE 1898** 42386

LLANFAIRFECHAN, THE BEACH 1890 23212

LLANFAIRFECHAN

THIS pleasant stone-built Victorian seaside resort just west of Conwy clusters beneath the steep craggy slopes of the coastal mountains on Conwy Bay, and looks across the broad eastern approaches of the Menai Strait to Anglesey. The resort is described thus in an 1890s guidebook: 'It has a wooded and well-sheltered situation and a singularly lovely seaward prospect. No great crowds of holiday-makers are seen here, but the astute observer may discern significant signs of the rising watering-place'. This marvellous image (23212, above) encapsulates the changes taking place in Llanfairfechan and similar villages at this time: the more recent terraced buildings are rising behind the few smaller cottages that still remained when this photograph was taken.

MENAI

Above: **THE MENAI SUSPENSION BRIDGE 1890** 23187t

Below: **THE MENAI SUSPENSION BRIDGE DURING RECONSTRUCTION 1938** M62304

The gentle, low-lying, undulating landscape of the island of Anglesey offers a complete contrast to the rugged, mountainous mainland to the east. Crossing between the mainland and Anglesey could be hazardous: vicious rip tides up and down the strait earned Menai the nickname 'the British Bosporus'.

Thomas Telford's Menai suspension bridge was opened in 1826 as part of an important scheme to improve communications between London and Holyhead on Anglesey. It was not only a pioneering engineering achievement, but a beautiful and elegant structure, the gateway into Anglesey, which soon became a tourist attraction in its own right. The strait was bridged at the highest point because of the Admiralty's requirement that a fully rigged sailing vessel should be able to pass underneath. The bridge roadway was at 100ft above the straits, and was the first structure of its type to carry heavy traffic. The pedestal towers were designed in the then-fashionable Egyptian style, and the bridge is 1,000ft long with a central span of 539ft.

A HURRICANE AND A SHIPWRECK

The road deck of the Menai Bridge was damaged by gales and replaced several times during the bridge's lifespan. The bridge was designed for horse-drawn transport, and as motor traffic increased a weight limit had to be introduced. After the bridge was damaged by a hurricane in 1936, the firm of Dorman Long modernised and strengthened the bridge in 1938 (M62304, below left). The currents and eddies in this part of the Menai Strait can be treacherous. HMS 'Conway' was a training ship run by the Mercantile Marine Services to train officer cadets. She was moved to the shelter of the Menai Strait in 1941 to avoid air raids. As she was being towed back to Birkenhead in April 1953 by two tugs, an unexpectedly powerful tide brought her aground near the Menai Bridge (M62118, below). Three years later the wreck burnt to the waterline in a mysterious fire.

THE MENAI BRIDGE, THE WRECK OF HMS 'CONWAY' 1953 M62118

❝ *It is perhaps at the best when the hour of sunset is approaching, and the glow of evening begins to flush the west. Then the Straits, like a broad river, reflect the amber tints of the sky; above them the opposite shore rises steeply, clothed with wood to the water's edge, and beyond it green fields and copses undulate inland till the Carnarvonshire mountains close the view.*

VICTORIAN GUIDEBOOK

It was evening when I first caught sight of the castle ... I lingered amongst those ruins till the last vestige of light was withdrawn, except such as is bestowed by a clear firmament emblazoned with burning stars ... Vast, irregular, and more shattered than its exterior grandeur would lead us to suppose, this giant fortress stretches far along the west of the town ... Its time-worn and ivy-covered bulwarks are now fast yielding, like the interior, to the assaults of time.

JOHN HICKLIN, 'EXCURSIONS IN NORTH WALES' 1847

CAERNARFON

Above: **CAERNARFON, THE CASTLE 1891** *29499*

KNOWN today for its massive castle, one link in Edward I's chain of fortresses built to subdue the Welsh, Caernarfon on the shore of the Menai Straits at the mouth of the River Seiont is now staunchly Welsh-speaking. It was formerly an important harbour, shipping a variety of goods. It is an ancient place, originally Segontium, a Roman fortress constructed in AD 78. The massive castle, begun in 1285, remains unchanged since this picture was taken. The structure covers two and a half acres and is roughly oblong, with 13 massive many-sided towers along the walls. The banded masonry and polygonal towers of Caernarfon Castle are strikingly similar to the Byzantine walls of Constantinople.

At the time of this photograph (29499, above) the Welsh slate industry was at its peak of production; the busy harbour at Caernarfon was often full of slate ships, with rows of roofing slates stacked on the quay ready for loading. Here, schooners, including the 'Catherine' in the foreground, lie alongside the slate quay, waiting to be loaded with Snowdon slate for transportation to Europe.

BEAUMARIS, THE PIER 1911 63294

BEAUMARIS

BEAUMARIS, on the Anglesey side of the Menai Straits, is one of Anglesey's best-known sailing resorts, but it began its life as the last and most technically advanced of Edward I's chain of north Wales castles, a superb example of a concentric castle, which took advantage of a flat marshy site – Beaumaris means 'beautiful marsh'. However, it was never finished, and the redundant castle gained new importance as a tourist attraction. The town developed around the castle, and was thought of as fashionable and elegant, with a number of wealthy gentlefolk living in the neighbourhood. It offered fine bathing grounds, pleasant walks and a ferry to Bangor.

From medieval times until the 19th century, Beaumaris was Anglesey's main harbour; 111 sailing vessels and 8 steamers were registered here in 1893. Copper ores, slate and marble were exported. In 63294 a paddle steamer approaches the pier, one of many vessels plying the coastal waters between Bangor and Liverpool.

Beaumaris enjoys a most beautiful and sublime prospect, with the distinguishing pecularity, that the eye at the same time rests on a noble expanse of ocean, and an extensive range of some of the loftiest mountains in Wales ... seaward, at full tide, it presents to the eye an infinite variety, in numbers of trading vessels, yachts, and smaller pleasure boats, constantly passing close to the beach, whilst at low water the sands afford many delightful and extensive drives.

JOHN HICKLIN, 'EXCURSIONS IN NORTH WALES' 1847

THIS exceptional lighthouse is situated to the north-west of Anglesey on the South Stack rock. Although the rock is about 106ft above sea level, it is dwarfed by its neighbour, Holyhead Island. The island, faced by formidable granite cliffs over 400ft high, is separated from the South Stack rock by a 100ft chasm, where the sea erupts in a spectacular fashion.

The lighthouse was designed by Daniel Asher Alexander in 1808. Welsh quarrymen were employed to produce the masonry from the hard South Stack rock. The 92ft-high lighthouse was completed in 1809; its light is recorded as being set at 197ft above the highest spring tide level, and was visible from 19 nautical miles away. At this time, no fog signal was needed because of the ever-present noise from hundreds of sea birds that nested around the rock.

The most arduous task given to the stone-cutters and quarrymen was the formation of 400 steps carved out of the granite face of Holyhead Island. At the bottom of these steps a 100ft-long hemp cable was stretched across to the South Stack rock, and stores, equipment and keepers were hauled over to the rock in a basket. This system lasted until 1828, when an iron suspension bridge was built. On 12 September 1984 the keepers left the South Stack lighthouse following its automation.

THE 'ROYAL CHARTER' GALE

As she crossed the Irish Sea towards Milford Haven on 25 October 1859, the steamship 'Royal Charter' was hit by tremendous waves and high winds, which blew her off course and into the South Stack rock. The keepers were powerless to help, and could only watch in total disbelief as 500 people drowned. This dreadful storm (200 other ships were either blown ashore or foundered in the high seas) became known as the 'Royal Charter' gale. On the same night as the 'Royal Charter' was wrecked, one of the keepers was making his way across the iron bridge when he was hit on the head by a rock that had broken away from the cliff. Covered in blood, he tried to climb the steep path to the lighthouse, but collapsed a short distance from the bridge. He was not found until the early hours of the following morning. This unfortunate keeper died three weeks later from his horrendous injury.

Left: **SOUTH STACK, THE LIGHTHOUSE 1892** 30299

BARDSEY ISLAND

Below: **BARDSEY ISLAND, THE FERRY BOAT** c1930 B668016p

Bottom right: **SEAL COLONY**, COURTESY OF BRENDAN GOGARTY

'THE LAND of indulgences, absolution and pardon, the road to Heaven, and the gate to Paradise': this is how Welsh bards described Bardsey, a Christian refuge from the 5th century and the site of an abbey from the 6th century. For hundreds of years pilgrims flocked here – the journey (and the crossing from the mainland) was so hard that three pilgrimages to Bardsey counted the same as one pilgrimage to Rome. Many pilgrims decided to stay on the holy island, and died and were buried here; Bardsey was known as 'the holy place of burial for all the bravest and best in the land' and 'the Isle of Twenty Thousand Saints'.

Medieval pilgrims once congregated on the mainland by Aberdaron, before undertaking the treacherous passage across the sound to Bardsey Island; in photograph B668016 (above), a party of trippers has just disembarked. The weather looks calm, but winds and tides make the crossing dangerous; Bardsey's Welsh name, Ynys Enlli, means 'island in the great currents'. Today, nature lovers come here to see shearwaters, curlews, and seals, as well as many other birds and animals – Bardsey is now a nature reserve.

CRICCIETH

THIS resort on the south side of the Lleyn peninsula became popular in Victorian times and has remained so ever since. The two sandy beaches are separated by a headland crowned by a castle. The statesman Lloyd George (1863–1945) was born nearby in Llanystumdwy. This magnificent view (84755, left) was taken from the east. The stooks lend period atmosphere to the harvest scene; the view today is far more built-up. Criccieth was once a modest market town, but it grew into a select watering-place when the Cambrian railway reached it. Its unspoilt beach, coastal vistas and village atmosphere drew the more discerning visitor.

Criccieth was a Welsh fortress, and was probably completed in the early 13th century. It was captured by the English in 1283, who immediately set about improving its defensive capability; Edward Longshanks committed a great deal of money to the project. The towers were heightened during the reign of Edward II. Criccieth became something of a hybrid: an English inner ward inside the earlier Welsh outer ward. In 1326 the garrison stood at ten men, armed with crossbows. These fired a heavy bolt that could penetrate armour at ranges up to 250 yards.

PORTHMADOG

Above: **CRICCIETH AND CARDIGAN BAY 1931**   84755

Right: **PORTHMADOG, THE HARBOUR c1870**   1837G

PORTHMADOG was a comparatively new town, which had developed as a major slate port on land reclaimed from the sea. It was a busy commercial centre rather than a tourist resort. Hotels like the Royal Commercial Hotel were frequented by salesmen and commercial travellers rather than by holidaymakers.

Photograph 1837G (right) was taken during the heyday of the Welsh slate industry, which reached its peak in 1873; tons of slates from the Ffestiniog area's slate caverns were exported from these wharves – indeed, the photograph shows rows of roofing slates lined up on the quay ready for loading. In 1836, a narrow gauge railway nine miles long had opened to connect the quarries at Blaenau Ffestiniog with Porthmadog harbour. The Porthmadog ships, some of which we see moored at the quays, traded all over the globe, and were noted for their beauty and speed.

Later in the 19th century, the Porthmadog schooners were able to call upon the services of a tug for towing either in or out of the harbour. Though paddle tugs were built for manoeuvrability, they lacked the power of screw tugs, and they were becoming expensive to operate as coal and labour costs increased. The Porthmadog-based paddle tug 'Snowdon', built in 1885, was sold off in 1900 to John Dry of South Shields. She served with various north-east tug companies until she was finally withdrawn in 1949.

HARLECH

Above: **HARLECH, THE CASTLE AND THE GOLF LINKS 1908** 60251

Thee have I met, on Harlech's castled verge,
Soothed by the music of the plaintive surge,
When evenings vocal wind, in mournful sport,
Waved the dark verdure of the mouldering court,
While falling fragments shook the echoing tower,
And flitting forms forsook their twilight bower.

THOMAS LOVE PEACOCK,
FROM 'THE PHILOSOPHY OF MELANCHOLY' 1811

❝ *The walls, now clad in ivy, are lofty and of great thickness, from the summit of which a most splendid and sublime prospect may be commanded, including a vast extent of marine and mountain scenery.*
JOHN HICKLIN, 'EXCURSIONS IN NORTH WALES' 1847

THE TOWN clusters around the castle, clinging to the steep slopes along steep roads. Harlech Castle, imposingly set on its crag overlooking the sands of Morfa Harlech and the famous golf course, is little changed today from this view (60251, above). Here, golfers can still enjoy the picturesque prospects of the castle and the headland as they walk between holes. The links were created on the Morfa (marsh), a tract of well-drained land from which the sea has receded. The greens are well-protected by sand dunes, which in places assume fantastic shapes.

When Harlech Castle was built in 1283, the sea lapped around the base of the rocky crag upon which it stands. At sea level was the water gate, which allowed the fortress to be reinforced or supplied by ship. Any attacker capturing the water gate then faced a climb of 108 steps up the side of the crag to the next objective, an intermediate turret with a drawbridge. Attackers also had to run the gauntlet of artillery fire from the castle walls. Harlech was indeed a formidable stronghold. The song 'Men of Harlech' relates to its eight-year siege during the Wars of the Roses.

Above: **BARMOUTH, THE QUAY 1889** 21701

Below: **BARMOUTH, THE RAILWAY BRIDGE 1908** 60208

BARMOUTH

The town of Barmouth is seated near the bottom of some high mountains, many of the houses being built on the steep sides; and viewed from the sea, it resembles a fortress of some strength, hanging immediately over the sands. The town stands near the sea, at the mouth of the Maw or Mawddach, and takes its name of Barmouth, ie. Abermaw or Mawddach, from that circumstance. At high water, the tide here forms a bay above a mile over (sic), but the entrance is rather hazardous, on account of the sand-banks.

JOHN HICKLIN, 'EXCURSIONS IN NORTH WALES' 1847

THIS well-known holiday resort, which has an excellent sandy beach, stands on the west coast of Wales at the mouth of the Mawddach estuary. Both Charles Darwin (right) and John Ruskin enjoyed stays here. The old harbour was formerly of some importance. Nearby, the viewpoint of Dinas Oleu ('Fortress of Light') was the first piece of land to belong to the National Trust. The old town clings to the steep hillside (21701, left); the beginning of the famous Barmouth Bridge is visible on the right. The coming of the railway here in 1867 sounded the death knell for commercial shipping. The bridge spans the Mawddach estuary (60208, below) – a steam train is heading south. Its original design, as shown in this picture, included rolling sections that could be opened for river traffic to sail through. It is half a mile long, and has a road for foot passengers, who can enjoy the freshness of the air and the sublime vistas of Cadair Idris. The railway was built as part of the Cambrian railway. Northwards the line went to Harlech and Afonwen, where it joined the L & NWR.

ABERDYFI

Above: **ABERDYFI, THE QUAY 1901** 46974   Right: **ABERDYFI, THE FRONT 1895** 36507

THIS small seaside town overlooks the wide sandy expanse of the Dyfi estuary. It is sheltered from the north wind by hills rising to the sombre Welsh mountains south of Cadair Idris. Aberdyfi was an important sea port during the 19th century; earlier, smuggling had been rife. This picture of the front (36507, right) shows a cargo vessel and numerous small fishing boats beached opposite the church. St Peter's, the Victorian church on the left, was Aberdyfi's first church, though the song 'The Bells of Aberdyfi' suggests that an earlier church lies drowned beneath the waves of Cardigan Bay.

In 46974 (above), note the railway line alongside the quay for the transportation of slate from the quarries. Many of the seafront terraces would have been built by local speculators as lodgings for visitors – the mildness of the climate made the town popular as a winter residence. The scene of the front and the hills behind remain much the same today; boating and water sports have grown ever more popular in the Dyfi estuary, which is fringed by wooded banks.

It is rapidly rising in estimation as a bathing place. The beach is highly favour-able for bathing, being composed of hard firm sand, affording a perfectly safe carriage-drive of about eight miles in length, along the margin of the sea. The ride to Towyn along the sands at low water, is extremely delightful. Several respectable houses and a commodious hotel (the Corbet Arms) have of late years been erected for the accommodation of visitors.

JOHN HICKLIN, 'EXCURSIONS IN NORTH WALES' 1847

BORTH

Right:
BORTH, THE DONKEYS 1952 B147223

Below: **BORTH, THE BEACH 1921** 71541p

CHILDREN enjoy a donkey ride at the south end of the beach (B147223, above). Beyond them is the headland on which the Borth War Memorial was built after the First World War. There are said to be smuggler's caves in the rocks below it. Beneath the sands at Borth are the remains of a forest that grew here at the end of the Ice Age before the sea rose to its present level. The stumps of massive trees and the peat they grew in are sometimes exposed by heavy seas.

It is said that almost every boy from Borth went to sea. Some of the older houses in the village were owned by sea captains who had returned from a life at sea having made their fortunes. However, the two other main occupations of the people of Borth were farming and tending to the needs of holidaymakers. A number of caravan sites were established in Borth after the Second World War, multiplying the population of the village in summer by many times its winter number.

ABERYSTWYTH

ABERYSTWYTH became a popular resort for the gentry, who came here to bathe and socialise from the late 18th century. At the beginning of the 19th century a number of new streets were built following the grid pattern of the medieval town. Once the railway arrived in 1864, many more visitors came, and a variety of activities were arranged for them, including swimming from bathing machines, taking trips around the bay in the rowing or sailing boats, or being entertained at the top of Constitution Hill (in the background of 77680t). This headland, known as Pen Dinas, is crowned by the clearly-visible double ramparts of an Iron Age hill-fort. The sea is calm in 77680t (below), unlike the huge breaking waves in A14010 (right). Storms are frequent along this coast, but these buildings are protected from the worst by Castle Point, from which A14010 was taken.

THE COLLEGE BY THE SEA

The magnificent neo-Gothic building on the promenade (A14010, above) began life as a triangular house designed by John Nash in about 1795. In 1865 the railway entrepreneur Savin began to build the Castle Hotel around it, but he became bankrupt in the process. It was bought by the fledgling Aberystwyth University in 1872. They made several alterations to it over the next 25 years, and in 1901 they agreed to allow the Town Council to build a promenade around it - on condition that the students were not disturbed by entertainers! The photograph shows the college buildings after the new promenade was built between 1901 and 1904. This wonderful location must have been rather distracting for the students of 'the College by the Sea'.

Above: **ABERYSTWYTH, A ROUGH SEA c1930** A14010

Left: **ABERYSTWYTH, THE PROMENADE 1925** 77680t

NEW QUAY became an important ship-building settlement from the late 18th century (244 ships were built here between 1779 and 1882), and since it was well protected from south-westerly gales, it was one of the few places along the coast where larger ships could shelter during storms.

This view (N151069, below), taken from the end of the stone pier, shows the four-story Custom House surrounded by the rowing boats used by both local fishermen and holidaymakers. The pier was built in 1835 with stone from a nearby quarry – it was transported here on a tramway. The three terraces of houses on the far right of the photograph provided accommodation for ship builders and ancillary workers. Fishing was an important local industry, particularly during the 18th century, when vast shoals of herring arrived in the autumn. The harbour now serves a few local fishing boats and many leisure boat owners; the regatta, which is held annually, dates back to 1868.

FISHGUARD

NEW QUAY

FISHGUARD, STRUMBLE HEAD LIGHTHOUSE c1960 F28045

THIS important lighthouse perched on top of this windswept point on the Pen Caer peninsula is Pembrokeshire's nearest point to Ireland; it cost £40,000 to build in 1908. Run by Trinity House, it was automated in 1980. Nearby is Carreg Wastad Point, where, in 1797, a French invasion force of 600 troops, 800 ex-convicts, 100 emigrés and three Irish officers led by William Tate, an Irish-American, attempted their farcical 'invasion'. This so-called 'Légion Noir' (so called because their uniforms were dyed black) looted nearby farms to discover plentiful stocks of Portuguese wine 'recovered' from a recent wreck – and set about consuming as much of it as they could. They were subsequently no match even for the local militias. These soldiers, so the legend has it, were supported by a troop of local Welsh ladies who, in their tall black hats and with red petticoats on show, looked to the Légion Noir (perhaps thanks to their somewhat impaired vision) rather like British troops in scarlet uniform. This large 'army' successfully saw off the invaders.

NEW QUAY, THE HARBOUR c1935 N151069

MILFORD HAVEN, THE SWIMMING POOL c1955 M77018

MILFORD HAVEN

MILFORD was once described as 'the finest port in Christendom' – it is a vast flooded valley, a harbour renowned for its safety. It was once a significant fishing port, landing all kinds of fish, including skate, hake and conger. During the Civil Wars it sheltered the Parliamentary fleet, which prevented the Royalist capture of Pembroke Castle. According to Defoe in the 17th century, one Mr Camden previously described the haven thus: 'It contains 16 creeks, 5 great bays and 13 good roads for shipping, all distinguished as such for their names; and some say a thousand of ships may ride in it and not the topmast of one be seen from the other.' Lord Nelson laid the foundation stone of the parish church, and his mistress Lady Hamilton once stayed in the town. The docks have a long history, with both Royal Navy and seaplane connections.

In M77018 we see interesting juxtaposition of leisure and commerce – docks, cranes and steamers form the background to the swimming pool, a typical open-air lido in a vaguely Art Deco style.

PHOTOGRAPH COURTESY OF MARIEKE KUIJPERS

BOSHERSTON

BOSHERSTON, STACK ROCKS c1955 B468002

BOSHERSTON is reputed to be the smallest harbour in Britain; it was built to import coal and export limestone. The land hereabouts belonged to the Stackpole estate (which came into the ownership of the Earls of Cawdor). The estate created Bosherston's famous lily ponds during the 18th and 19th centuries by blocking three narrow limestone valleys; they are now a nature reserve, and as well as beautiful water lilies, it is possible to see otters, rare birds, and dragonflies here.

The spectacular rock formations in B468002 (above) were crafted by the waves from a collapsed arch. They are home to colonies of guillemots, razorbills and kittiwakes.

ST GOVAN'S HEAD

St Govan's Chapel (32819) is rich in legend. It is thought the original chapel dated from the 5th century. Was it the retreat of Cofen, wife of a king of Glamorgan? Or is this where Sir Gawain became a hermit after King Arthur's death? H Thornhill Timmins, writing in 1895, had another theory: 'Here, according to a curious old legend, St Govan sought shelter from his pagan enemies; whereupon the massy rock closed over him and hid him from his pursuers, opening again to release the pious anchorite as soon as the chase was overpassed.' Yet another legend says that the chapel's silver bell was once stolen by pirates; their ship was promptly wrecked, killing all on board. The bell was recovered and encased in rock, which would ring out when struck. The present chapel is 13th-century, and contains an altar, a bench and a cell hewn out of the rock. Note the steps leading from the cliff top – it is said that they never count the same going up as going down.

The story goes that Huntsman's Leap (32821) is named after a rider who was galloping on his horse along the cliffs; unaware of the formidable drop into the sea, he leapt across the chasm. He landed safely on the other side, but looking back and realising what he had done, promptly died from sheer fright!

Above: **ST GOVAN'S HEAD, HUNTSMAN'S LEAP 1893** 32821   Below: **ST GOVAN'S HEAD, THE CHAPEL AND STEPS 1893** 32819

❝ An exudation from the floor of the chapel is held to be of sovereign efficacy in complaints of the eyes; and the saint's well, a short distance below the chapel, has long since enjoyed a high reputation. Not so many years since 'crippled patients' came hither to bathe their limbs from the remotest inland parts of the Principality, and leave their crutches behind as a votive offering on the altar.

VICTORIAN GUIDEBOOK

MANORBIER

MANORBIER, THE CASTLE 1890 27981

❧ *Within a short distance of the sea lies the ruin of Manorbeer Castle, situated, as Fenton describes it 'in a very sequestered*

vale, ending in a little creek of the sea below it' … [It is] the perfect model of an old Norman baron's residence, with all

its appendages – church, mill, dove-house, ponds, park, and grove – still to be seen and traced, and the houses of his

vassals at such a distance as to be within his call. VICTORIAN GUIDEBOOK

MANORBIER is five miles from Tenby, lying in the valley of a west-facing bay. The name of the town and castle almost certainly derive from the Welsh 'maenor Pyr', meaning 'a holding of land in the ownership of Pyro' – Pyro was the first Abbot of Caldey in the 6th century. Manorbier was the birthplace in c1145 of one of Wales's most interesting churchmen, Giraldus Cambrensis (or Gerallt O Gymru) the historian; he thought Manorbier one of the most pleasant places in the country.

The castle (27981, above) was erected on a red sandstone spur from locally quarried limestone. It occupies an excellent defensive position overlooking the sea and the beach beyond. In 1890, the date of our photograph, it would appear that fields immediately adjacent to the castle were grazed, whereas today the fields to the right and foreground are covered with trees, bushes and undergrowth. The gatehouse was built in the 13th century. It stands next to the earliest parts of the castle, the Old Tower on the right, built in the 12th century, and a fighting gallery and curtain wall to the left, built c1230. In days gone by smuggling was rife here, and Manorbier Castle is rumoured to have tunnels and hiding places for contraband.

THE PEMBROKESHIRE coastline is dramatic and beautiful, and its rocks and caves have been popular with holiday makers over the centuries – Gosse, writing in 1886, called Lydstep 'the sweet little cove'. There are tunnel caverns in these limestone cliffs with large natural skylights and both landward and coastal entrances. Lydstep caverns are only accessible at low tide, with the exception of the Smugglers Cave – which was probably so named because of the high incidence of smuggling along the rocky coastline of Pembrokeshire, particularly in isolated bays where contraband could be stored.

This beach became a most popular excursion from Tenby – perhaps the well-dressed party in 28010 (below) are staying in one of the resort's better hotels. The Droch, or Cave of Beauty (28006, right), is regarded as the finest at Lydstep; it has a smaller secondary entrance as well as the magnificent opening we see here. Also popular with keen Victorian botanists was the abundance of interesting plants and ferns to be found here, including the sea spleenwort.

Above: **LYDSTEP, THE CAVE OF BEAUTY 1890** 28006

Below: **LYDSTEP, THE BEACH 1890** 28010

LYDSTEP

The birds here are mostly guillemots, puffins, and razor-bills, the last locally bearing the name of 'eligugs'. Several rare birds are from time to time noted in the cliffs between these rocks and St Gowan's Head. The Cornish chough occasionally makes its nest among them. A few species of the hawk tribe still linger here, such as the kestrel and the sparrow-hawk; but the peregrine falcon is now extinct on this coast, having been harried to death by the game-keepers and pheasant preservers. In olden days Pembrokeshire was famous for these hawks, and Giraldus Cambrensis gives an account of the fate of a Norwegian hawk, which was let fly at a peregrine falcon by Henry II, and was struck dead by the peregrine at the feet of the king. From that time the king sent every year about the breeding season for the falcons of this country, which are produced on the sea-cliffs.

VICTORIAN GUIDEBOOK

TENBY has a long history: Castle Hill (centre top in 77263, above) has a commanding view of both its landward and seaward approaches, and was almost certainly the location of an Iron Age promontory fort. The beaches, caves and rock pools around Castle Hill and especially St Catherine's Island have been a favourite haunt of the serious and amateur naturalist for generations. Above, the old fort, having never fired a shot in anger, remains a reminder of the threat posed to Pembrokeshire by Napoleon III.

Fishing and especially dredging for oysters was an important part of Tenby's economy. Oysters from the Caldey Island beds were so large that a single specimen was considered too much for one person. A common sight in the harbour was the shallow-drafted clinker-built Tenby lugger, peculiar to the town, a three-masted open boat used mainly for drift-net fishing and oyster dredging. However, over the years the oysters declined, and subsequently Tenby depended more and more on the new industry of catering for seasonal visitors. Today, its harbour, fringed by colour-washed fine Georgian and Victorian houses, is a magnet for visitors.

THE FISHWIVES OF LLANGWM

Each day women from the village of Llangwm would walk 11 miles cross-country to Tenby to sell prawns, cockles and oysters, which they carried on their backs in their baskets and panniers. Here we see a group of fishwives who became the subject of many photographic portraits – they were paid well for their work as models. They are posed on Goscar Rock on Tenby's North Beach. Note the basket of shrimps, the hats and scarves of their traditional dress, and the larger basket one woman has on her back.

TENBY

In the graveyard of Tenby's parish church rests Walter Vaughan, of Dunraven Castle (in the Vale of Glamorgan), of whom evil stories are told. He was said to have been in the habit of hanging out false lights to mislead passing ships, in order that he might enrich himself with the spoils of the wrecks. So, for a time, he prospered, but at last a fearful doom overtook him. He had three children, of whom he was bereft in a single day. Two were drowned before his eyes, and the third was scalded to death. In this terrible visitation he read a judgement on his evil deeds. Broken down by unavailing sorrow, childless as he had made others, he sold Dunraven, and betaking himself to this extremity of the kingdom, died in obscurity.

VICTORIAN GUIDEBOOK

Top left: **TENBY, THE HARBOUR 1925** 77263

Left: **TENBY, FISHWIVES 1890** 28091

Above: **DREDGING FOR OYSTERS**

THIS attractive seaside resort with its sandy beach has been a magnet for holidaymakers for a long time. It is hard to believe from the tranquillity of photograph S64243 (below) that Saundersfoot was once a busy industrial port. As long ago as 1325 there was a reference in the accounts of the Earl of Pembroke to a coal mine at Caytrath (the wooded area behind Saundersfoot). The coal mined hereabouts was known for its good heating qualities and low ash. It was brought here by bullock wagon for loading on to the ships.

By the 19th century, the coal industry was conducted on a relatively large scale; in 1829 the harbour was built, and various mineral railway lines made their way to the town. By 1864 some 30,000 tons of coal were being shipped from here every year, as well as large quantities of pig-iron (made from iron ore extracted from the cliff faces between here and Amroth). Bonville's Court Colliery nearby employed 300 men at its peak and closed in 1930. The last mine closed in 1939, and the harbour has since been developed as an excellent yachting harbour.

SAUNDERSFOOT

One of the most delightful spots in Wales, either for a long holiday or for a mere trip from its pretentious neighbour [Tenby] close by.

VICTORIAN GUIDEBOOK

SAUNDERSFOOT, THE HARBOUR c1965 S64243

THE VILLAGE of Ferryside stands on the east side of the river Towy where the river breaks out to sea through a widespread expanse of sandbanks at low tide. This can be partially seen in photograph 77309; the spits are appearing, indicating that the tide is on the ebb.

The man pushing off from the shore, his sizeable skiff equipped with both sails and outboard engine, is no fisherman. By the look of the boarding plank and the amount of seating, he is more likely to be a ferryman. He would need both sails and engine to manoeuvre across the dangerous currents of the river Towy whilst carrying his passengers across from Ferryside to Llanstephan. A lifeboat was deemed necessary by the local authorities in view of the dangerous channels and sandbanks. Many small craft, both working fishing boats and pleasure vessels, regularly experienced difficulties here.

FERRYSIDE

FERRYSIDE, THE COAST AND A BOATMAN 1925 77309

THE NAME 'Mumbles' actually derives from the French 'mamelles', meaning 'breasts'. Strictly speaking, the name actually refers to two islets near here which are only accessible at low tide, but the name has come to refer to the whole promontory.

The Mumbles railway began as a tramway authorised by an Act of Parliament in 1804; it carried limestone and coal. Then one of the original shareholders, Benjamin French, used a horse-drawn wagon to carry passengers on it, thus making it the first passenger railway service in the world. It became very popular in 1879 when steam power was introduced, and it was extended to Mumbles Pier (40925, right) when it opened in 1898 – could this photograph have been taken on the pier's first day of business?

With the Mumbles Railway carrying as many as 40,000 passengers on a bank holiday, many on excursions from nearby Swansea, the village prospered. The rail system was electrified in 1929, but the railway was closed in 1960. Now cyclists and walkers use the track, which has been paved to make a popular pathway from Swansea marina and along the length of Swansea bay.

The beautiful and varied landscape of the Gower Peninsula was in 1956 the first place in Britain to be designated as an Area of Outstanding Natural Beauty. Bounded by the Bristol Channel and the Atlantic, it has an astonishing range of scenery, habitats and species. In its hills and valleys, beaches and clifftops, dunes, heathland, marshes, and woodland, the visitor can find hares, newts and choughs, rare butterflies and moths, and seldom-seen orchids and ferns. The Gower has a long and fascinating history too. There are over 1,200 archaeological sites here, including caves, standing stones and hill-forts, as well as castles, churches, a lighthouse, a lead mine, and a Second World War radar station.

MUMBLES

Above: **MUMBLES, THE PIER 1898** 40925

Below: **MUMBLES, THE LIGHTHOUSE AND THE NATURAL ARCH 1893** 32732

A LIGHTHOUSE, PIRATES, AND A VANISHED ARCH

The Mumbles lighthouse (32732, right), first built in 1793, had a coal-fired beacon; later, oil and then gas were used. Nowadays a solar-powered 100-watt quartz iodine electric lamp provides the light. Tradition says that a called pirate Bob kept his plunder in the large sea cave at the end of the island, and the pirate John Avery was hanged near here in 1731. The natural arch of rock on the right was destroyed during a bitter winter's storm in 1910; this photograph is a poignant reminder that nothing is permanent on the picturesque Gower peninsula.

SWANSEA

SWANSEA, GENERAL VIEW 1893 32719

TO THE casual visitor, Swansea today appears to be a modern town, but its history stretches back many centuries. Its feeling of modernity is mostly attributable to the extensive rebuilding programmes of the 1950s and 1960s after the February 1941 blitz. Much of the city's architectural heritage was destroyed, and there are now only two remaining medieval buildings still surviving (the Castle and the Cross Keys inn). It has to be said that the Victorian town planners also played their part by comprehensively demolishing entire streets to make way for developments.

Photograph 32719 (above) looks out into the hills, which play such a part in defining Swansea. Notice the factory chimneys and their smoke. Sailing ships on the river Tawe and the long lines of terraced workers' cottages tell the tale of Swansea in its heyday as a major industrial centre. Swansea's maritime tradition has always been vital to the town. The South Dock (54952, opposite left) opened in 1859, serving cargo vessels for regular services to London, Bristol, Liverpool, Dublin and Cork. The ship pictured here is the 'Talbot', and the rail carriages linked the port facilities to the GWR network. The shed survived the blitz, and now houses the Maritime Museum; the dock is now a marina.

SWANSEA, SOUTH DOCK 1906 54952p

SWANSEA BLITZED

As a Channel port, Swansea was an obvious target in the Second World War – docks, industry, flour mills and the large grain stores were considered vital to the war effort. The German High Command obviously agreed. Swansea was attacked 44 times during the war, but her worst moments came on 19, 20 and 21 February 1941, when thousands of bombs and incendiaries were dropped on the town. These incendiaries caused the majority of the damage, claiming some notable victims, and the fires acted as a homing beacon for successive waves of German bombers to locate the town and deliver still more mayhem. The fires could be seen from as far away as Pembrokeshire and North Devon. The death toll was 230, with 400 injured.

Near Swansea we visited the copper and iron works. They were just opening a smelting furnace; the fused copper, in a little stream of liquid fire, flowed along a channel towards a cistern full of water; we saw it approach with terror, expecting an explosion; instead of which the two liquids met very amicably, the water only simmering a little. The workmen looked very sickly: we found, on inquiry, their salary was but little higher than that of common labourers. It is remarkable, that, much as men are attached to life, there is no consideration less attended to in the choice of a profession than salubrity.

LOUIS SIMOND, 'JOURNEY OF A TOUR AND RESIDENCE IN GREAT BRITAIN' 1810

BRITON FERRY

Below: **BRITON FERRY, THE NEW BRIDGE 1959** B398019

THIS sea-port at the mouth of the Nedd derived its importance from its docks and from its steel and tin works. The former steelworks at Briton Ferry, just across the River Neath from Swansea and downstream from Neath, can be seen on the left of photograph B398019 (below). The elevated road bridge, which sweeps across the picture carrying the M4 motorway, has a surprisingly modern look. The M4 motorway is South Wales's arterial route to the south of England, connecting South Wales almost as far as Carmarthen with London. As well as servicing the industrial coastal heartland of Neath, Port Talbot and Swansea, it also forms a vital link for the mainly agricultural areas of South and West Wales.

Above:
**MONKNASH, THE BEACH
AND THE CLIFFS 1936** 87820

MONKNASH

MONKNASH Beach is situated near the villages of Wick and Broughton (pronounced 'Bruffton'), and from them a pretty path through the woods leads down to the beach. As we can see from photograph 87820 (above), the dramatic cliffs rise from rock ledges – it is possible to fish for bass and cod from here – and sand is only exposed at low tide. There are fossils embedded in the limestone rocks, including gryphea (devil's toenails - actually an ancient shellfish).

THE MONKS' BREWERY

As one might expect from the name, there was an abbey at Monknash, a daughter-house, built in the 12th century, of the great abbey at Neath. The monks of Monknash were farmers, producing grain, fish and other produce so as to keep Neath Abbey well stocked. The forge where the monks shod their farm horses still stands. The story goes that the monks of Monknash did not spend all their time at work and prayer; they had their own brewery, and enjoyed a drink. When the Abbot of Neath found out, he sent a messenger to ban the brewing and drinking, but the monks sent him back to the abbot with a succinct message: 'No beer, no grain'! So the abbot was forced to let the brewery remain.

BARRY

BARRY, WHITMORE BAY 1900 45548p
Right: **BARRY, THE DOCK 1899** 43450

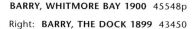

THE BARRY Dock & Railways Company, the largest dock and railway company in Great Britain, was formed in 1884. Colliery owners, dissatisfied with increased costs at Cardiff, had decided to open a dock at Barry, and built it between the mainland and Barry Island. It was opened in 1889 and became the greatest coal shipping port in South Wales (43450, above), handling 11 million tons in 1913. The prime mover involved in building the docks was David Davies of the Ocean Coal Company Ltd – his statue stands in front of the dock offices. He was known as 'Davies the Ocean' and also as 'Top Sawyer', a nickname earned from his youthful employment at a saw-pit.

In 1896 the railway was extended to Barry Island, which thus ceased to be an island, now that there was a road and railway built on the causeway. Photograph 45548p (left) conveys the pleasure to be gained from a day at the seaside with rocks to sit on, a driftwood fire to heat water for a picnic, and parasols to prevent damaging that fashionably pale complexion. We are looking towards Nells Point. The bay is mainly sandy, but at this point a rock fall allows the ladies a natural seating area.

THE PRICE OF POPULARITY

After the First World War, some residents of Barry Island resented the crowds of trippers that arrived in charabancs at the weekends; nearly 100,000 people would descend on Barry, including thousands of miners enjoying their annual fortnight away from the pits. A Mr Austin Beynon complained in a letter to the press that he had bought a large house on the island in 1899 when the location was the 'fairest place on earth', but now with vast crowds, silver bands, roundabouts and so on, who would want to buy it? An answer was printed from 'Anonymous Bandsman', reminding him that many ex-servicemen were forced to live in filthy conditions packed in houses like sardines in a box, and suggesting that he should have bought the whole island and fenced himself in.

Penarth, a few minutes to the west of the capital and with fine views over Cardiff Bay, has been a magnet for holidaymakers and day-trippers for more than a century. Its Victorian and Edwardian founders created a resort of great elegance and beauty, and their legacy is an attractive, bustling town of charm and character. From the Esplanade, an attractive coastal path leads out to Lavernock Point, an important site in the history of communications. It was from here in 1897 that Marconi sent the first radio transmission over water to the islet of Flat Holm.

The famous Penarth Pier (38467, left and 38464t below), 658 feet in length, was built in 1894; the pier included the usual entertainment for the time, such as a ballroom, tea-rooms and amusements, and in this case, even an art gallery. Here we see a crowded paddle steamer leaving the pier head. Now completely restored and re-furbished, the pier is a regular port of call during the summer months for the cruise ships heading up and down the Bristol Channel.

Left: **PENARTH, THE PIER AND THE STEAMER 1896** 38467
Below: **PENARTH, THE PIER 1896** 38464t

GUGLIELMO MARCONI

PENARTH

CARDIFF

THE GROWTH of Cardiff's docks was to some extent a symptom of their own success. There was simply too much coal coming down the valleys from Merthyr for the wharves to cope with. Hence, ships of all sizes and from all ports had to berth in the outer docks and wait their turn. The port kept abreast of technology: it had massive cranes on tracks which could lift an entire coal wagon and dump it into a ship's hold. Steam took over from sail; small paddle steamers, such as the 'Success' in the foreground of 32696 (above left), were developed especially for Cardiff. They sat high in the water, and could work in tidal estuaries where the water level became very low. Many were used as pleasure craft, but these were working boats, used as tugs and pilot boats.

In 77422 (below left) we see an ocean-going tug heading out of Bute docks towards the open sea. The sailing lugger, probably a fishing smack, seems to be in trouble; no sails are rigged, and thus she is needing a tow from the tug, the 'Norman'. In the background the paddle steamer 'Waverley' is churning the surf as she sets off on her next cruise.

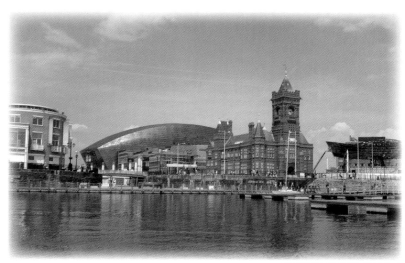

COURTESY OF RHYS GREGORY

CARDIFF'S NEW DOCKLAND DEVELOPMENT

At the old docklands, the waterfront development – one of the world's largest – is transforming Butetown, perhaps better known as the legendary Tiger Bay, Shirley Bassey's birthplace.

It is a perfect juxtaposition of old and new. The beautifully restored Pier Head building (centre) is flanked by Roald Dahl Plass (Oval Basin) and the stylish leisure and retail facilities of Mermaid Quay – all products of periods of economic boom.

With the destruction of important wildlife habitats by flooding, the completion of a barrage proved the most controversial aspect of the bay development. Environmental concerns aside, the costly futuristic structure is stunning. The construction impounds the rivers Taff and Ely, but three navigation locks allow through traffic – the largest is able to manage 12 yachts at a time.

Top: **CARDIFF, THE DOCKS 1893** 32696

Above: **CARDIFF, BUTE DOCKS 1925** 77422

NEWPORT

THIS spectacular transporter bridge (54935p, above, N25175, left) was designed by the engineers R H Haynes of Newport and the Frenchman F Arnodin, and it cost £98,000 to build. The impressive span is 645 ft. It transported vehicles and pedestrians across the river Usk by means of a cradle, thus preventing any obstruction to water-borne traffic. Photograph 54935p was taken the year the bridge opened. The cradle is in movement, transporting pedestrians and vehicles high across the Usk, thus preventing any disruption to the shipping channel. The platform is capable of carrying six vehicles and 100 passengers. A platform allowed pedestrians who were brave enough to walk across 242 ft above the ground and admire a panoramic view of Alexandra Docks. In 1958 the bridge featured in the film 'Tiger Bay', starring Hayley Mills.

Left: **NEWPORT, VIEW FROM THE TRANSPORTER BRIDGE c1955** N25175
Top: **NEWPORT, THE TRANSPORTER BRIDGE 1906** 54935p
Above: **NEWPORT, A FLOATING CRANE c1955** N25181p

CHEPSTOW

CHEPSTOW, THE CASTLE FROM THE BRIDGE 1893 32495

CHEPSTOW'S Welsh name is Cas Gwent, Castle of Gwent. It has generally been believed that the earliest part of Chepstow Castle, the Great Tower, was built by William fitz Osbern, Earl of Hereford. However, in recent years historians have cast doubt on this assumption. Whatever the case, Chepstow Castle is one of Britain's earliest stone castles and is certainly impressive, standing as it does on precipitous cliffs high above the river Wye (32495) – the young J M W Turner was inspired to paint it in 1793.

By late Victorian times the castle was already a tourist attraction and was the setting for grand local pageants which took place annually. Today, the local people organise an ambitious biennial festival in which the castle often plays a prominent part as the setting for a spectacular son et lumiere in the lower bailey, and a medieval fair is held here in front of the castle. In 32495 there is evidence of the timber trade on the quay while two boys watch people working beside the 'Alice'. Goods were taken by boat and barge from Chepstow up the Wye as far as Hereford.

SALMON FISHING ON THE WYE

The River Wye played a major role in the commercial life of Chepstow, and besides trade and shipbuilding, there was a flourishing salmon fishing industry as far back as medieval times. During the 18th and 19th centuries, salmon was being shipped to London, among other places. With the coming of the railway in the middle of the 19th century, the market for salmon was greatly expanded, as many large cities became accessible. Indeed, Stuart House, the one-time headquarters of Wye Valley Fisheries, took its name from an important London buyer of salmon. In front of the building was a bay hedge from which people could pluck a few bay leaves with which to cook their salmon. Both the Wye and the Severn are also fished for elvers, tiny eels, which are used both for food and for restocking eel fisheries in Europe and Asia.

Nowadays drivers enter this part of South Wales across the river Severn on one of two motorway bridges, but before the first bridge was opened in 1966, the only road link was via Gloucester. However, in 1931 the Aust to Beachley ferry was inaugurated, making the journey shorter if somewhat precarious on occasion. There were three ferryboats operating here (C77097, above): the 'Severn Queen', the 'Severn Princess', and this one, the 'Severn King'. Both the 'Severn King' and the 'Severn Queen' were scrapped, but the 'Severn Princess' had a different fate ahead. She was eventually taken to Ireland and used as a coastal freighter. In 1998 a local resident found the ferry in Kikieran harbour in a dilapidated state, and the people of Chepstow rallied together to fund her journey home; she is now being restored. The slipway used by the ferry at Chepstow is still in existence, but it is primarily used for water skiing. The whole scene is now completely overshadowed by the second Severn crossing bridge (left).

Top left: **CHEPSTOW, THE 'SEVERN KING' FERRY BOAT AT BEACHLEY c1950** C77097
Below left: **THE SECOND SEVERN CROSSING 2006 (COURTESY NEIL HOBBS)**

GLOUCESTER

GLOUCESTER, THE DOCKS 1912 65114

Queen Elizabeth I gave Gloucester the formal status of a port in 1580, but it was not until the Gloucester & Berkeley Canal was built in 1827 that the city began to equal Bristol in importance as a grain port - it is the furthest inland port in Great Britain, and the canal connects the city to the Severn estuary. Then, during the railway expansion of the mid 19th century, even more produce found its way to the docks, especially timber.

In photograph 65114 (above), note the many warehouses all around the docks, and the barges to the right, heavily loaded with sacks of grain. Moored in the foreground is a little pleasure steamer ready to take weekend revellers for a trip on the river – a pleasure boat builder was located at Westgate Bridge in the early 20th century. Today some of the warehouses are home to Gloucester's National Waterways Museum, and another contains an antiques centre. The popular television series 'The Onedin Line' was filmed here.

BRISTOL

AS LONG ago as 1752, a certain William Vick had left money in his will for a bridge over the Avon gorge, and by 1829, Bristol's Merchant Venturers were advertising for designs for a bridge. The 23-year-old Isambard Kingdom Brunel knew the area well – he had been staying (and sketching) in Bristol the year before – and he submitted drawings of a bridge in the then fashionable Egyptian style. Older and more experienced engineers also submitted designs, including the distinguished Thomas Telford, but it was Brunel's design that was accepted. The cost of building the bridge was a massive £57,000 – building did not start until 1836, and the project was not completed until 1864, after Brunel's death. The chains that hold up the roadway were second-hand – they came from Brunel's Hungerford Suspension Bridge (1841–45) over the Thames at Charing Cross.

In photograph 20169 (below left) we can see clearly how the tower on the Bristol side (left) stands on rock, but the one across the river is supported on a vast brick buttress; in this photograph and in 45555 (opposite) we can appreciate the dizzying height of the seemingly fragile roadway above the Avon.

SKETCHING IN LEIGH WOODS

As we can see in photograph 20175, the Avon gorge is flanked by beautiful woodland, which is threaded through by charming paths and streams. It was in picturesque spots such as these that Bristol's many artists loved to sketch and paint. Bristol was fortunate to have so many local artists in the early 19th century, including the genius Francis Danby, William Muller, who died tragically young, Danby's followers and friends Samuel Jackson and James Johnson, and many minor artists. In Bristol's City Art Gallery there is a charming watercolour by Samuel Jackson of a sketching party in Nightingale Valley, Leigh Woods: men and women lounge and sketch among the trees in a rocky valley, while a young girl plays her guitar.

❝ *Well then I have to say that of all the wonderful feats I have performed since I have been in this part of the world I think yesterday I performed the most wonderful – I produced unanimity amongst 15 men who were quarrelling about the most ticklish subject – taste. The Egyptian thing I brought down was quite extravagantly admired by all – unanimously adopted and I am directed to make such drawings, as I in my supreme judgement may deem fit.*

ISAMBARD KINGDOM BRUNEL, LETTER TO HIS BROTHER-IN-LAW 1831

Opposite: **CLIFTON, THE RIVER AVON AND THE BRIDGE 1900** 45555
Top: **CLIFTON, LEIGH WOODS AND THE GORGE 1887** 20175
Above: **CLIFTON, THE SUSPENSION BRIDGE 1887** 20169

BRUNEL'S GREAT STEAMSHIPS THAT REVOLUTIONISED THE CROSSING OF THE ATLANTIC OCEAN

Brunel's steamships the 'Great Western' and the 'Great Britain' were both built at Bristol. The 'Great Western' (1838) was the first steamship to cross the Atlantic; she was a wooden paddle steamer 236ft long of 1340 tons. She took 15 days to reach New York. The 'Great Britain' (1845) was the first ocean screw steamer, fitted with a six-bladed propeller; an even larger vessel, and built of iron, she was immediately based at Liverpool. Brunel's last steamer, the 'Great Eastern', remained the largest vessel ever built until 1899. An iron paddle steamer, she was designed to carry 4,000 passengers. While watching her trials in 1859, Brunel suffered a seizure and died.

The SS 'Great Eastern' arriving at New York in 1860

The launching of the SS 'Great Eastern' in 1857

BRISTOL, THE DOCKS 1953 B212285

BRISTOL has been a major port since medieval times, when wool was exported from here. Over the next four centuries, Bristol flourished, continuing to export wool and leather and importing wine and tobacco. The port was heavily involved in the slave trade too. By the 19th century, Bristol was the second most important port in Britain after London.

However, it had long been a difficult port to leave and enter – the tidal Avon, very narrow at this point, is only navigable for a few hours on each side of high water. In 1802 the engineer William Jessop made huge improvements by damming the Avon and diverting it to form new docks with an area of 70 acres, which made it far easier for ships to load, unload and manoeuvre. Jessop constructed Cumberland Basin, locks from the Avon, and the Floating Harbour. Isambard Kingdom Brunel was made chief engineer of Bristol Docks in 1831, and made further improvements.

Bristol's associations with the slave trade brought it a great deal of money. However, after William Wilberforce's successful campaign the port went into a decline, and it was not until the 20th century, after the development of the Avonmouth docks at the seaward end of the Clifton Gorge, that the city managed to return to something approaching the bustling days of the 18th century. In 1890 it was selected as the UK port for the fortnightly Imperial West Indies mail service and from 1921 liners from Rangoon and Colombo were making scheduled calls at Avonmouth. An important boost came in 1901 when Elders & Fyffes inaugurated their fortnightly service to Port Limon, Costa Rica. For over sixty years the banana ships would berth at Avonmouth.

CLEVEDON

ALTHOUGH less popular than neighbouring Weston, Clevedon's devotees valued its refined quietness. Among its distinguished visitors were Tennyson, Thackeray, Sir John Betjeman and Coleridge, who came here on his honeymoon.

The pier (31251, below right) was opened in 1869, and in comparison to that at neighbouring Weston, its construction is light and graceful, looking far too delicate to survive the storms that periodically wreak havoc along the coast. Below the fishing boats are some bathing machines drawn down to the water's edge, ready for use. Various additions and alterations were made to the pier, but its luck ran out in 1970 when two spans collapsed; however, following restoration, it is again open for business.

This delightful and fashionable watering-place is about fifteen miles from Bristol. As a health resort it occupies a very prominent place, whilst its immunity from the heavy excursion element which affects many seaside towns renders it a veritable haven of rest, commending itself each year more and more to professional men and others from Bristol. Clevedon is snugly situated with the broad expanse of the Bristol Channel open to its western front. The most popular and fashionable part of the promenade is that known as the Green Beach [31252, below left]. It consists of an extensive plateau of greensward, about 40ft above the shelving beach, and provided with an elegant band-stand, a plantation, and a very handsome drinking-fountain.

VICTORIAN GUIDEBOOK

Top left: **CLEVEDON, THE BEACH 1923** 74008t

Below left: **CLEVEDON, GREEN BEACH 1892** 31252

Below right: **CLEVEDON, THE PIER 1892** 31251

WESTON-SUPER-MARE

WITHIN a century, the Victorian enthusiasm for the seaside and the railways transformed Weston from a village of 100 inhabitants into a resort of 20,000. Today it has a population of 70,000. The Grand Pier now dominates the bay (74009, above); it opened in June 1904. The extension to the Grand Pier was removed in 1916, as the currents had proved too dangerous for steamers to safely berth there. The church in the foreground is Holy Trinity, built in the 1860s. The town is pictured here just before the big developments of the 1920s and 1930s: the Winter Gardens would be built at the landward end of the pier in 1927, soon to be joined by the marine lake, the open air pool, and the airport. We can see how defined the boundaries of the town were before the sprawl of development in the 20th century.

Top: **WESTON-SUPER-MARE, THE VIEW FROM THE ENCAMPMENT 1923** 74009

Above: **WESTON-SUPER-MARE, THE SANDS 1887** 20318p

BREAN DOWN

ALL THE way north from Burnham to Brean Down, the six miles of road behind the sand dunes and beaches has a straggle of bungalows, chalets, shops, caravan parks, amusement parks and holiday camps, as well the odd older building, including Berrow's medieval church in the dunes.

It is a relief to reach the archaeologically rich and beautiful headland of Brean Down (dominating the background of 68585), a carboniferous limestone outlier of the Mendips reaching 300 feet high, from whose bare grassy slopes are long views to Wales, Glastonbury and along the Somerset coast. Closer in, you can look down on Weston Bay and Weston-super-Mare to the north; it is probably better not to look too closely at the holiday sprawl along the road back to Burnham-on-Sea. In prehistoric times a camp was built on this high stretch of land, but there are few traces now left of the fortifications. The photograph shows the ferry carrying visitors from the coast a little south of Weston-super-Mare.

Above left:
**BURNHAM-ON-SEA,
DONKEYS ON THE SANDS
1907** 58698

Below left:
**BURNHAM-ON-SEA,
THE BEACH 1913** 65379

BURNHAM-ON-SEA

BURNHAM-ON-SEA is situated on the east side of the estuary of the river Parrett. Nowadays it has views north-west to Steep Holm island and depressing views west to the troubled Hinckley Point nuclear power station. Before the 19th century Burnham was little more than a village, and it was not until the fashion for sea-water cures and seaside holidays arrived that it developed as a town.

Looking southwards, view 65379 (left) is terminated by the elaborately Italianate Queens Hotel. From the plain late Georgian stuccoed terraces in the foreground, the architecture gets more 'seaside Victorian' in style, with a profusion of bay windows and the use of various building stones; the four gabled houses date from 1897. The sea wall, recently here completed in reinforced concrete, has since been robustly and massively replaced to repel rising sea levels.

BREAN DOWN, THE FERRY 1918 68585

EAST QUANTOXHEAD

THIS pretty village has a long history; there are records of it in Saxon times. The estate was granted to the Paganel family after the Conquest, and in 1207 Geoffrey Luttrell married the Paganel heiress. It still belongs to the Luttrell family, and thus has one of the longest recorded tenures in the country. Since the village is part of the estate, little has changed here over the years, and there has been no development. The Court House, the home of the Luttrell family, is a stone Elizabethan manor set in beautiful gardens, Near it lies this tranquil pond (82153, left), constructed to hold water for a mill, now home to ducks.

A path leads from the tiny village across the fields to low cliffs above this quiet beach (82148, below). The thin strata of the rocks form attractive patterns in the headland, but they are soft and readily eroded by the sea. Embedded within the layers are numerous fossils: ammonites and gryphea, sometimes called 'devil's toenails', are commonly found here.

Left:
EAST QUANTOXHEAD, THE MILL POND 1929
82153

Below:
EAST QUANTOXHEAD, THE CLIFFS 1929 82148

A MINIATURE PAINTER – IN MORE THAN ONE SENSE

East Quantoxhead was the birthplace in 1784 of Sarah Biffen, the daughter of estate workers; she was born without arms and with very small legs, and she was only 37 inches tall. Despite her humble birth and crippling disabilities, she became a famous painter, creating miniature portraits of the celebrities of the early 19th century. She painted with her brush hooked to her shoulder, and a contemporary advertisement proclaims how she 'executes her drawings by her shoulder with the assistance of her mouth'. Sarah Biffen's life was long and eventful; she married a man who deserted her when her patron's monetary contributions ran out. Fortunately, she was granted a small income and given a house in Liverpool where she died aged sixty-six in 1850. Sarah Biffen's paintings reveal her concentration on detail. She was particularly skilled at painting lace and richly-textured dress materials such as silk and brocade.

Above: **ST AUDRIES, THE BEACH AND THE CLIFFS 1903** 50463

Right: **ST AUDRIES, THE WATERFALL 1903** 50464

ST AUDRIES

ST AUDRIES occupies a natural bowl looking out over the sea above the cliffs of St Audries Bay. This spectacular waterfall (50464, right) terminates the course of a stream that crashes onto St Audries' beach from the cliffs: such picturesque natural phenomena were popular with Frith photographers. The beaches hereabouts are rich hunting grounds for fossils, and many of the cliffs display remarkable folded strata. The tusks of a mammoth were once found here.

The sea, so much less lovely than the name Severn Sea suggests, comes rolling, brown-grey and sullen, towards the towering cliffs. On a summer day it sometimes takes on a faint tone of blue, but in Somerset you get no really blue sea except at Porlock in bright weather. But when the sun shines it brings out variegated colours in the cliffs at St Audries: blue, grey, the red of sandstone, streaks like alabaster, layers of malachite green. Whorled fossils are washed up on the beach. Over one steep cliff-face pours a cold cascade from a Quantock steam that has run across the fields: small children stand in its spray on a hot afternoon. At the top of one cliff there is a hollowed 'look-out' called the Grotto. But as warning notices tell you, nobody should sit in the shadow of the cliffs, for all along this coast … the sea is gnawing at the coastline so that lumps of rock may fall on the beaches at any moment.

BERTA LAWRENCE, 'QUANTOCK COUNTRY' 1952

Above: **WATCHET, THE HARBOUR 1927** 80595
Below: **WATCHET, THE BEACH 1927** 80604

WATCHET

WATCHET was one of medieval Somerset's most important towns. A major export from the town after 1855 was iron ore, which was mined in the Brendon Hills. It arrived at the harbour (80595, left) by rail for loading onto boats and transportation across the Bristol Channel to smelting furnaces in Newport. The trade came to an end in 1910, with the import of cheaper ore from Spain. The harbour remained important into the 20th century, always busy with commercial traffic, and to guide the boats in, the entrance is marked with a lighthouse. In 1900 a great storm hit the coast, severely damaging the harbour and hindering the shipping. Coleridge apparently used Watchet as the inspiration for the port from where his Ancient Mariner set sail.

Watchet's shingly beach (80604, below left) has long been an attraction for children, who here search for curiosities along the tide line. The girls have tucked their skirts inside their knickers, which preserves their dignity and at the same time allows them some freedom to paddle. The soft lias rocks of the cliffs are rich in fossils, and ammonites are commonly found.

FROM GUSTAVE DORÉ'S 'ANCIENT MARINER' 1875

❝ *And here is where he shall set out on his fateful voyage.*

COLERIDGE ON THE SETTING FOR
'THE ANCIENT MARINER'

PORLOCK

AT ONE time the sea extended to Porlock itself, but a retreating shoreline has left it a mile inland and the harbour is now at Porlock Weir (82188, left). This is a charming place with a harbourside pub and whitewashed cottages. The place was once a thriving fishing port; Porlock Weir is named from the old fish weir or trap on the beach. As fishing declined, the fishermen's wives sold teas from their cottages. The fishing stores and salting sheds are now craft workshops. In 82188 (left) we see the cottages on the seashore from the former fish market. Porlock Weir was also busy with coastal trade from Wales, importing coal and limestone and exporting woodland products, including pit props, in return. The harbour was improved in the 19th century by the addition of lock gates (foreground), which allowed cargoes to be handled at all stages of the tide.

Left: **PORLOCK WEIR, THE HARBOUR 1929** 82188
Below: **PORLOCK, HIGH STREET 1919** 69270t

❝ *The ceaseless movement of the sea during the long procession of centuries has worked a marked change in places. In front of the stony beach at Porlock and at Minehead – the 'chesil' of the old records – are still to be seen between high and low water marks the semi-fossilized remains of what was once a forest of large trees. The marsh lands of Porlock were formerly covered in the whole by the sea. As time rolled on the waters left them, but there is reason to believe that as late as the fourteenth century the sea formed a creek, or haven, like the Hawn at Dunster, where nowadays in wet seasons the water lies in a wide shallow pool ... Constantly moving, heaping itself high above the low lands, encroaching here and there upon the grazing ground, [the beach] still protects the marshes. Open a breach through the huge mound and a large part of the low-lying land below the town would be submerged.*

C CHADWYCK HEALEY, 'HISTORY OF PARTS OF WEST SOMERSET' 1901

NEAR the coast, in a steep wooded combe 400 feet above the sea (82193, below left), Culbone's church is well-known to walkers along the Somerset and North Devon Coast long-distance footpath – it is inaccessible by public road. The tiny church of St Beuno (82194, left) is cupped in the sylvan cleft. The church measures only 35 feet long by 12 feet 4 inches wide, and has the distinction of being the smallest complete parish church in England. Its most unusual feature is the spire which rises straight from the nave roof, but its chief charm is its peaceful setting. The woodland provided a living for the villagers, who coppiced the oaks for tanbark, charcoal and timbers; it is said that the original charcoal burners were a colony of lepers.

Above left:
CULBONE, THE SMALLEST PARISH CHURCH IN ENGLAND 1929
82194

Below left:
CULBONE, CHURCH COMBE 1929 82193

CULBONE

WHERE ALPH, THE SACRED RIVER, RAN

The poet Samuel Taylor Coleridge often visited this spot; he would walk here all the way from his cottage at Nether Stowey, 20 miles away. This was a favourite walk for him and for his friends William and Dorothy Wordsworth, who were living in Somerset at the time; walks as long as this and longer were nothing to them. On one occasion, in 1798, Coleridge walked here by himself, and spent the night at nearby Ash Farm.

It was there that he began his great poem 'Kubla Khan', 'composed in a sort of reverie brought on by two grains of opium', his writing of it so tragically interrupted by the visit from 'a person from Porlock'. So perhaps these woods at Culbone were the woods:

> *'Where Alph, the sacred river, ran*
> *Through caverns measureless to man,*
> *Down to a sunless sea.'*

LYNTON

THIS 'convulsion of nature', close by Lynton, was highly popular with Victorian artists and writers, and other early seekers after the sublime and picturesque. Huge rocks lean precariously, the many stacks forming fantastic shapes that worked on the poetic fancy of early visitors like Wordsworth and Coleridge.

It is believed that the Valley of the Rocks was created during the last Ice Age. It is now a wild landscape of crags and pinnacles, occupied by a famous herd of wild goats. On a clear day the mountains of Wales can be seen from here.

Left: **LYNTON, THE VALLEY OF THE ROCKS 1907** 59384

❧ *The traveller ... will not omit the extraordinary Valley of Rocks, reached by a grand walk along the face of the cliff which overhangs the sea to the west of Lynton. At a break in this path he suddenly comes to a gigantic gateway, formed of two rocky pyramids, and enters upon a scene which, to his first view, appears strewn with the fragments of some earlier world. 'Imagine', says Southey, 'a narrow vale between two ridges of hills, somewhat steep: the southern hill turfed; the vale which runs from east to west covered with huge stones, and fragments of stone among the fern that fills it; the northern ridge completely bare, excoriated of all turf and all soil, the very bones and skeleton of the earth; rock reclining upon rock, stone piled upon stone, a huge terrific mass. A palace of the pre-historic kings, a city of the Anakim, must have appeared so shapeless, and yet so like the ruins of what had been shaped after the waters of the flood subsided ... I never felt the sublimity of solitude before'.*

THE REV SAMUEL MANNING 1885

THE NORTH Devon coast is exposed to the might of the Atlantic and swept by powerful tides, and in the lee of Lantern Hill (above the jetty, to the right of 56783a, below) – probably once an island at high tide – ships could find a safe haven, practically the only one east of the estuary of the Taw and Torridge.

Here we see Ilfracombe at the height of its popularity, with paddle-steamers clustered round the pier. The railway had arrived in 1874, the year after Sir Bourchier Palk Wrey's building of the Promenade Pier, and the stage was set for what many regard as Ilfracombe's golden age.

Nothing typifies Ilfracombe's success more than the paddle-steamers. Before the building of the pier the paddlers had been regular visitors, but docking was difficult, and often the passengers had to be ferried off by rowing boat. Now the steamers could tie up alongside, and disembarking passengers was merely a matter of pushing up the gangplank. The ship-owning Campbell family moved from the Clyde to Bristol in 1880 to take advantage of the potential of the Bristol Channel trade, and their white-funnelled vessels soon became a common sight; the first Campbell paddle-steamer, the 'Waverley' (right), arrived in Ilfracombe in 1887. Trips were run to Ilfracombe from Swansea, Barry and Cardiff, carrying day-tripping miners and steel workers, and the sheer volume of passengers disembarked is hard to believe. On the August Bank Holiday of 1905 the 'Britannia', the 'Westward Ho!', the 'Albion', the 'Brighton', the 'Normandy', the 'Ravenswood' and the 'Gwalia' all visited, carrying between 400 and 800 passengers each to a resort which at the time had a population of around 8,000. In 1906, 164,745 passengers disembarked.

ILFRACOMBE

FISH, SHIPBUILDING, LIMESTONE, BRICKS

Alongside the tourist trade, the old industries of Ilfracombe carried on. Fishermen landed huge catches of herrings and pilchards, and when the fishing was poor they could always supplement their income by taking out the more adventurous visitors to, say, Hele Bay. Shipbuilding carried on until the latter part of the 19th century, with the 'Duchess of Clarence', launched in 1828, being the largest home-built vessel at 274 tons. The trading ketches, too, were busy. For centuries they had brought Welsh limestone for the limekilns, but increasingly they carried building materials: the yellow bricks that are such a feature of Ilfracombe's Victorian villas and hotels, and limestone, not for burning but to construct the stout walls of the harbour and pier.

Above: **ILFRACOMBE, THE VIEW FROM HILLSBOROUGH 1906** 56783a   Above right: **ILFRACOMBE, 'THE 'WAVERLEY'** (COURTESY IAN MURRAY)

WESTWARD HO!

WESTWARD HO!, THE PEBBLE RIDGE 1906 55961

CHARLES Kingsley's novel 'Westward Ho!' (1855) was so popular that it brought hordes of visitors to this part of North Devon, and so the resort town of Westward Ho! was founded in 1863. There were grand plans for development. A pier was built, but was soon washed away by the force of the waves surging in from the Atlantic. After the initial flush of planned development, the resort never became as successful as had been hoped; it was bought by a local investor and sold off in small lots during the 1900s. The result is the present hotchpotch of buildings.

The glorious three miles of sands at Westward Ho! are backed by the astonishing Pebble Ridge, a huge bank of enormous pebbles rounded by the sea and washed here by the force of the waves in a process known as longshore drift. The pebble ridge has been driven inland by more than 120 yards during the past century, and it is still retreating by about one yard each year. The girls in photograph 55961, who have been driven up onto the ridge from the sands by the incoming tide, will have found that walking on the pebbles in bare feet can be painful!

KIPLING'S STALKY ON THE DELIGHTS OF WESTWARD HO!

Rudyard Kipling's 'Stalky & Co' was published in 1899. It tells of the exploits of Stalky and his friends at school, drawn from Kipling's experiences at the United Services College in Westward Ho!. Kipling based one of the boys, Beetle, partly on himself. The friends built makeshift lairs in the prickly gorse on the hill behind the school:

He parted the tough stems before him, and it was as a window opened on a far view of Lundy, and the deep sea sluggishly nosing the pebbles a couple of hundred feet below. They could hear young jackdaws squawking on the ledges, the hiss and jabber of a nest of hawks somewhere out of sight; and, with great deliberation, Stalky spat on to the back of a young rabbit sunning himself far down where only a cliff-rabbit could have found foot-hold. Great grey and black gulls screamed against the jackdaws; the heavy-scented acres of bloom round them were alive with low-nesting birds, singing or silent as the shadow of the wheeling hawks passed and returned; and on the naked turf across the combe rabbits thumped and frolicked. 'Whew! What a place! Talk of natural history; this is it,' said Stalky, filling himself a pipe. 'Isn't it scrumptious? Good old sea!' He spat again approvingly, and was silent ...

They looked out over the sea creaming along the Pebble Ridge in the clear winter light. 'Wonder where we shall all be this time next year?' said Stalky absently.

RUDYARD KIPLING, 'STALKY & CO' 1899

CLOVELLY

THE ONLY safe anchorage on the inhospitable, craggy coastline between Appledore and Boscastle, Clovelly lived for centuries from the herring fishery. However, Charles Kingsley's use of the village as a location in 'Westward Ho!' alerted the new breed of holidaymaker to the charm of its steep, cobbled streets; by 1890 there were three hotels. Clovelly grew organically. The houses were built (mostly of cob) by the fishermen as and when they were needed, and display a remarkable variety of sizes, shapes and styles which somehow manage to harmonise perfectly together, thanks to the precipitous setting. In 1890, 34 men of Clovelly held master's tickets, a reflection of the little port's long maritime history. Famous for its herrings, it was also busy with boat building, pilotage, and supplying ships anchored in the roads offshore.

Clovelly's remarkable state of preservation is due to the philanthropic Hamlyn family, who acquired the manor in 1740. Christine Hamlyn took charge of things in 1886 and founded the Clovelly Estate Company, which runs the village to this day.

Donkeys (61016, below) were (and still are) used to transport everything up and down Clovelly's steep street: herring, coal and lime came up the hill from the harbour, along with tourists who could not face the walk, while mail and provisions went down the hill. There was even a donkey refuse collection.

> ❧ The street is cut in steps and paved with cobbles, and up it comes a string of donkeys limping from the quay, straying into the cool shade of every open doorway which they pass, while the women come out and hang over the green balconies above and scold and chatter at the luckless driver, who defends himself in his slow western speech, and at last with many thwackings sets the head of the poor patient donkey straight again, and goes up three steps more when the same process is repeated.
>
> A H NORWAY, 'HIGHWAYS AND BYWAYS IN DEVON AND CORNWALL' 1897

Opposite left: **CLOVELLY, THE HARBOUR 1906** 55953
Above: **CLOVELLY, THE STREET 1890** 24766p
Below: Clovelly, **'UNEMPLOYED - BUT ALWAYS READY FOR WORK!' 1908** 61016

Three fishers went sailing away to the West,
Away to the West as the sun went down;
Each thought on the woman who loved him the best;
And the children stood watching them out of the town;
For men must work, and women must weep,
And there's little to earn, and many to keep,
Though the harbour bar be moaning.

Three wives sat up in the lighthouse tower,
And they trimmed the lamps as the sun went down;
They looked at the squall, and they looked at the shower,
And the night-rack came rolling up ragged and brown.
But men must work, and women must weep,
Though storms be sudden, and waters deep,
And the harbour bar be moaning.

Three corpses lay out on the shining sands
In the morning gleam as the tide went down,
And the women are weeping and wringing their hands
For those who will never come home to the town;
For men must work, and women must weep,
And the sooner it's over, the sooner to sleep;
And good-bye to the bar and its moaning.

CHARLES KINGSLEY (1819–1875),
'THE THREE FISHERS'

BUDE

THE BUDE Canal (35 miles long, from Bude to Launceston) was something of an oddity. For its first two miles, it was a barge canal, as we see here (23782 and 31893). Then, freight was trans-shipped into tub boats, small, square-ended boats which were towed along by horses in strings of up to six boats. Each tub boat had four wheels, which allowed the boats to run in the rails of the canal's inclined planes, which were used on this canal instead of locks to negotiate the changes in contour. At the inclined planes, water-powered engines drove a chain to which each boat was attached so that it could be hauled up and down.

The Bude Canal was commissioned by Lord Stanhope, a local landowner; engineered by James Green, the canal was completed in 1823. This was the only English canal to open directly into the Atlantic Ocean. The sea lock (its seaward side is clearly visible in 31893) was restored to working order in 2001, although the rest of the canal was abandoned in 1896. However, the barge section was retained as a water channel.

View 23782 (left) shows a fine view of sailing ships awaiting high tide. Note the activity on the beach (in the distance on the right): sand was loaded into carts and brought to the quayside to be loaded into the barges - the sand was used to lighten the heavy agricultural soils hereabouts. On their return trips through the canal, the barges brought oats and slate to the trading vessels in the harbour.

The harbour is somewhat altered today. Part of the quay is now a car park, and what used to be a blacksmith's forge is now a museum with a fascinating exhibition showing the canal as it used to be.

Above left:
BUDE, THE CANAL AND THE HARBOUR 1890
23782

Below left:
BUDE, THE LOCK AND THE BREAKWATER 1893
31893

Below right:
BUDE, ON THE CANAL 1920 69564p

> The shore and country about 'Castle Boterel' is now getting well known, and will be readily recognized. The spot is, I may add, the furthest westward of all those convenient corners wherein I have ventured to erect my theatre for these imperfect little dramas of country life and passions; and it lies near to, or no great way beyond, the vague border of the Wessex kingdom on that side, which, like the westering verge of modern American settlements, was progressive and uncertain. This, however, is of little importance. The place is pre-eminently (for one person at least) the region of dream and mystery. The ghostly birds, the pall-like sea, the frothy wind, the eternal soliloquy of the waters, the bloom of dark purple cast, that seems to exhale from the shoreward precipices, in themselves lend to the scene an atmosphere like the twilight of a night vision. One enormous sea-board cliff in particular figures in the narrative; and for some forgotten reason or other this cliff was described in the story as being without a name. Accuracy would require the statement to be that a remarkable cliff which resembles in many points the cliff of the description bears a name that no event has made famous.

THOMAS HARDY, FROM THE PREFACE TO 'A PAIR OF BLUE EYES' 1899

THE DEEP inlet of Boscastle Harbour is one of the few safe anchorages on this exposed coast. Its narrowness and the fact that it is surrounded by high cliffs make it very difficult to spot from the sea, and a winding inlet has to be negotiated before the harbour can be reached – indeed, the fishermen of Boscastle were said to be Cornwall's best navigators, thanks to the skills they acquired in plotting their course through the harbour. Boscastle was once a thriving fishing port, but during the 19th century the jetty was also used for the landing of cargoes of coal.

Around the harbour mouth there are many under-sea caves which seals are known to frequent. Here too is a blowhole, which at certain times of the tide produces an explosive booming sound that can be heard clear across the harbour. Water cascades from the hole high in the air, and on a sunny day makes rainbow after rainbow.

In August 2004 Boscastle suffered a catastrophic flash flood that caught it completely by surprise. The Valency, normally a tranquil stream, flows down into the valley and through the village. However, a sudden surge of rainwater falling on the hills around ran off into the stream, causing it to swell and break its banks. The speed and force of its flow increased dramatically, causing widespread damage, and the raging waters demolished many buildings in the village and swept cars away into the harbour wash. A total of 75mm of rain fell in two hours, which is normally the average rainfall for the entire month of August.

It was once possible to descend to Pentargon caves (36978A, below right). However, landslides in the 1930s destroyed the path. A large cave known as Double Doors extended 200 feet under the cliff and was a great tourist attraction in Victorian and Edwardian times. (Information courtesy of Boscastle Visitor Centre).

BOSCASTLE

Top left: **BOSCASTLE, THE HARBOUR AND PROFILE ROCK c1871** 5964
Top right: **BOSCASTLE, THE HEADLAND 2007**
Above: **BOSCASTLE, PENTARGON CAVES 1895** 36978A

NEWQUAY

NEWQUAY'S harbour was developed in the 19th century for the export of minerals and china clay, and at that time a railway ran out onto the island pier in the centre. Today it is a safe haven for fishing and pleasure boats, while summer visitors find more tranquil water here than at the town's surfing beaches – Fistral Beach is one of Britain's most popular places to surf. Behind, the coastline stretches as far as Trevose Head.

The little building known as the beacon in 1894, situated just south of the Atlantic Hotel (which is in the background of 33525, below left), was once a coastguard lookout. Originally it was the Huer's Hut, where the huers watched for the pilchard shoals. It is identical today, even down to the granite railing posts. Sited up on the headland near the harbour, this is where the huer, who had to have very good eyesight, waited to spot the purple stain on the sea that heralded an incoming pilchard shoal.

He would raise the alarm by crying 'hevva! hevva!' ('here they are!') through his trumpet, or loud hailer, and would use signals made with two 'bushes' (originally gorse bushes) to direct the fishing fleet to the shoal out in the bay. The steps on the outside of the hut gave the huer an even better vantage point. Wilkie Collins, the 19th-century novelist, thought that the huer waving his bushes would resemble 'a maniac of the most dangerous character' to an outsider. The huer was paid a guinea a week, and also a percentage of the value of the fish taken. The hut offered rather basic accommodation for the huer, who would take up his post several days before the shoals of pilchard were expected. Here he would live during the hours of daylight for up to four months of the year. The 'hue and cry' was an exciting sound for the whole fishing community, and many traditional rhymes reflect the fact:

> *The pilchards are come, and hevva is heard,*
> *And the town from the top to the bottom is stirred.*
> *Anxious faces are hurrying in every direction.*
> *To take a fine shoal they have no objection ...*
> *We see the huer with bushes in hand*
> *Upon the white rock he now takes his stand.*
> *While 'Right off,' 'Win tow boat,' 'Hurray' and 'Cowl rooze'*
> *Are signals no seiner will ever refuse.*

Top: **NEWQUAY, THE HUER'S HOUSE 1907** 59333

Above: **NEWQUAY, THE BEACON 1894** 33525

PERRANPORTH

PERRANPORTH takes its name from St Piran, patron saint of Cornish miners, for it was originally a mining community. It received its first taste of tourism as early as the 1800s, when Truronians used to come here to paddle.

The sandhills to the north of Perranporth are constantly shifting; they are held in check by marram grass, reputed to have been introduced by Sir Walter Raleigh. The dunes hide St Piran's Oratory, Cornwall's famous 'lost church', built in the 7th century and covered by the sands.

The cliffs to the south of Perranporth are riddled with the adits of old mine workings, which followed the rich veins of tin and copper that ran from the granite intrusion of Cligga Head into the surrounding killas slate (64386, left). Around Perranporth many old engine houses from the tin mines are prominent features in the landscape, while Wheal Towan is what is left of an old copper mine.

This is Poldark country: Winston Graham was living in Perranporth when he wrote the first Poldark novel.

Left: **PERRANPORTH, THE ROCKS 1912** 64836
Above: **SURFING** (COURTESY CHRISTOPHER BRUNO)

GODREVY LIGHT

GODREVY Island is the closest and largest of a group of rocky outcrops located about four miles off shore from St Ives. Close by is the treacherous Stones reef; its notorious reputation for shipwrecks is only beaten by the Manacles near Falmouth.

Strangely, the pleas for a light close to St Ives Bay were long ignored, despite the growing catalogue of shipping disasters. In 1854 a public outcry followed the loss of the 700-ton steamer 'Nile' (see below).

The wreck of the 'Nile' became the prime reason for a light to be established near St Ives. Within 2 months of her loss, eight petitions were presented to Trinity House. Eventually, in 1857 the building company of Eva & Williams, from Helston in Cornwall, was awarded the contract to build a lighthouse. The accommodation for the builders on Godrevy Island was extremely basic and consisted of waxed canvas tents. It was not until the following March that a wooden barrack was built.

James Walker designed the Godrevy tower in the typical octagonal style of this period. Rubble stone masonry quarried from the island was used to construct the lighthouse. It had a cavity wall, and its external surface was plastered with sand and cement rendering. Its foundation was excavated out of the sloping rock surface to a depth of 3ft. The first course of masonry was set at 21ft in diameter, with the walls nearly 4ft thick. The walls were tapered externally to the gallery, where the tower was 19ft in diameter. The tower was just over 56ft in height.

On 1 March 1859 the Godrevy light was lit for the first time; it was maintained by a principal keeper and two assistants. Their tours of duty were two months on and one month off.

By 1932 the Cornwall mining industry had collapsed, and this brought about a dramatic fall in sea trade. Trinity House converted the Godrevy light to acetylene; this only required a visit by the keepers once a week and the fuel to be changed every six months. It became one of the first Cornish lights to be automated.

TRAGEDY AT SEA ON THE 'NILE'

The 'Nile' seemed to be burdened with bad luck. On 4 July 1854 a Cornish miner, who was on his way home from Liverpool, fell through the engine room skylight when a guard rail broke. A month later, the

'Nile' collided with the brigantine 'William & Anne' close to the Plymouth breakwater. Although badly damaged, the 'Nile' managed to return to Plymouth harbour, but the brigantine sank within 15 minutes of the collision and took her captain to a watery grave.

By 26 November 1854, the 'Nile' was back in her home port of Liverpool after extensive repairs. However, even with a north-westerly gale churning up the Irish Sea, her master, Captain Moppet, refused to be held up any longer, and on 28 November the 'Nile' left Liverpool. On the night of 30 November, the 'Nile' was spotted by the keepers on Lundy Island – she was clearly battling against heavy seas. Over the next few hours, the 'Nile' was sailing dangerously off course; at 2.30am on 1 December she hit the Outer Stones Rocks, which pierced her port side like a sieve. She took on water so rapidly that no one had any chance to lower the lifeboats, and all 60 passengers and crew perished.

Left: **GODREVY ISLAND, THE LIGHTHOUSE 1890** 24195

HERE we see the gaunt remains of a once thriving industry. Perched on the cliff edge, this is the engine house and lofty chimney of one of Cornwall's many mines. Tin and copper have been mined here for centuries: Phoenician merchants came to Cornwall for tin in the 5th century BC, and the Romans extracted ore from shallow open-cast mines – deep mines were not viable, because they would fill up with water. Then in the early 18th century Newcomen's steam engine enabled the pumping of water from the mines, and Cornwall's boom years began. Trevithick's Cornish beam engine meant that mines could be dug even deeper - Dolcoath, near Camborne, reached 3,300ft, the deepest metal mine in Britain. In the 19th century, three-quarters of the world's copper was mined in Cornwall. However, competition from mines abroad led to a slump, and few mines survived into the 20th century.

Wilkie Collins describes his visit into the mine at Botallack in 'Rambles Beyond Railways' (1852): 'The process of getting down the ladders was not very pleasant. They were all quite perpendicular, the rounds were placed at irregular distances, many of them were much worn away, and were slippery with water and copper-ooze. Add to this, the narrowness of the shaft, the dripping wet rock shutting you in, as it were, all round your back and sides against the ladder – the fathomless-looking darkness beneath – the light flaring immediately above you, as if your head was on fire – the voice of the miner below, rumbling away in dull echoes lower and lower into the bowels of the earth – the consciousness that if the rounds of the ladder broke, you might fall down a thousand feet or so of narrow tunnel in a moment – imagine all this, and you may easily realise what are the first impressions produced by a descent into a Cornish mine.'

Left: **PENDEEN, WHEAL EDWARD AT BOTALLACK** **c1960** P273003

LAND'S END

LAND'S End is much busier than the Lizard; there is now a tourist complex set back from the headland along with the old First and Last House (61285, left). This must be the most photographed house in Cornwall. At this date, souvenirs (perhaps including model lighthouses carved from serpentine stone) and postcards (perhaps Frith's) are displayed outside the most westerly house in England. William Thomas, named on the sign, was listed in a directory of the time as a carpenter and proprietor of the Land's End 'refreshment house'.

However, the 19th-century art critic John Ruskin ignored the tourist attractions and characteristically only paid attention to the geology; he saw only disorder here, 'a dizzy whirl of rushing, writhing, tortured, undirected rage, coiling in an anarchy of enormous power'.

Right: **LAND'S END, THE FIRST AND LAST HOUSE 1908** 61285

MARAZION

MARAZION, ST MICHAEL'S MOUNT 1895 36179

MOUNT'S BAY takes its name from this famous rock, an island at high tide, surmounted by the site of a Benedictine monastery and castle, now a National Trust property. St Michael's Mount has been the home of the St Aubyn family since the 17th century, with the south-east wing added by Piers St Aubyn in 1875–78. Beautiful landscaped gardens nestle among the rocks below the house. The distinctive silhouette of St Michael's Mount is unmistakable. It is from Marazion that visitors make the centuries-old pilgrimage, either by boat at high tide or on foot across the causeway at low tide.

In the foreground men are collecting kelp for use as fertiliser. Seaweeds have been used as a fertiliser for hundreds of years; farmers collected weed brought in by the tides, as we see in this photograph, or would cut weed from the rocks with sickles. After about three weeks composting, the seaweed would be ready to be dug into the fields.

FERTILITY FROM THE SEA

Why does seaweed make such a good fertiliser? It is high in potassium, and also contains nitrogen and phosphate. It is beneficial for germinating and growing crops, giving them increased resistance to damage from frost and parasites. Its salt content deters slugs. Seaweed also improves clay soils, a highly important consideration in Cornwall; it helps the clay in the soil to form crumbs, improving the soil's water retention.

Today, the ready availability of chemical and processed seaweed-based fertilisers means that most farmers no longer gather cartfuls of seaweed, but some National Trust properties still use seaweed fresh from the shore.

THE LIZARD is a remote peninsula set at the southernmost point of Cornwall. Its coast is characterised by a chaos of jagged rock ridges fringing the sea. Much of the Lizard's grandeur derives from its unique serpentine rock, which assumes extraordinary shapes and colours. At Kynance the brilliantly-hued rough green stone forms spectacular caves in the cliffs. Their very names conjure up the ancient romance of this mysterious county: the Devil's Frying Pan, the Devil's Mouth, the Bellows.

THE DEVIL'S FRYING PAN

The serpentine stone reveals yet greater wonders when it is polished. The rich colouring it attains has been compared to the sinuous skin of a snake. In the 1850s there was a considerable local industry devoted to turning and forming the stone into a variety of sought-after gift objects. The Penzance Serpentine Works employed twenty craftsmen, and held a stock of 160 tons of rock in their yard. They supplied chess tables, chimneypieces, vases and flower stands, and boasted that 'orders were constantly received from the nobility and gentry at home and abroad'. Prince Albert commissioned decorative serpentine slabs for his Isle of Wight residence at Osborne.

Serpentine souvenirs have been very popular ever since. This photograph is hard to date, but the simple equipment on show – the lathe and various chisels and scrapers – would be the same as were used a century ago. The tall object on the right is the first stage of a model lighthouse. These were made in sizes from a few inches to several feet, and were popular with visitors.

THE LIZARD

Left:
**THE LIZARD,
IN A SERPENTINE
WORKSHOP c1950** L62019

CHARLESTOWN

BUILT by Charles Rashleigh and designed by the ubiquitous engineer John Smeaton, Charlestown was once one of Cornwall's busiest ports, shipping tin from the Polgooth Mine which in 1790 was the biggest in Cornwall. Between 1794 and 1874, 28 ships were built here, the largest being the 'Pride of the Channel' at 175 tons.

The principal export from the tiny south Cornish port of Charlestown was china clay, much of it bound for Runcorn; from there it would be forwarded on to the Potteries. The principal import was Lancashire and North Staffordshire coal from Runcorn. A vessel arriving from Runcorn would discharge at a coal berth and then move over to a china clay berth to load. That was the theory, but the harbour could be so jammed up with ships that the move could involve several other vessels all being shunted around in a series of moves choreographed by the dock master.

THE CHINA CLAY INDUSTRY AROUND ST AUSTELL

'[St Austell] is a place of some bustle from the continual transit through its streets of heavy waggonloads of china-clay for the harbours of Par and Charlestown'.

'MURRAY'S HANDBOOK FOR TRAVELLERS' 1865

By the early 1860s, tin and copper mining were suffering a decline; it was fortunate, therefore, that some miners could transfer to the expanding china clay industry. There is no doubt that china clay and china stone were responsible for St Austell's prosperity and growth in the 19th and 20th centuries. In about 1746, William Cookworthy discovered their properties for porcelain manufacturing, first in West Cornwall and then at St Stephen near St Austell. He took out a patent in 1768. From the 1770s, Josiah Wedgwood and others from the Staffordshire potteries took an interest in the St Austell area. The china clay industry dates from that time; over the years the whole landscape has been remodelled by Cornwall's major extractive industry. China stone and china clay result from the decomposition of feldspars in granite. The china stone is less altered, and was quarried in the traditional way; china clay (kaolin) was washed out by a stream of water and pumped to the surface to be settled and dried. In the 20th century, high-powered hoses (monitors) took over the job of washing clay from the pit face. In the days before pollution control, much waste – clay, mica and sand – went into the rivers; that is why the St Austell River was called the White River. The disposal of waste has always been a problem, because every ton of china clay produced leaves up to 8 tons of sand, gravel and rock. By the late 19th century, the disposal method was to carry the sand in special skips up inclined tramways to be discharged at the top of conical skytips. These white tips, spreading over the landscape, gave the area the name of the Cornish Alps.

Left: **CHARLESTOWN, THE HARBOUR 1912** 64784

FOR TRAVELLERS to Cornwall, crossing the broad, sweeping waters of the Tamar deepened the sensation that they were entering a foreign land. Some took the chugging chain ferry, and others rattled over Brunel's curious bridge in the carriages of the Great Western Railway. Brunel's celebrated masterpiece across the Tamar estuary (76023, right) made the first direct rail link between Cornwall and the rest of England when it was opened by Prince Albert in May 1859. The bridge is only 31 years old in this view; it was taken from the Devon bank, looking over to Saltash with its railway station, left, and ferry slipway below the bridge.

The estuary a little down river at Plymouth presents a maritime face, with expansive stretches of water that are the province of ocean-going ships and naval vessels. Yet here at Saltash the Tamar threads a narrower, serpentine course between wooded banks up to Gunnislake.

SALTASH AND PLYMOUTH

DOWNDERRY, CAVE DWELLERS 1901 47803

DOWNDERRY

FRITH may have been guilty of a little artistic licence in describing these women as 'cave dwellers' – there are indeed plenty of caves on the beach here, but all are sea-washed at high tide with even a small swell running, and thus not habitable. Perhaps these hard-looking women only spent the odd couple of days in the caves gathering flotsam and jetsam.

SALTASH, THE FERRY AND THE ROYAL ALBERT BRIDGE 1924 76023

❝ *We have time to finish the game, and beat the Spaniards afterwards ...*

DRAKE'S ghost haunts the Hoe. It is difficult to cross this wide, breezy promenade without thinking of him. Sailor, circumnavigator, mayor, MP, bowls player, facial hair consultant to an Iberian monarch, scourge of the Spanish – he crammed a lot into his fifty-one years. On the Hoe stands a statue of him, where we can almost hear him saying: 'We have time to finish the game, and beat the Spaniards afterwards'. The tide was against him, so he could not have sailed just then anyway, but the gesture was typical of the man, and cemented his place in history - one gets the impression that he was well aware of it.

The Hoe that Drake knew was a very different place from the one we know today. The same limestone ridge endures, of course, from which the name is derived – 'hoe' comes from the Saxon for 'high place'. But long ago the Hoe was mostly devoid of buildings, and cattle and sheep grazed on the grass slopes, into which two enormous white figures were cut. These were Gogmagog and Corineus, two giants who had fought on the Hoe. Their origin is unclear, but they remained there until 1671.

PLYMOUTH, THE HOE AND SMEATON'S TOWER 1913 65978t

PLYMOUTH, THE HOE, SMEATON'S TOWER AND THE BANDSTAND 1913 65980

PLYMOUTH, ONION SELLERS 1907 59208p

❝ *Where else can one see a spot trodden like the Hoe by so many generations of the greatest men our country ever saw, and retaining still almost the same aspect as it bore when their eyes looked back upon it from the decks of departing ships which were bearing them to seas unassailed before, and by coasts which were never mapped or charted, through those far regions of the West whose very peril was their great attraction.*

A H NORWAY, 'HIGHWAYS AND BYWAYS
IN DEVON AND CORNWALL' 1897

Leisure and lookout have been the Hoe's lot for hundreds of years. Drake used it for both purposes, but not in the way that immediately springs to mind. The idea of him shading his eyes, squinting into the distance, and seeing the sails of the Armada looming on the horizon, romantic though it might be, does not hold water. In fact the Hoe has a very limited field of view, and Drake, like defenders of the city down the ages, would have been looking towards the beacons of Staddon Heights and Maker for warning. The fleet was in fact commanded by the Lord High Admiral Charles Howard, Drake's bowls opponent; Drake was vice-admiral commanding a flotilla of smaller, more manoeuvrable vessels, which no doubt suited his nature far better.

The lighthouse once occupied the feared Eddystone Rock, 14 miles south of the Hoe. Built by John Smeaton, it was the third lighthouse on the rock; it shone from 1756 to 1890, when the present lighthouse, designed by Douglas, was completed.

Photograph 59208p (below right) reminds us that Plymouth's importance was not purely naval – it was a trading and fishing port too. The onions on the shoulders of these two boys, photographed at the Mayflower Steps, may well have been French. Breton onion sellers were once a common sight on the streets of Plymouth.

BIGBURY-ON-SEA

BIGBURY-ON-SEA, THE TRACTOR c1950 B92055

BIGBURY-ON-SEA stands on a promontory above the River Avon, which rises high on southern Dartmoor. Bigbury has a long history – in the post-Roman era, Mediterranean traders brought wine, oil and spices here in exchange for tin.

Burgh Island, which is linked to the mainland by a broad spit of sand, stands just off the mainland opposite Bigbury. There was a monastery here in the Middle Ages, and in later centuries Burgh Island was a base for smugglers and wreckers. In 1895, a music hall performer, George Chirgwin, built a hotel here. Then in 1927 Archibald Nettleford built the present hotel, a Grade II listed Art Deco masterpiece visited by Noel Coward, Agatha Christie and Winston Churchill. It is possible to walk out to the island and its hotel at low water, but when the tide is in, a weird contraption like the one we see in B92055 (above) takes visitors out to the island. This particular machine no longer exists, but its replacement serves the same purpose.

The Devonian purple and green slates which make up this part of the coast can erode into all sorts of odd shapes. They are also very reflective: the cliffs near Challaborough, on the western side of Bigbury Bay, sometimes appear to shimmer silver in bright sunlight.

TORCROSS stands on the banks of Slapton Ley, a 270-acre fresh water lake dammed by the shingle bank of 'the Line', as it is known. The Line is thought to be about 3,000 years old, and the Ley about 1,000 years old. Slapton Ley is famed for its bird life. Fed by two streams, the Gara and the Start, it is a fine fishing ground – in 1905 two men staying at the Torcross Hotel caught 21 pike and 1,812 perch and rudd (with rod and line, not nets!) during a four-day stay.

At the end of 1943, the whole area was requisitioned by the military so that the US forces could practise the D-Day landings on the sands - more died training here than were killed on Utah Beach on D-Day. A mouldering old Sherman tank, lost during the 1944 rehearsals, and only recovered in 1988, stands as a memorial to those US servicemen who lost their lives.

Torcross's fishermen kept Newfoundland dogs, which were trained to swim out and help tow the boats ashore in heavy weather. The boats were dragged up the beach on baulks of timber known as ways; their catch of crabs, for which the area was famous, was sent to London daily.

Below: **TORCROSS, SLAPTON SANDS 1907** 58788

TORCROSS

BRIXHAM became a major fishing port ranking alongside Hull, Grimsby, Fleetwood, Lowestoft and Fraserburgh. It was from here that some of the biggest smack and ketch-rigged trawlers sailed to fishing grounds in the North Sea, the Irish Sea and the Western Approaches. The dimensions of these vessels varied, but many were around 80ft in length and registered at about 70 tons. They made full use of equipment such as steam capstans that considerably reduced the time it took to bring the trawl in.

In 21558 (below left), we see smacks dry their sails within the protection of the outer harbour. These beam trawlers, so called because the trawl was kept open by a wooden beam across the mouth of the net, rarely ventured beyond the confines of the English Channel. They sailed fast, and needed to, as their catches often had to be landed in time to be loaded on to scheduled express fish trains.

The statue in 78492 (left) commemorates the landing of William of Orange in 1688. His aim was to depose the Catholic King James II and to herald 'a glorious revolution'. William and his Dutch troops received a hearty welcome from local families. It is the only statue in the country to have an inscription in Dutch.

BRIXHAM

Above left:
**BRIXHAM,
THE HARBOUR
1925** 78492

Below left:
**BRIXHAM,
THE FISHING FLEET
1889** 21558

Below right:
BRIXHAM 2006
(COURTESY MELVIN
GREEN)

PAIGNTON

UNTIL the 1840s Paignton was a farming village half a mile inland, producing cider and the then famous Paignton cabbage, but it became popular with convalescents, and its beach – longer and better than Torquay's - started to attract family holidaymakers. Soon it had expanded east to meet the sea: marshy land behind the beach was reclaimed, and the wealthy barrister Hyde Dendy built the pier in 1879.

Although one could hardly call Isaac Merritt Singer a true entrepreneur, he certainly was a very wealthy man. He bought an estate at Paignton near Preston, in part to escape the air pollution in London which affected his wife Isabella's health. Contrary to general belief, he did not actually invent the sewing machine, but amassed his fortune through his ingenious invention of the shuttle and by his amazing salesmanship in America. Eventually he produced his own sewing machines, complete with his patented shuttle. Keenly interested in cars and aviation, Isaac Singer's younger son Paris had his own hanger built on Preston Green. Later Captain Truelove used the hanger to house his Avro seaplane (68533) for tourist flights around Torbay.

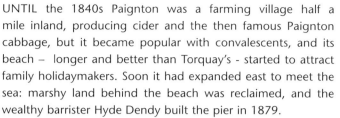

Above: **PAIGNTON, PRESTON SANDS 1918** 68533
Left: **PAIGNTON, THE BATHING BEACH 1896** 38545

❝ *This watering-place may be described as a handsome and extensive suburb of Torquay. Of late it has been greatly improved; a promenade pier has been erected, and the Esplanade - on which there is a bandstand - greatly extended. This charming resort should be visited in the apple blossoming season, for the cider apple is largely cultivated in the neighbourhood, and cider is manufactured on a large scale. Originally some distance from the sea, Paignton has now approached it, and like its fashionable neighbour, Torquay, it is rapidly extending in every direction. The town is, however, very old, having belonged to the See of Exeter from a period before the Conquest. The remains of the Bishop's Palace adjoin the churchyard. Like Torquay, Paignton possesses splendid climate and remarkably fine sands. The bathing, too, is excellent; the surrounding country is fertile and well wooded, abounding in the combes which are so characteristic of the district.*

VICTORIAN GUIDEBOOK

DAWLISH, FROM LEA MOUNT 1896 37614

DAWLISH

THE COVES around Dawlish were used extensively by smugglers until Isambard Kingdom Brunel built his railway and the accompanying cliff tunnels in the first half of the 19th century, making the landing of cargoes more difficult.

Brunel originally conceived this line as an 'atmospheric railway': it worked on a vacuum principle, with the carriages propelled by atmospheric pressure. Air was pumped from a pipe by engines installed in pumping stations along the track. The first passenger trains ran in September 1847. However, the atmospheric system proved troublesome. There were frequent breakdowns, and passengers were expected to get out and push! After only a year, it was decided to run the railway with conventional steam locomotives.

This engineering miracle still thrills travellers to Devon and Cornwall as it runs right next to the sea under the sandstone cliffs; lashed by the waves in rough weather, trains can arrive at Exeter with carriages adorned with seaweed. How much longer can it last? Global warming now brings rising sea levels and strong ocean surges, and maintenance of the track is becoming more and more expensive.

❝ *The climate has almost an Italian geniality, and the tender myrtle and other delicate plants bloom freely in the open air.*
VICTORIAN GUIDEBOOK

EXETER

THE EXETER Ship Canal, five miles long, reaches the sea at Topsham, and was built between 1564 and 1566 after the building of a bridge at Countess Wear stopped the use of the river for trade. The city's wool merchants, eager for more profits, had commissioned John Trew to make the Exe navigable to the estuary. However, Trew came up with a different scheme: he proposed to build a canal deep enough to allow barges of up to 16 tons to dock at the city wharf. The transfer of goods between barges and sea-going ships would take place in the estuary, thus cutting out both the middlemen at Topsham and the need for packhorse trains.

Exeter City Basin (38035) opened in 1830 as the final stage of the canal development. The completion of Turf Lock enabled vessels to enter the canal and proceed up to Exeter regardless of the state of the tide. Just out of the picture is a warehouse advertising Newfoundland fish, a trade which had started in 1563. Fishermen from all over Devon and Cornwall worked the cod stocks of the Grand Banks, and Topsham sent more ships across the Atlantic than any other port.

Left: **EXETER, IN THE PORT 1896** 38035

Above: **EXETER, FROM THE CANAL 1896** 38033

SIDMOUTH

SIDMOUTH, THE ESPLANADE 1918 68739t

SIDMOUTH was one of many towns that became popular during the Napoleonic wars when the rich could not travel to Europe. As the railway did not arrive until 1874, the town remained unspoilt by mass tourism, especially as the beach was shingle. Thus the charming Regency buildings have retained their character, and much of the town remains untouched by modern development. Sidmouth was considered rather a select resort in Victorian times; it was frequented by royalty, and Queen Victoria had her first view of the sea here as a child.

It was around 1700 that the Royal Glen (S129052, below) was built by a Mr King of Bath. It was then a modest farmhouse with a dairy, outhouses, a hayloft and a well that still exists in the centre of the house. It was first known as King's Cottage, taking the name of the owner. When in 1817 it was purchased by Major General Edward Baynes, he added considerably to the grounds, made several general improvements, and changed the name to Woolbrook Cottage; it was sometimes known as Woolbrook Glen. The house was converted from a farmhouse into Regency splendour with delightful castellated pediments, a tent-roofed veranda, and Gothic casements complete with painted drip moulds. The inside was as charming, especially the elegant and graceful drawing room. The royal coat of arms is proudly depicted on the plaque above the Gothicised porch.

Right: **SIDMOUTH, THE ROYAL GLEN HOTEL c1955** S129052

PORTLAND

PORTLAND, CHESIL BEACH 1890 27328

AT FIRST glance, Portland, with its quarries and penal establishment, seems a harsh and unforgiving landscape. But for those who seek out its quiet corners and hidden delights, it is a place of considerable charm. The Isle of Portland is more properly a peninsula, which Thomas Hardy described as 'the Gibraltar of Wessex'. Portland gives shelter to the westerly approaches of Weymouth Bay and is visible for many miles both up and down the English Channel. Chesil Beach (27328, above) is a great ridge of shingle eight miles long with a lagoon of brackish water between it and the mainland. A hard walk along the stones takes some hours to complete, but provides an interesting route between Portland and Abbotsbury.

Above right:
**PORTLAND,
PORTLAND BILL
1898** 41149

Below right:
**PORTLAND,
QUARRYING 1894**
34553

Left: **PEBBLES ON
CHESIL BEACH**

❝ *The sea off this island, and especially to the west of it, is counted the most dangerous part of the British Channel. Due south, there is almost a continued disturbance in the waters, by reason of what they call two tides meeting, which I take to be no more than the sets of the currents from the French coast and from the English shore meeting: this they call Portland Race; and several ships, not aware of these currents, have been embayed to the west of Portland, and been driven on shore on the beach, and there lost.*

DANIEL DEFOE (1661–1731), 'FROM LONDON TO LAND'S END'

❝ *The island is sufficiently fruitful of grain, and famous for the nicety and smallness of its mutton: having no wood, they are obliged to burn the dung of cattle … The inhabitants are well govern'd by their own (naturally framed) laws; never suffer'd a press-gang; intermarry with each other, dreading the alliance of foreigners; and have hitherto from their detach'd and remote situation continued an hardy, honest, industrious people – but now that an high road is open to the great world, I should fear that vices and depopulation will take place, with all the other improvements of this refined age: and to accomplish this glorious work in the grandest style, it was lately proposed to employ the convicts at the stone quarries, to the total extirpation of the virtue and support of the natives.*

JOHN BYNG, 'RIDES ROUND BRITAIN' 1782
(EDITED D ADAMSON, FOLIO SOCIETY)

Portland stone is known throughout the world as a prime building material, renowned for its durable qualities. Sir Christopher Wren used a great deal of it in the construction of St Paul's Cathedral. Apart from the privately-run quarries, a great deal of stone was broken by convicts from the nearby prison in times past (34553, below). In 41149 (above), we can see blocks of quarried stone waiting to be loaded on to ships. The unusual stone formation at the end of the headland at Portland Bill is known as Pulpit Rock.

WEYMOUTH

Above: **WEYMOUTH, THE PROMENADE 1918** 68114t

Below: **WEYMOUTH, THE HARBOUR 1904** 52861

Right: **WEYMOUTH, THE PARADE 1904** 52855

WEYMOUTH owes its origins as a resort to the patronage of George III, who came here for the new 'cure' of sea bathing. As the king plunged into the waves a brass band, discreetly hidden in a bathing machine, played 'God Save the King!' King George is commemorated by a statue in the town and by a chalk figure on the hills beyond the bay.

Many of the buildings along the Parade (52855, left) date back to this period. Queen Victoria's reign brought huge changes for the town, which expanded considerably during the 19th century to cater for the large increase in tourists. In this photograph we see the Parade, with the red brick of Royal Terrace followed by the late Victorian exuberance of the Royal Hotel. Beyond it the terraces stretch on for half a mile – 'Has any coast town a more spectacular seafront than Weymouth?' says Pevsner. In the distance is the Jubilee Clock Tower, built to commemorate the long reign of Queen Victoria.

In 52861 (opposite, below) we see a fine sailing vessel moored near Weymouth Bridge. The heyday of sail was almost over, for steam vessels were replacing the ocean-going ships, but some sailing vessels continued to trade from Weymouth well into the 1920s.

> *Budmouth is a wonderful place – wonderful – a great salt sheening sea bending into the land like a bow – thousands of gentlepeople walking up and down – bands of music playing – officers by sea and officers by land walking among the rest – out of every ten folk you meet nine of 'em in love.*
>
> THOMAS HARDY, 'THE RETURN OF THE NATIVE' 1878

❝ *I saw on the shore a little fishar towne caullid Lilleworth, where is a gut or creke out of the se into the land, and is a sucour for smaul shippes.*

JOHN LELAND (1506–1552)

Left:
LULWORTH, DURDLE DOOR 1903 49148

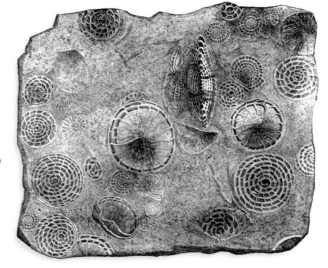

THE FOSSIL-RICH Jurassic coast from Exmouth to Studland now carries the ultimate accolade of being England's first Unesco-designated World Heritage Site. The beauty of Lulworth cove has always attracted writers and artists. John Keats spent some of his last days in England here, as did Rupert Brooke, who returned several times before sailing away to the First World War. Thomas Hardy immortalised the cove in poems and novels.

Durdle Door (49148, above left), an arm of Portland-Purbeck limestone, was formed by the sea breaking through to the soft chalk rocks behind, with strata uplifted from the horizontal to vertical (left) by the collision of the Earth's tectonic plates.

Paddle-steamers returned to Lulworth Cove after the Great War. The one we see in 78804 (left) is the 'Victoria'. She was bought by Cosens & Company of Weymouth in 1884, and for decades she was one of the most familiar vessels along the Dorset coast. For a time she was active all year: the 'Victoria' inaugurated a daily winter service at Bournemouth on Boxing Day, 1902.

Stair Hole (34576, opposite), where the downlands of Dorset meet the sea, is hollowed out by vast caverns, many used by smugglers for centuries.

Left: **LULWORTH, THE STEAMSHIP 1925** 78804

LULWORTH COVE

LULWORTH, STAIR HOLE 1894 34576

SWANAGE, THE PROMENADE 1925 78791

SWANAGE

❝ *He descended and came to a small basin of sea enclosed by the cliffs. Troy's nature freshened within him; he thought he would rest and bathe here before going farther. He undressed and plunged in. Inside the cove the water was uninteresting to a swimmer, being smooth as a pond, and to get a little of the ocean swell, Troy presently swam between the two projecting spurs of rock which formed the pillars of Hercules to this miniature Mediterranean. Unfortunately for Troy a current unknown to him existed outside, which, unimportant to craft of any burden, was awkward for a swimmer who might be taken in it unawares. Troy found himself carried to the left and then round in a swoop out to sea.*

THOMAS HARDY, 'FAR FROM THE MADDING CROWD' 1874

THOMAS Hardy described Swanage as '… a seaside village, lying snugly within two headlands as between a finger and thumb'. The town may get its name from Swene's Wic, the Bay of Swene, perhaps commemorating the great naval battle fought nearby between the Saxons and Danes in 877. For hundreds of years smuggling was a major industry in Swanage, the smuggled goods being hidden in the local caves and quarries. Prominent coastguard stations were built along the coast to act as a deterrent. The 40-ton Portland stone Great Globe (31357, right) stands at 111ft above sea level on Durlston Head. It was carved in fifty sections at John Mowlem's famed Greenwich works in 1887. Educational, biblical and poetical inscriptions set around the globe include quotations from the works of Pope, Shakespeare, Milton, Dryden and Tennyson.

Right: **SWANAGE, THE GLOBE 1892** 31357

SWANAGE

WESTWARDS from Durlston Head, George Burt turned disused cliff quarries at Tilly Whim Caves (43775, left) into an early Victorian tourist attraction noted by early guidebook writers, who nevertheless deplored the graffiti left by Victorian visitors. From the narrow ledge, visitors could enjoy magnificent views across the sea to the Isle of Wight and Old Harry Rocks. The caves are now closed to the public through safety concerns.

TILLY WHIM CAVES

The caves are a strange mixture of erosion and quarrying. The Purbeck marble quarried here was used for ornamental purposes in many of our finest cathedrals, including Salisbury, Canterbury and Westminster Abbey. The stone was worked in underground galleries and lowered into boats moored below.

The apt quotation (on the wall top left) is from Shakespeare's 'The Tempest' (the play was inspired by the Bermuda shipwreck of Sir George Somers from Lyme Regis):

> *'The cloud-capped towers, the gorgeous palaces,*
> *The solemn temples, the Great Globe itself,*
> *Yea, all which it inherit, shall dissolve,*
> *And, like the baseless fabric of a vision,*
> *Leave not a rack behind.'*

THURSDAY, 14 SEPTEMBER: *Fine, warm, windy. Trip in steamer ... We ran past the Needles, touched at Bournemouth Pier and took in new passengers, then came the cliffs of Swanage Bay, the Old Harry rock, with tossing and seasickness. Landed at Swanage, an out-of-the-world place, houses roofed with large gray stones, narrow crooked street. Many stonemasons here. Beyond, a valley with trees and brook. Lunched at 'The Ship', kept by Mrs Diddlecomb, and back to steamer — more tossing and discomfort, of which I had a little.*

WILLIAM ALLINGHAM 1865

Above: **SWANAGE, TILLY WHIM 1899** 43775

Right: **SWANAGE, OLD HARRY ROCKS 1897** 40316

THIS low-tide view shows the outer chalk stack at Handfast Point, where coastal erosion has claimed the site of Studland Castle, built as part of Henry VIII's coastal defences of the entrance to Poole Harbour. A double arc of fire was achieved from a fort in the basement of the present Branksea Castle on Brownsea Island. Old Harry's wife collapsed in the same gale that swept away the old chain pier at Brighton in the 1890s. Old Harry Rocks and the Needles are all that remain of a chalk ridge that ran from the Purbecks to the Isle of Wight – 10,000 years ago the sea level was about 40 metres lower than it is today, and prehistoric man lived in what is now Poole Harbour.

AN EXPLOSIVE LANDSCAPE

Throughout the Second World War, heather-clad Ham Common, the site of Rockley Sands caravan camp after the war, hid underground fuel tanks for the civilian and military flying-boats of the BOAC and RAF Hamworthy. The secret nearly exploded one night when Luftwaffe bombs set the common ablaze. Photograph P72243p looks northwards from Rockley Jetty, which carried a railway siding from the Royal Naval Cordite Factory on Holton Heath.

POOLE Harbour is one of the world's great natural anchorages. The town of Poole prospered from medieval times as its merchant adventurers traded with ports across the world. One Poole privateer, Harry Page, brought home 120 prize ships during raids on the continent in the Middle Ages.

The Custom House (52814t, right) was built in about 1788, a little later than the similar-looking Guildhall. Outside is the Town Beam, which was used for weighing. HM Customs has now relinquished the building, and it has become a wine bar and restaurant. On the quay a steamship is being loaded.

Rockley Sands caravan camp (P72243p, above right) covered some 600 acres of harbourside heathland and pine wood; it was one of the earliest holiday camps, with high-tide fun including water-skiing up the arm of Wareham Channel leading into Lytchett Bay. By the 1960s, about 100,000 visitors a year were holidaying at Rockley Sands. For years this was Poole Council's only concession to the tourism industry. These caravans are on the west side of the wood just above Rockley Point. Behind is Bay Hollow; there are now some trees on the cliff, and the path to the right has become steps.

Right: **POOLE, THE CUSTOM HOUSE 1904** 52814t

Above right: **POOLE, ROCKLEY SANDS, WATER SKIING c1957** P72243p

POOLE

THIS wooded valley was known to young Winston Churchill when he stayed with his aunt Lady Wimborne at her nearby holiday house. Three years after the picture was taken, 18-year-old Winston injured himself whilst trying to slide down a pine tree in the next door Branksome Dene Chine. It was during his convalescence that he resolved to enter Parliament.

Alum Chine, a little further to the east towards Bournemouth, is named after a short-lived alum works opened in 1564 by Poole's lord of the manor, Lord Mountjoy of Canford.

6 *This fashionable watering-place, with its eastern and its western stations, its piers, its groves of pines, its promenades, and its covered gardens, was, to Angel Clare, like a fairy place suddenly created by the stroke of a wand.*

THOMAS HARDY,
'TESS OF THE D'URBERVILLES' 1891

Above:
BOURNEMOUTH, BRANKSOME CHINE c1890 B163301

Left:
BOURNEMOUTH, INVALIDS' WALK 1900 45226p

BOURNEMOUTH

UNLIKE resorts which had grown up around older industries such as fishing and merchant shipping, Bournemouth dedicated itself from the start as a venue for holiday pleasures, spurred on by the enterprising Sir George Gervis, a wealthy landowner. Under his guidance the first real hotels began to appear, a library and reading room were established, and the first villas – available for hire at four guineas a week – began to line the cliff-tops. An early travel writer expressed his approval: 'The magic hand of enterprise has converted the silent and unfrequented vale into the gay resort of fashion, and the favoured retreat of the invalid'. Bournemouth Pier (centre right of 19529, left) stands above the original mouth of the Bourne Stream. Its construction marked the town's commitment to its role as a resort.

THE INFLUENTIAL DR GRANVILLE

The whole project to promote Bournemouth as a resort might have foundered had it not been for the timely arrival of the famous Dr Granville, eventual author of the standard Victorian guide, 'Spas of England and Principal Sea-Bathing Places'. Bournemouth's wily planners gave a dinner in the good doctor's honour, seeking his help in keeping the momentum going. Granville responded magnificently, announcing that the resort was superb for the treatment of consumption, but urging the gathered dignitaries not to allow the burgeoning new town to go downmarket. On his advice the flowing waters of the Bourne Stream were captured and transformed into the decorous brook we see today. The wilder parts of the vale were turned into gardens and walkways. Villas sprang up along the slopes of the hills and the cliff-tops, each one standing in its own health-giving grounds – just as the doctor ordered. Grateful (and well-off) valetudinarians flooded into the area. The results probably were conducive to better health, even if, as the consumptive Robert Louis Stevenson put it some years later, life there 'was as monotonous as a weevil's in a biscuit'.

BOURNEMOUTH, FROM WEST CLIFF 1887 19529

❛ *Do not allow mere brick-and-mortar speculators … to build up whole streets of lodging houses, or parades and terraces interminable, in straight lines facing the sea, the roaring sea, and the severe gales, that make the frames of an invalid's bedroom casement rattle five days a week at least, and shake his own frame in bed also.*

DR GRANVILLE, 'SPAS OF ENGLAND AND PRINCIPAL SEA-BATHING PLACES' 1843

CHRISTCHURCH

THE PRIORY tower and Place Mill, also known as Town Mill (centre), are the historic backdrop to the view across Clay Pool (68053, left); here the waters of two great rivers, the Stour (left) and the Avon (right), merge and mix before flowing into Christchurch harbour. The yacht club headquarters (right of centre) was a familiar landmark until its replacement in the 1960s. The club was founded in 1883 and the clubhouse opened in 1896.

View 45045 (below) shows Wick ferry. Bicycling was clearly popular. The young woman is a picture in her ankle-length skirt, long-sleeved blouse and straw boater. The boat on the left is a fishing punt of the type known as a marsh tub, once used for carrying tubs of smuggled spirits over shallows where the keel boats of the customs authorities could not follow. The boat in the centre is a marsh punt of the type used for wildfowling; the large calibre punt gun it carried required the punt be aimed rather than the gun. The ferry today is still a punt, but with a motor. In fact this is the south bank of the River Stour, opposite what became Fred Pontin's holiday camp on the meadow – he and Billy Butlin pioneered the post-war holiday business, and both retired with knighthoods.

SUNDAY, 13 DECEMBER: *Walk from Lymington to Christchurch, by cliffs and beach—mean, straggling little Town among flat watery fields, by a broad muddy estuary. It has a huge and striking old gray Church, part Norman, much decayed, and full of coughs and rheumatisms for the worshippers, being very unfit for the Protestant service.*

WILLIAM ALLINGHAM 1863

Above: **CHRISTCHURCH, THE PRIORY CHURCH AND THE QUAY, FROM WICK 1918** 68053

Right: **CHRISTCHURCH, WICK FERRY, WEST LANDING 1900** 45045

HYTHE

LOCATED on the western bank of Southampton Water, in the shadow of an oil refinery and heavy industry, Hythe was once the port of the New Forest. A settlement survived here after the Conquest, despite the excesses of William the Conqueror.

The 'Hotspur III' (H372077, below) was launched at the end of January 1938. She joined 'Hotspur I' and 'Hotspur II', and these ferries ran from Southampton to Hythe every half an hour during the day. They would drop and collect passengers from Hythe pier, where an electric railway (H372076, below left) connected to the mainland. Let us hope that the child's pushchair, towed by the train, has not been forgotten! Hythe pier is the longest on the south coast, jutting out into Southampton Water opposite Netley. It was opened to the public in 1881, and is one of only a couple in this country with a railway. The track was electrified in 1922. In July 1952, 50,000 people crammed onto the pier to witness the world's fastest liner and Blue Riband winner, the 'United States', arrive in Southampton.

Flying boats (H372015, left) remained a common sight on Southampton Water during and after the Second World War. In that conflict they were used mainly for anti-submarine duties, though a minor passenger service using these craft existed in the peaceful days of the 1950s.

Above left: **HYTHE, FLYING BOATS c1955** H372015

Below left: **HYTHE, THE PIER RAILWAY c1960** H372076

Above right: **HYTHE, THE FERRY c1960** H372077

SOUTHAMPTON

ACTING as a symbolic gateway to the world, Southampton is situated on the wide estuary of two great rivers – the Test and the Itchen. In the golden days of ocean-going travel, this internationally famous waterway provided first-time visitors to these shores with one of the first glimpses of English soil. Today, the waterfront is more heavily industrialised, and the great passenger liners are certainly fewer. But the sense of maritime history is still tangible as one recalls the names of the great liners that once plied these historic waters – the 'Mauretania', the 'Aquitania', the 'Queen Mary' and the 'Queen Elizabeth' among them. The ill-fated 'Titanic' sailed from Southampton in 1912, and the 'Great Eastern' was moored in Southampton Water before her maiden voyage in 1861. To serve these ships, Southampton had dry docks (60442, opposite), graving docks and a foreign animals wharf.

The Pilgrim Fathers' Monument (76264, left) is built of Portland stone and rises 50ft above the ground. Just visible at the top is a beacon surrounded by Greek pillars, and the monument is crowned by a copper model of the 'Mayflower' in the form of a weathervane. The ship set sail from nearby West Quay.

Left:
SOUTHAMPTON, THE PILGRIM FATHERS' MONUMENT 1924 76264

Below:
SOUTHAMPTON, ABOVE BAR 1900
S151001t

A BUSY PORT

Southampton was the port of destination or call for such lines as Union Castle, North German Lloyd and American Lines. At noon every Saturday an American Line liner left the Empress Dock bound for New York. It was also from the Empress that the Cape Line mail boats for South America and the West Indies departed. From the Outer Dock there were services to the Channel Islands and London (thrice weekly); there was a daily sailing to Le Havre, and Tuesday, Thursday and Saturday departures for St Malo and Cherbourg. Packets for Dublin, Falmouth, Plymouth, Glasgow, Liverpool and Cork used the Town Pier, as did the ferry for Hythe, while those for the Isle of Wight, Southsea and Portsmouth left from the Royal Pier.

Can you help us with information about any of the Frith photographs in this book?
We are gradually compiling an historical record for each of the photographs in the Frith archive.
It is always fascinating to find out the names of the people shown in the pictures, as well as
insights into the shops, buildings and other features depicted.

If you recognise anyone in the photographs in this book, or if you have information not already
included in the author's caption, do let us know. We would love to hear from you, and will try to
publish it in future books or articles.

Our production team
Frith books are produced by a small dedicated team at offices in the converted Grade II listed
18th-century barn at Teffont near Salisbury, illustrated above. Most have worked with The
Francis Frith Collection for many years. All have in common one quality: they have a passion for
The Francis Frith Collection.

For further information, trade, or author enquiries please contact us at the address below:
The Francis Frith Collection, Frith's Barn, Teffont, Salisbury, Wiltshire, England SP3 5QP.
Tel: +44 (0)1722 716 376 Fax: +44 (0)1722 716 881 Email: sales@francisfrith.co.uk

www.francisfrith.com

Voucher for **FREE** and Reduced Price Frith Prints

Please do not photocopy this voucher. Only the original is valid, so please fill it in, cut it out and return it to us with your order.

Picture ref no	Page no	Qty	Mounted @ £8.50	Framed + £17.00	Total Cost £
		1	**Free of charge***	£	£
			£8.50	£	£
			£8.50	£	£
			£8.50	£	£
			£8.50	£	£
			£8.50	£	£
			* Post & handling		£3.50
			Total Order Cost		£

Please allow 28 days for delivery. Offer available to one UK address only.

Title of this book . . . .

I enclose a cheque/postal order for £ . . . .
made payable to 'The Francis Frith Collection'

OR please debit my Mastercard / Visa / Maestro card, details below

Card Number

Issue No (Maestro only)   Valid from (Maestro)

Expires   Signature

Name Mr/Mrs/Ms/Miss . . . .

Address . . . .

. . . .

. . . .

. . . . Postcode . . . .

Daytime Tel No . . . .

Email . . . .

Britain's Coast Readers Digest
ISBN: 978-0-276-44303-9

Valid to 31/12/09

Free Print - see overleaf

FREE PRINT OF YOUR CHOICE

Choose any Frith photograph in this book.

Simply complete the voucher opposite and return it with your remittance for £3.50 (to cover postage and handling) and we will print the photograph of your choice in sepia and supply it in a cream mount with a burgundy rule line (overall size approx 14 x 11 inches). (The picture ref. no. can be found at the end of each caption in the book).

Offer valid for delivery to UK addresses only.

PLUS: Order additional Mounted Prints
at HALF PRICE £8.50 each (normally £17.00)

If you would like to order more Frith prints from this book, possibly as gifts for friends and family, you can buy them at half price (with no additional postage and handling costs).

PLUS: Have your Mounted Prints framed

For an extra £17.00 per print you can have your mounted print(s) framed in an elegant polished wood and gilt moulding, overall size approx 16 x 13 inches (no additional postage and handling required).

Mounted Print
Overall size 14 x 11 inches (355 x 280mm)

IMPORTANT!

These special prices are only available if you use this form to order.

You must use the ORIGINAL VOUCHER on this page (no copies permitted).

We can only despatch to one address.

This offer cannot be combined with any other offer.

Send completed voucher to:
The Francis Frith Collection, Frith's Barn, Teffont, Salisbury, Wiltshire SP3 5QP

BRITAIN'S COAST
Compiled and edited by Eliza and Terence Sackett
Designed by Terence Sackett
Reader's Digest Edition
First published 2007

Original edition first published in the United Kingdom in 2007 by The Francis Frith Collection
Text and Design copyright The Francis Frith Collection®

Reader's Digest Association Limited
11 Westferry Circus, Canary Wharf, London E14 4HE
www.readersdigest.co.uk

®Reader's Digest, The Digest and the Pegasus logo are registered
trademarks of The Reader's Digest Association, Inc., of Pleasantville,
New York, USA.

The Francis Frith Collection
Frith's Barn, Teffont, Salisbury, Wiltshire, SP3 5QP
Tel: +44 (0) 1722 716 376
Email: info@francisfrith.co.uk
www.francisfrith.com

The Frith® photographs and the Frith® logo are reproduced under
licence from Heritage Photographic Resources Ltd, the owners of the
Frith® archive and trademarks.
'The Francis Frith Collection', 'Francis Frith' and 'Frith' are
registered trademarks of Heritage Photographic Resources Ltd.

A CIP catalogue for this book is available from the British Library.

Printed in Singapore by Imago

Front cover: Southwold, the Beach 1919 *69118t*

The colour-tinting in this book is for illustrative purposes only, and is not intended to be historically accurate.

Every attempt has been made to contact copyright holders of illustrative material. We will be happy to give
full acknowledgment in future editions for any items not credited. Any information should be directed to
The Francis Frith Collection.

As with any historical database, the Francis Frith archive is constantly being corrected and improved, and
the publishers would welcome information on omissions or inaccuracies.

Book code: 410-708 UP0000-1
Oracle code: 250011063H
ISBN: 978-0-276-44303-9